FEAR OF FEAR
A Survey of Terrorist Operations
and Controls in Open Societies

CRIMINAL JUSTICE AND PUBLIC SAFETY

Series Editor: Philip John Stead
John Jay College of Criminal Justice
The City University of New York
New York, New York

FEAR OF FEAR: A Survey of Terrorist Operations and Controls
in Open Societies
John B. Wolf

FEAR OF FEAR

A Survey of Terrorist Operations
and Controls in Open Societies

John B. Wolf

John Jay College of Criminal Justice
The City University of New York
New York, New York

PLENUM PRESS • NEW YORK AND LONDON

Library of Congress Cataloging in Publication Data

Wolf, John B.
  Fear of fear.

  (Criminal justice and public safety)
  Bibliography: p.
  Includes index.
  1. Terrorism. 2. Terrorism—Prevention. I. Title. II. Series.
HV6431.W6   363.3′2   81-13816
ISBN 0-306-40766-3   AACR2

© 1981 Plenum Press, New York
A Division of Plenum Publishing Corporation
233 Spring Street, New York, N. Y. 10013

Printed in the United States of America

To the women in my life:

the one who bred me,
the one who wed me,
and the one who led me

PREFACE

Terrorism, continuing unabated in the contemporary world, is having a serious impact on the lives of people and nations. Once, only governments and ruling classes possessed the power to coerce large segments of the world's peoples. Today, a handful of thugs, covered and concealed by a collection of terrorist organizations, are disturbing people everywhere by perpetrating dramatic criminal acts—bombings, kidnappings, assassinations, etc.—on an almost daily basis, in places specifically chosen for their vulnerability: a railroad train, a pub, a beachfront apartment, a bus, a restaurant.

Furthermore, a few of the world's most notorious terrorist groups are associated in a loose coalition, which has left around the earth a trail of violent crimes against humanity of the most heinous type. Among these outrages are random murder, including the killing of innocents, and barricade and hostage situations involving the elderly and young children. Many of the victims of these terrorists are randomly selected for the sole purpose of obtaining maximum shock action calculated to attract widespread exposure via the communications media. A dramatic example is the assassination of Lord Louis Mountbatten, one of the most distinguished soldier-statesmen of the century, by terrorists of the Provisional Wing of the Irish Republican Army (I.R.A.).

Moreover, the kind of terrorism favored by these gangs is replete with a "philosophy" of self-justification whose logic transcends all political borders and ideologies. Contemporary acts of terrorism (unlike the Algerian variety of 1957, which impacted only upon the peoples involved: Muslims, Colonials, and Mainland French) are frequently committed across both national and continental boundaries. It is no longer uncommon for the press to report the activity of a sniper, presumably motivated by anger at the treatment of Jews in the Soviet Union, who has perpetrated an act endangering the lives of sleeping children at the Soviet mission to the United States in New York City, or to report the seizure of a busload of school children on a dust-filled street of an African city by terrorists bent on liberating the Somali Coast. Contemporary terrorism is an international problem.

In today's world, any person could become a victim of a terrorist regardless of his or her innocence or neutrality. Many terrorist actions are intended to appear indiscriminate, but are purposely designed for the sole reason of strewing a certain number of bodies on the street for "all the world to see." By these actions, the terrorists seek to enhance the fearsome reputation of the organizations which they represent.

The deliberate use of this diabolical variety of terror as a weapon to achieve social change in Western society originated in the twisted thought processes of the nineteenth-century Russian anarchists, who advocated a theory known as the propaganda of the deed: "A single deed is better propaganda than a thousand pamphlets." Consequently, in the street, at work, at home, a citizen who lives in areas of actual or projected terrorist activity is continually under the threat of violent death, and often experiences the depressing feeling of being an isolated and defenseless target. Unhappily, this distress is neither self-induced nor unwarranted: in some instances, the police are powerless to ensure protection.

It is evident that today's terrorist tries to influence behavior by extranormal means through the use or threat of violence, while simultaneously creating an atmosphere of perpetual and escalating terror conducted by zealous patriots whose only options are the "bullet or the bomb." Thus, the terrorist carefully avoids undertaking any action which might fall beyond the ambit of a real or a contrived popular cause. Despite this camouflage, a terrorist is nothing more than a criminal who tries to exploit any available and natural social pathology in accordance with a formula utilized by Lenin, Hitler, Stalin and other twentieth-century practitioners who relied on random violence to achieve their ends. The techniques used by these totalitarians to recruit people for murder and terror operations have been defined by the Soviet KGB who advised their operatives to search for people who are hurt by fate or nature—the ugly, those suffering from an inferiority complex, craving power and influence but defeated by unfavorable circumstances. The sense of belonging to an influential, powerful organization often provides people of this type with a feeling of superiority over the handsome and prosperous people around them. For the first time in their lives they experience a sense of importance.

Once a terrorist group forms, it already has access to a vast body of literature of "social demolition," including the works of Marx, Lenin, Mao Tse-tung, Che Guevara, Carlos Marighella, and others. These books are dissected by would-be reformers, turned revolutionaries, in library reading clubs, prison cells, college cafeterias, urban flats, and elsewhere, and are readily exploited to provide a radical group with a manipulative popular grievance to use as a trigger for an armed terrorist campaign. Frequently, the grievance usurped by a terrorist group may have been in existence for years, and "old hands" may tend to dismiss it as unimportant. But terrorists of the new breed, a few of whom have advanced degrees in the behavioral sciences and urban politics, are alert not to dismiss any cause as unimportant, particularly if it can be associated with a gap in communication between the persons in positions of power, "the establishment," and discontented elements.

This book does not suggest that an outbreak of terrorism may not arise from issues associated with deprivation or genuine grievances. But gaps between people have always existed, and will continue to separate, for example, management from labor, power elites from students, and the urban areas from the countryside. Much of this discord, nevertheless, has existed for years without serving as a catalyst for terrorist campaigns. The contemporary terrorist has identified these issues, and does not act until he has made a careful and rational analysis of the general conditions and manipulative causes which are latent within his society, as well as of the present and potential strength of his group. The organization and extension of a terrorist campaign, therefore, are predicated on a supportive propaganda message designed to attract and condition people to serve as followers and supporters of an extremist organization. The terrorist could not otherwise openly involve or sustain himself in a protracted program of terror designed to influence society as a whole.

After twenty years of researching the use of terror as a weapon, I am convinced that adequately funded and properly managed campaigns of social, economic, or political reforms will not satisfy the psychobiological urges of terrorists because, for the terrorist, organizing an entire population or class is not a necessary prerequisite for a terror campaign. Instead, I have concluded that these persons recognize that the essential element is to have a group of specialists in a terrorist organization. These cutthroats understand that the ingredients needed to sustain a campaign of terror are the recruitment of a charismatic leader with destructive tendencies, ideas which can be extracted from the literature of social demolition, swindles, bank robberies, or kidnapping to raise funds, and self-serving politicians who can be duped into lending their support to a seemingly good cause.

Part I of this book is intended to provide the reader with a description of the techniques and tactics used by terrorist groups and their relevance to the urban environment of the industrialized democracies. Factors limiting the extension of police power within the framework of a free society, and thereby impairing the efficiency and effectiveness of the police as a social control agency, are also discussed in this section.

The author, however, does not believe that an internal passport system, forced quartering, labor camps, or other methods associated with totalitarian governments are reasonable solutions to the problem of terrorism; their implementation would signal the demise of democracy itself. Thus, part of the price paid by the people of a free society for their freedom is the requirement to work within the framework of established laws when attempting to control terrorist and other elements who manipulate their constitution and other legal safeguards. The legal systems of a democratic state regard a terrorist as just another criminal. But the terrorist, on command of superiors, will kill without hatred people in whom he has no personal interest, while claiming to be a patriot and a soldier. When apprehended, the terrorist is punished for a crime, and is only asked details about himself and his act. His rights concerning the divulging of information are protected, and precise information about his organization is not usually obtained.

Part II of this book tenders a basic system of antiterrorist measures which are compatible with the framework of a free society and useful for the control of this menace. These measures should be of particular interest to members of the police services of the world, the criminal justice community as an entity, the personnel of intelligence services, students, and the general reading public. This section contains the author's view of intelligence operations: the focus for antiterrorist operations as a system that removes the cloak of invisibility from those who perpetrate terrorism, and thereby makes them more fearful of apprehension by the police. Fear, the basic weapon of terrorists, is used by society against terrorists themselves, and forces their organizations to constrict themselves and eventually vanish.

Some of the control measures described in this book may be viewed in some circles as impairing the freedoms of the people of a free society. The mass production of automobiles nevertheless made it mandatory that a traffic system be developed and installed, drivers licensed, and vehicles registered. The technological vulnerability of modern society to terrorism obviously requires the institution of control measures for the similar purpose of protecting the commonwealth. I personally have no objection to a magnetometer check of my person and luggage at an airport, for example, as it enhances one of my most basic freedoms— freedom from fear. Furthermore, I sincerely believe that a terrorist, whose organization and techniques are based on fear, cannot survive in a society free of fear. For those who fear the imposition of antiterrorist measures, the words of Franklin Delano Roosevelt, often reiterated during the American depression years of the 1930s, might be reassuring. Mr. Roosevelt remarked, "The only thing we have to fear is fear itself." Terrorists are human beings with human fears, although many of them would have the rest of us forget that point.

My most grateful thanks are due to all those who have helped me conceive and complete this book, particularly my wife, and the many associates and students, military, police, and civilian, whose enthusiasm and needs have so often served to stimulate my interest. To Professor Halford L. Hoskins, my friend and mentor at American University, Washington, D.C., who introduced me to a unified system of research techniques, and to Professor Philip John Stead, my colleague at John Jay College of Criminal Justice in the City University of New York, who encouraged me to publish my papers, I owe a particular debt of gratitude.

JOHN B. WOLF

ACKNOWLEDGMENTS

Although all the material contained in this book has been revised and updated, the substance of the information contained in Part I and Chapters 6 and 10 of Part II was written by the author during the period April 1975 through August 1978, and published as follows:

- Chapter 1: "A Global Terrorist Coalition: Its Incipient State," *The Police Journal*, LI, no. 4 (October–December 1977): 328–39.
- Chapter 2: "Urban Terrorist Operations," *The Police Journal*, LI, no. 3 (July–September 1977): 221–30.
- Chapter 3: "Organization and Management Practice of Urban Terrorist Groups," *Terrorism: An International Journal*, I, no. II (1978): 169–86.
- Chapter 4: "Terrorist Manipulation of the Democratic Process," *The Police Journal*, XLVIII, no. 2 (April–June 1975): 102–12.
- Chapter 5: "Prisons, Courts and Terrorism: The American and West German Experience," *The Police Journal*, LI, no. 3 (July–September 1977): 221–30.
- Chapter 6: "Controlling Political Terrorism In a Free Society," *ORBIS: A Journal of World Affairs* (Winter 1976): 1289–1308.
- Chapter 10: "An Analytical Framework For the Study and Control of Agitational Terrorism," *The Police Journal*, XLIX, no. 30 (July–September 1976): 165–71.

CONTENTS

PART II: CONTROLS

Chapter 6 • Controlling Political Terrorism in a Free Society 73

Chapter 7 • Approaches to Antiterrorism 89

PART I
OPERATIONS

1

THE GLOBAL TERRORIST COALITION

Terrorism, when employed on an international or a transnational scale, is intended to convince major world powers that there is a real and urgent need for them to correct the conditions responsible for its utilization.[1] The terrorists attempt to manipulate the publicity generated by their activities to emphasize that moderation over an extended period is not capable of bringing about the required political change, be it the termination of a colonial situation or the achievement of social equality. Thus, the terrorist tries to show that his actions are clearly a response to the denial of basic freedoms to a politically identifiable and deprived people, whom the major powers, in the interests of their own national security, should "liberate." Without a credible publicity campaign skewed to this consideration, the terrorist risks not having his activities accepted as logical and tolerable behavior. The transnational terrorist, particularly, seeks to demonstrate to the world that he is grimly determined to use violent means to end the injustice and humiliation of his people.

In the pursuit of this objective, the terrorist seeks to demonstrate his capability to be militant, and to withstand prolonged suffering. Con-

[1] Transnational terrorism is defined as terrorist action carried out by basically autonomous nonstate actors, whether or not they enjoy some degree or support from sympathetic states. International terrorism is defined as action carried out by individuals or groups controlled by a sovereign state.

3

sequently, the environment for terrorism is dominated, not by terrain and physical factors, but mostly by human beings and political and psychological issues. It is the emphasis placed on these factors that lends credence to the terrorist threat: a strategy which makes sense only when it is understood that terrorism is not so much a military technique as the creation of a political condition. The strategic intent of the transnational terrorist, therefore, is to manipulate the major world powers into accepting the premise that his plight must be resolved in the interests of world peace.

The Palestinian terrorist groups are examples of transnational terrorist organizations whose structure, strategy, and operations closely conform to the theoretical aspects pertaining to the worldwide utilization of terror as a weapon. The bombing campaigns of the Irish Republican Army (I.R.A.) in England are not examples of transnational terrorist activity. Other contemporary terrorist groups, among them the E.T.A. (Euzkadi Ta Askatasuna in the esoteric Basque language of northeastern Spain), the Italian Red Brigades, and the inactive National Liberation Movement in Uruguay, better known as the Tupamaros, a prototype for many contemporary extremist groups, should also be regarded as domestic groups, as their operations are undertaken in a particular locale. Additionally, their causes are related to a somewhat isolated domestic political situation, which in no immediate way has ramifications which pose a threat to the existing international balance of power. But the Palestinian terrorist groups, whose activities have a dramatic impact on the Middle East where both the United States and the Soviet Union have vital but opposing national interests, are movements which represent a cause with a direct impact on world stability, ostensibly the plight of the Arab refugee.

PALESTINIAN TERRORIST ORGANIZATIONS

The Palestinian terrorist organizations have been unable to redeem their lost lands inside Israel through the vehicle of diplomacy, conventional warfare, or Maoist-oriented guerrilla warfare. Consequently, they employ the tactics of terror against Israeli people and their international supporters everywhere.

They have used terror to intimidate the world community by raising the specter that the cost of maintaining the status quo is an eventual nuclear confrontation between the United States and the Soviet Union. Palestinian terrorism, therefore, complements conventional Arab diplomacy, which emphasizes that a lasting peace in the Middle East is dependent on a resolution of the "Palestinian Question."

It seems that some youthful Palestinians, once aware that their people were unable to prevail over the Israelis when employing either the tactics of conventional warfare or those of the guerrilla, shifted to the tactics of terror. These tactics were defined by Leon Trotsky as measures which *"kill individuals* and *intimidate thousands."*[2] Today the Israeli people themselves and their supporters everywhere are the targets of Palestinian organizations whose purpose in unleashing these forces is to intimidate the world community by raising the costs of maintaining the status quo, thereby forcing concessions. Consequently, most Palestinians regard the terrorist organizations as an expression of their national liberation movement. The origin and operations of this movement are the natural outgrowth of a repressed people's struggle for independence, which has been marked by abysmal failure, and whose pleas for restitution are viewed by most other people as unrealistic.

The tactics employed by the Palestinian terrorist organizations include aircraft hijacking, political kidnapping, assassinations, letter bombings, and the slaying of innocent people at airports in the Middle East and Europe. In the United States, they are believed to be responsible for placing explosive rigged vehicles in front of Israeli-owned installations in New York City, and for the murder of an Israeli official in Washington, D.C.

A COMMON TERRORIST IDEOLOGY

The ideology of these terrorist movements contains a curious mix of the ideas of not just one theorist, but many. The Palestinian groups share, along with the Tupamaros, who exploited Uruguay's chronic unrest for 8 years, and others, the Marxist doctrine that the revolution will emerge after a period of "armed struggle," which is to include political kidnappings, bank robberies, and assassinations. They have disregarded, however, the Marxist caution against embarking on the course of insurrection unless sufficient forces are mobilized to overcome a well-organized, disciplined enemy. Instead, they have adopted the Maoist notion that infiltration, conspiracy, agitation, and terror can create and prolong a revolutionary situation.

[2] Bertram D. Wolfe, *Three Who Made a Revolution* (New York: Dell Publishing, 1964), pp. 88–89.

Also, the ideas of the Brazilian theoretician of urban guerrilla warfare, Carlos Marighella, have had a great impact on Palestinian terrorists, and most other contemporary terrorist groups. In his *Minimanual of the Urban Guerrilla*, Marighella remarks:

> Today to be an assailant or a terrorist is a quality that ennobles any honorable man because it is an act worthy of a revolutionary engaged in armed struggle against shameful military dictatorship and its monstrosities.[3]

Additional explanations are used by revolutionaries to celebrate the tactics of terror employed by Palestinian terrorists as positive virtues. Violence, they say, promotes the "manhood" of oppressed people, and leads to freedom and unity. Obviously, this notion is gathered from the Algerian Existentialists, Albert Camus and Frantz Fanon. Fanon's book *The Wretched of the Earth*, a chronicle of his experiences and reflections during the Algerian uprising in the 1950s, envisaged a new alliance between revolutionaries and the lumpenproletariat—the criminals and the idlers of society. Fanon saw "all the hopeless dregs of humanity, all who turn in circles between suicide and madness" as marching "proudly in the great procession of the awakened nation."[4]

This concept of Fanon's is now a reality, as some of the Arab terrorist groups have made common cause with groups which are representative of other people with real or supposed grievances which have been translated into a popular cause. For example, an article in *ACTION*, a publication of Arabic–English Newspapers, Incorporated, sees a certain similarity between the activities of the militant Oglala Sioux at Wounded Knee and Black September in Khartoum:

> In Munich and Khartoum small groups of Palestinians, members of the militant Black September movement, took hostages, offering their release in return for the release of imprisoned Palestinians.
>
> In Wounded Knee, a small group of Oglala Sioux took hostages and offered to release them in return for, among other things, official investigation into treaties made and broken by the United States government.[5]

"In short," exclaims *ACTION*, "the Oglala Sioux and the Palestinians have resorted to direct and violent action for precisely the same reason nobody would listen."[6] Frustrated by this lack of attention and infuriated by decades of neglect and failure, the Arab terrorists, and some individuals associated with the relatively obscure group called the American

---

[3] Carlos Marighella, *For the Liberation of Brazil* (Harmondsworth, England: Penguin Books, 1971), p. 93.
[4] Frantz Fanon, *The Wretched of the Earth* (New York: Grove Press, 1968), p. 18.
[5] H. Ben Isaac, "Munich, Khartoum and Wounded Knee," *Action*, April, 16, 1973, p. 3.
[6] Ibid.

Indian Movement (A.I.M.), having nothing to lose, are committed to the idea that violence is the only language the world understands.

COMBINED TERRORIST OPERATIONS

Reports of an international exchange of ideas and pooling of weapons and information among terrorist groups emerged during the early spring of 1972, when information filtered into the press about American Weathermen, I.R.A. people, terrorists from Turkey's Dev Genc group, and Sandanista guerrillas from Nicaragua attending joint summer training sessions at Palestinian commando bases in Jordan. In May 1972, additional evidence became apparent when members of Japan's Red Army Group, in the interest of the Palestinians, took weapons out of suitcases and opened fire in Tel Aviv airport, killing 26 persons and wounding 80. Also, in July 1973, the hijackers of a Japan Air Lines jumbo jet were identified as three Palestinians, a Japanese, and a blond Latin American woman about 30 years old who was killed accidentally when a grenade in her handbag exploded.[7]

Most alarming, also, are other developments which point to the growth of "joint action" agreements between various terrorist groups. In December 1974, a French guerrilla group known as the "Raul Sendic International Brigade" killed the Uruguayan military attaché in Paris, and stated that they were not Uruguayans, but French committed to avenging tortures of imprisoned guerrillas. The guerrillas, who named their groups after the organizer of the Uruguayan Tupamaros, said that their victim once headed military intelligence in Uruguay, and had recently been assigned to pursue Uruguayan political refugees in France. Over the years, the Tupamaros have been reported to have connections with Palestinian, Cuban, and Japanese terrorists, and with the Black Panther Party (B.P.P.) in the United States.

Furthermore, the urban guerrilla warfare techniques of the Tupamaros and the massive publicity generated by some of their more spectacular propaganda actions have made them the most popular and imitated revolutionary group in the world. The Weathermen, the Front de Libération du Québec (F.L.Q.), the Baader–Meinhof gang in Germany, and the Symbionese Liberation Army (S.L.A.) all duplicate Tupamaro-devised tactics of propaganda actions and direct actions. For example, on Christmas day 1954, the Tupamaro "hunger commandos" hijacked

---

[7] "The Terrorist International," *Newsweek*, September 18, 1972, pp. 33–34.

trucks from food stores and dispensed their contents to slum dwellers. Publicity generated by this activity had the same calculated impact that was caused when the Hearst Corporation agreed to an S.L.A. demand for a multimillion-dollar food handout in Oakland, San Francisco, Richmond, and East Palo Alto, California. Both these operations are classic examples of propaganda actions undertaken by terrorist groups.

Therefore, because of the proliferation of joint-action agreements and the obvious tactical similarity, various antiterrorist specialists have concluded that certain terrorist organizations realize that their strikes are more effective and deceptive when they are coordinated on an international level. In December 1972, for example, the Italian Interior Minister mentioned that an investigation conducted by the Italian police pointed to the presence of a shadowy extremist group which had organized and was responsible for terrorist actions at airports situated in Rome, Athens, Zurich, and Tel Aviv. Collectively these actions involved terrorists of various national origins and movements, acting as a team, and responsible for the deaths of approximately 80 persons.

TACTICAL AND LOGISTICAL ASPECTS OF COMBINED TERRORIST OPERATIONS

Italian police sources also report that Rome's metropolitan area once served as the center of a clandestine arms network operated by international terrorists, with hideaway apartments, an arsenal, and resident operators acting under plausible cover with large amounts of cash. On December 12, 1973, an automobile, driven by a Palestinian and equipped with secret compartments for smuggling arms, was stopped near the Italian border by French customs officials. Although the secret caches used for the transport of arms were empty, follow-up investigation led French police to a villa (safe house) in southwest Paris, where grenades and explosives were found along with equipment for making bombs, false identity cards, and passports. Reportedly, the villa had been rented several months earlier for use as a relay point and dormitory for the terrorists. The French sources also said that eight Turks, including two women, were inside the villa when the police arrived. Additionally, plastic explosives and hollowed out books for use as letter bombs by these terrorist groups were uncovered in Paris by the French police.[8]

---

[8] "Paris Arrests 13 in Terrorist Plot," *The New York Times*, December 26, 1973, p. 6.

Other information indicative of a worldwide combination of terrorists was hinted at in July 1973 by American intelligence services which reportedly traced numerous connections between the Japanese terrorist "Red Army," the Uruguayan Tupamaros, the Irish Republican Army (I.R.A.), the Turkish People's Liberation Army, the Italian "Red Brigades," and a number of other but lesser-known terrorist organizations. Reportedly, formal links were forged between the I.R.A. and the Arab Black September Group at a secret meeting held in Dublin between May 26th and May 28th, 1972. Arab arms, therefore, have frequently been moved into Ireland through Belgium and West Germany, and I.R.A. men have received terrorist training at Arab guerrilla camps in Syria and Libya.[9]

According to Belgian governmental sources, Soviet SAM–7 missiles were also once circulated through the same northwestern European network of routes used by the smugglers of the I.R.A. weapons. The Belgians mentioned, further, that several similar small ground-to-air missiles of western manufacture were stolen at about the same time from European military depots. The disappearance of these missiles, which can be carried in suitcases, was related to the general alert that went into effect at a number of European airports during the first week of January 1974, when reports indicated that Arab guerrillas were planning to attack an Israeli or an American plane.[10]

Various intelligence agencies continue to report that clandestine contacts among terrorist movements are facilitated by the maintenance of the "safe house" networks situated in Tokyo and various Middle Eastern and European cities. These facilities are used as the sites of secret meetings convened for the purpose of formulating action plans that contain elaborate "exchange attack" systems. The bombings by the I.R.A. which took place in 1974 in downtown London, while the British Army and the police cordoned Heathrow Airport in anticipation of an Arab terrorist assault, exemplify such a combined and coordinated terrorist action. There are reports that terrorist groups execute "exchange" attacks against a target, obviously of no significance to themselves, because they expect it may be designated for destruction by another group with which the target is usually associated. The assassination of the Uruguayan official by members of the Raul Sendic International Brigade is the first documented incident of this type.

[9] "British Suspect Tie Between the I.R.A. and Palestinians," *The New York Times*, January 4, 1974, p. 4.
[10] "Terrorism, Missile Alert," *Newsweek*, January 21, 1974, p. 45.

PATTERNS OF TERRORIST COOPERATION

Patterns of terrorist cooperation are no longer rare. In its heyday, the West German Baader–Meinhof gang helped the Japanese Red Army set up its European operations center in a perfume shop situated on the elegant Avenue de l'Opéra in Paris, and allegedly provided logistical support for the Red Army's most notorious operation, the massacre of 26 passengers at Lod Airport in Israel. On that occasion, three Japanese terrorists who had been trained in Japan and Lebanon were given false credentials in West Germany and Czechoslovakian weapons in Rome, and boarded a French airliner for Israel. This event was an astonishing and a complex instance of transnational terrorism.

Also, a few terrorist movements actually like to boast of their international connections. The Japanese Red Army has long espoused the cause of the Palestinians, the Palestinian guerrilla armies have talked in glowing terms of the I.R.A., and in turn the Irish gunmen have sympathized with the Basque Homeland and Liberty organization (E.T.A.). The Basques have discussed political revolution with representatives of Uruguay's Tupamaro organization in Germany (1974), and with the I.R.A. in Dublin. Meanwhile, exiled members of the Tupamaros in Paris have formed the "Junta for Revolutionary Coordination," which includes displaced elements of three other Latin American extremist groups who now live in Western Europe.[11]

THE TUPAMARO MODEL

Unfortunately, this pattern of violent radicalism, utilizing Tupamaro tactics, has become the scourge of the 1980s. Groups of skilled terrorists, organized along Tupamaro lines into cells, columns, and action groups to insure compartmentalization and anonymity, are now undertaking in various countries specific operations, such as bank robberies, killing of police, raids on sources of weapons and ammunition, and "symbolic bombings." Their former strategy of fronting with a broadly based movement or a mass demonstration, both of which were effectively exploited by extremist elements during the Vietnam era, for example, is no longer productive, and for the present seems to have been abandoned as a terrorist ploy. According to reports attributed to the Federal Bureau of

[11] Robert Fisk, "The World's Terrorists Sometimes Are United," *The New York Times*, August 17, 1975, p. 3.

Investigation (F.B.I.), "Terrorist revolutionaries in this country are more sophisticated now than ever before, better trained in handling explosives and more dedicated to violence." The same F.B.I. spokesman mentioned that terrorists once had a protective network of safe houses in the United States, similar to that used by European and Latin American terrorists.[12]

During the 1970s, the now defunct Weather Underground, a residual group of associates who were once known as simply Weathermen and who divorced themselves from the broadly based Students For a Democratic Society (S.D.S.) in 1969, was the most active of the American terrorist groups. This group claimed responsibility for approximately 20 politically motivated bombings in the United States, and issued a manual entitled *Prairie Fire*, the first document devoted specifically to urban guerrilla warfare in the United States. Cuban, Puerto Rican, Croatian, and other terrorist groups associated with nationalistic and ethnic causes continue to pose a threat to residents of American cities.

LIBYA'S ROLE AS A SUBVERSIVE CENTER

Military assistance has been given openly to terrorist groups by some governments, particularly Cuba and Libya. Among the favored recipients of Castro's largesse are Latin American and North American terrorist organizations, whereas Libya supports Islamic insurgent groups, among which are included the Muslim rebels in Chad, Palestinian units, and Filipino groups. The Irish Republican Army (I.R.A.) also has been supplied with Libyan arms, as Libya's leader, Colonel Qaddafi, contends that it represents "a little people fighting for their liberty against a great state." Consequently, it was no surprise when on April 7, 1973, British newspapers revealed that the Tripoli government had forwarded three shipments of between 3 and 7 tons apiece to the I.R.A. since December, 1971.[13]

The newpapers said that evidence of the Libyan connection with the I.R.A. was revealed as a consequence of the seizure by Irish security forces of 5 tons of weapons aboard a Cypriot gunrunning ship off the coast of southeast Ireland on March 29, 1971. The owner of the ship said that weapons had been loaded in Tripoli by uniformed Libyan army personnel. Irish authorities arrested six men on board the vessel, including Joe Cahill, who was at the time listed by the British army in

---

[12] "Terror Takes a New Turn in U.S.," *U.S. News & World Report*, March 17, 1975, p. 26.
[13] "Britain Halts Arms Flow to Libya after Seizing Guns Sent to I.R.A.," *BRIEF: Middle East Highlights*, April 1–15, 1973, p. 2.

Belfast as its "most wanted man." I.R.A. gunmen also received training in guerrilla warfare at a camp situated near Benghazi, Libya.[14]

On April 21, 1975, a parliamentary delegation from the Irish Republic, visiting Libya, failed to obtain a promise from the Tripoli government to stop backing the I.R.A. with weapons, supplies, and financial assistance. Far from agreeing, the Libyans wanted Ireland to support participation by the Palestine Liberation Organization (P.L.O.) in scheduled talks between the Arab states and representatives of the European Economic Community—a pledge the Irish parlimentarians said they could not make.[15]

Libyan money, also, is believed to be the reason behind a bloody spate of infighting within the American Black Muslim community which developed in the early winter of 1973. At the time, President Quaddafi rejected the request of the Nation of Islam (N.O.I.) for additional money to supplement an almost three-million-dollar short-term loan which it received from Libya in 1972. President Quaddafi stated that the request was rejected because he was convinced that the N.O.I. did not profess the orthodox (Sunni) variety of Islam, since it denied membership to white people.[16]

Consequently, some observers speculate that a February, 1974 shootout in Brooklyn, New York was initiated by members of the N.O.I. who were angry with members of a rival black Sunni Muslim group who described themselves as authentic Muslims, and thus eligible to petition the Libyans for the financial help which the N.O.I. was denied.

Sunni Muslims are the primary branch of orthodox Islam, and, as a consequence, place ultimate authority in the Koran and the practices and teachings of the prophet Muhammad, who they believe was the last prophet and messenger of Allah. Their group is open to all races, and claims an estimated membership in the New York metropolitan area of fifteen thousand people, mostly black converts. They regard the deceased Elijah Muhammad, former leader of the N.O.I., as an exemplary figure but do not acknowledge his claim to direct descent from the Prophet.[17]

Although many in the American black community now view open

---

[14] Ibid.

[15] "Libya Refuses to End Support of I.R.A.," BRIEF, Middle East Highlights, April 16–30, 1975, p. 4.

[16] "Shoothout Fatal to 4 Traced to Quarrel over Libyan Funds," The Jewish Week and American Examiner, February 16, 1974, p. 1.

[17] C. Gerald Fraser, "Elijah Muhammad Dead; Built Religious Body," The New York Times, February 26, 1975, p. 1.

warfare between the Sunni Muslims and the N.O.I. as unlikely, the police in several American cities have noticed a steady deterioration in relations between the two groups since the 1965 assassination of Malcolm X, who had converted from the N.O.I. to Sunni Islam. Between 1965 and 1975, approximately 25 persons were slain as a consequence of the ideological feud that once unsettled the Black Islamic community of the United States.

CUBA'S SUBVERSIVE ROLE

A substantial volume of documentary evidence indicates that Castro's Cuba was the primary training center for the cadres of terrorist groups who have wrought great havoc over the past several years in the United States and elsewhere. In 1968, for example, Mark Rudd, Jordan Ford, and Ralph Featherstone were among the personalities who traveled to Cuba from the United States. Rudd (who surrendered to the authorities on September 14, 1977) had returned to New York City to play a key organizational role in the student riots at Columbia University, and in the formation of the Weathermen. Ford on his return became one of the leaders of the violent demonstration at San Francisco State University, and Feathersone, before blowing himself up in an automobile accident, was a close confidant of black militant leader H. Rap Brown. Bernadine Dohrn, still part of the underground and a founder along with Rudd of the Weathermen, is another graduate of the Cuban terrorist and urban guerrilla warfare schools.[18]

In the early 1970s approximately fifteen hundred young Americans spent time in Cuba as members of an organization known as the "Venceremos Brigade." Ostensibly assembled as a gesture of solidarity with the Cuban people by demonstrating its willingness to help with the sugarcane harvest, the "Brigade" was organized by the Weathermen, and indoctrinated by Moscow-controlled Tricontinental Organization in Havana. All the contemporary left-wing American extremist organizations which are committed to violence and terrorism have been openly supported by the Cuban-directed Tricontinental Organization, and have evolved from one or more of the following organizations active in the 1970s: the Black Panther Party (B.P.P.), the Young Lords, the Chicano

[18] Subcommittee to Investigate the Administration of the Internal Security Act and Other Internal Security Laws of the Committee on the Judiciary, United States Senate, *The Assault on Freedom* (Washington, D.C.: U.S. Government Printing Office, 1971), pp. 124–35.

Liberation Movement, the Weathermen, and the Puerto Rican Independence Movement.[19]

During the course of investigations conducted by the United States
Internal Security Subcommittee in the 1970s, commanders of police bomb
squads rendered additional evidence regarding Cuba's role as a subversive center. The police officers told the Committee that the California-
based Symbionese Liberation Army (S.L.A.) (no longer active) and some
Puerto Rican extremists who planted bombs in New York City learned
their bombing techniques from either Venceremos Brigade members or
Cuban instructors. "The Puerto Ricans," for example, remarked the police officers, "travel to Cuba as tourists or on good-will missions and
learn bombing." When they come back home, "you know what hap-
pens." Puerto Rican bomb-squad officers have confirmed the remarks
by the police officers to the Subcommittee.[20]

The most dangerous of the Puerto Rican terrorist organizations probably also has ties with Cuba. In October 1975, this radical underground
group, calling itself the Fuerzas Armadas de Liberacion Nacional Puer-
toriquena (F.A.L.N.)—Armed Forces For The National Liberation of
Puerto Rico—took responsibility for nine early morning bomb explosions
against government buildings, corporate offices, and banks in New York,
Chicago, and Washington. Its objective is immediate independence for
Puerto Rico.[21] However, on April 4, 1980, the police arrested 11 persons
suspected in bombings by the Puerto Rican group, and announced that
they had broken "the hard core of Chicago elements of the F.A.L.N."

TERRORISM AND COMMUNISM

Reports pertaining to cooperation between international terrorist
groups indicate that the cunning and fanaticism of revolutionaries from
all over the world, irrespective of political shadings, is being utilized in
the common cause of helping one another destroy what each does not
like. Various groups which have distinguished themselves by ruthless-
ness in their own respective countries are represented in this new coalition of international terrorist groups. Consequently, the membership
roster of this collection of thugs listed a number of people who had had
prior experience in undertaking kidnappings, assassinations, and bank
robberies in their area of operations.

[19] Ibid.
[20] "Left-Wing Bombing Is Linked to Cuba," *The New York Times,* October 26, 1975, p. 8.
[21] David Vidal, "F.A.L.N. Organization Asks Independence for Puerto Rico," *The New York Times,* November 9, 1975, p. 35.

Although the terrorist coalition does not cooperate as an entity with revolutionary communism, protection for Arab terrorists in Eastern Europe and the Middle East is provided by a communist front organization known as the Arab Front for Participation in the Palestinian Resistance. Emerging in December 1972 from the Arab People's Conference for the Support of the Palestinian Revolution, held in Beirut, Lebanon, this front also provides protection for other members of the international terrorist coalition who were present at the Beirut meeting; for example, representatives of the Tupamaros and the Vietcong.

Members of this international terrorist coalition are apparently not able to undertake a joint action anywhere over a sustained period of time. It is suspected, though, that they meet and exchange ideas on a regular and formal basis within the confines of cities such as New York, Paris, London, and Rome. It has been noted that all the diverse movements to which the terrorists belong are essentially nationalistic in nature, with only a thin overlay of common ideology. Consequently, in the past there has seldom been any continuing and profitable contact between them. But the most recent evidence of connections between terrorist groups seems to indicate the beginnings of regular contacts which, on occasion, lead to exchanges of ideas and general cooperation on a particular action.

Meanwhile, the worldwide rampage of terrorism conducted by groups resembling the Paris-based International Terrorist Collective, also known as the Arab Armed Struggle Organization, continues. A Lebanese magazine, *Al Dyar*, has said that the Armed Struggle Organization is part of the Popular Front for the Liberation of Palestine (P.F.L.P.), and is linked to such organizations as the Baader–Meinhof gang in Germany and the Japanese Red Army. A 26 year-old Venezuelan, Carlos Martinez, known also as "Carlos" and "the Jackal," is the leader of the Armed Struggle Organization, and is hunted by the police of twelve nations for a string of murders and terrorist attacks. Carlos led the group that kidnapped the Middle Eastern oil minister from Vienna in December 1975. European police sources tracked him to Libya. His whereabouts, at the time of this writing, are unknown.[22]

With groups led by men such as the "Jackal" on the prowl, it is imperative that civilized society be capable of responding effectively to their bitter challenge. Transnational terrorism, therefore, provides the rationale for all nations to make a greater effort to think cooperatively.

---

[22] Bernard Weinraub, "Carlos Said to Go to Libya in a Deal with Terrorists," *The New York Times*, January 1, 1976, p. 1.

2

URBAN TERRORIST OPERATIONS

The tactics of the terrorist are particularly effective in urban areas, although many of the most frequently quoted guerrilla theorists express an almost pathological fear of the city. Castro believed that "the city was the cemetery of revolutionaries."[1]

However, most of the writings of these men are rather more like memoirs than a theoretical analysis of insurrectionary techniques. They tend to ignore the fact that a strategy that was successful in their case may not be appropriate in others, because of unique political climates, environmental differences, and historical circumstances. To ignore these factors is to negate the very essence of strategy. In strategic analysis, the objectives to be attained are considered in light of "certain unique elements, conditions, characteristics or peculiarities of a situation." In military analysis, these refer to "the physical conditions of the terrain attending the application of means"; in political analysis, "the framework has to be expanded to include social, political and economic as well as physicalecological factors."[2] Thus, it appears to be extremely foolhardy

---

[1] Regis Debray, *Revolution in the Revolution* (New York: Monthly Review Press, 1967), p. 69.

[2] Andrew C. Janos, "The Communist Theory of the State and Revolution," in *The Strategic Use of Political Violence*, ed. Cyril E. Black and Thomas P. Thornton (Princeton: Princeton University Press, 1970), p.38.

for insurgents simply to import a strategy or a set of tactics. Something which has been eminently successful in one place may prove to be an abysmal failure in another.

THE DISADVANTAGES OF URBAN TERRORIST OPERATIONS

Yet there are many tangible reasons for the reluctance of terrorists to operate in large urban areas. Foremost is the principle that a terrorist campaign should not be opened unless the insurgents can hold the initiative, attack selected targets at a time of their own choosing, and avoid battle when the odds are against them.[3] It is only by such tactics that they can hope to offset the technical advantages of the incumbent's forces. It is absolutely necessary to avoid being boxed in by the counterinsurgent forces. When this occurs, the technological sophistication of the incumbent's troops becomes the decisive factor.

This fear of being limited to a tightly circumscribed field of operations carries the most weight in arguments against urban terrorist operations. It has become axiomatic that through technical advantage the incumbent can block all avenues of escape and force the insurgents to stand and fight, a most undesirable position due to their technical inferiority. Also, because of the closeness of life in some cities, there are extreme limitations on the number of people that can be assembled secretly. Such a situation increases the incidence of potential informers, and necessitates a sophisticated security system.[4]

It can justifiably be argued that the conduct of primarily urban operations may cut the terrorists off from the masses, thus placing them at a decided disadvantage *vis-à-vis* the incumbent, who is free to influence the population virtually at will. In conjunction with this, the anonymity imposed by terrorist activities is really not conducive to the establishment of a leadership that can become known and admired by the population as a clear alternative to the government in power. Furthermore, the operating methods of the urban terrorists fail to create an image either of benevolence or of leadership.[5]

---

[3] Sir Robert Thompson, *Defeating Communist Insurgency: The Lessons of Malaya and Vietnam* (New York: Praeger Publishers, 1966), p.115.

[4] Raymond M. Momboisse, *Riots, Revolts and Insurrections* (Springfield, Ill.: Charles C Thomas), p. 471.

[5] Walter Laqueur, *Guerrilla:A Historical and Critical Study* (Boston: Little, Brown, & Company, 1976), pp.326–381.

THE ADVANTAGES OF URBAN TERRORIST OPERATIONS

These liabilities notwithstanding, other theorists recognize the possiblities which the urban environment offers for terrorist actions, since they appreciate the strategic importance of the cities to the incumbent. Large cities are recognized by insurgents as the administrative and commercial centers of regions. Thus, a significant disruption in an urban area is apt to have both a regional and a national impact. Also, cities have a symbolic value: here, where his power is most concentrated, the incumbent should be least vulnerable and most capable of maintaining order. A government that cannot enforce its will in areas where it is most powerful is shown to be inadequate as a governing agent.

Throughout World War II, for example, urban resistance movements played a significant role by emphasizing that point. Operating both alone and in conjunction with rural forces and regular armies, these clandestine organizations proved to be particularly bothersome to the Germans. The activities of the Danish and the Dutch, although exclusively urban in nature, were heavily weighted toward operations in large cities. The urban activities of the French resistance movement were a significant element in the liberation of Paris.[6]

There are, however, other characteristics of the urban environment which favor the terrorist. The urban landscape is as geographically complex as that of any rural setting; physical cover is multidimensional, owing to the walls, roofs, basements, and utility passages.[7] These topographical characteristics give the urban environment a vertical acreage and horizontal mileage that offer terrorists tactical protection.[8] Because of these spatial relationships, fighting is likely to take place in confined areas, where small numbers of men are able to stand against numerically superior forces.[9] The labyrinth of buildings, courtyards, and alleys is just as inaccessible to a stranger as any more natural and equally unfamiliar terrain. Furthermore, the logistical problems are not so great as in the countryside, since food and medical supplies are readily available from the corner store.

Also, the enemy's communications system is most vulnerable at centralized urban switching centers. Although specific targets can be

[6] Aage Roussell, *The Danish Resistance Movement 1940–1945* (Copenhagen: Royal Danish Ministry of Foreign Affairs, 1964), p. 14.
[7] Raymond M. Momboisse, *Blueprint of Revolution: The Rebel, the Party, the Techniques of Revolt* (Springfield, Ill.: Charles C Thomas, 1970), p. 282.
[8] Donald C. Hodges, *Philosophy of the Urban Guerrilla* (New York: William Morrow and Company, 1973), pp. 261–265.
[9] Momboisse, *Blueprint of Revolution*, p. 283.

safeguarded, "collectively downtown is vulnerable." Traffic, cable conduits, and normal business activities can be disrupted at locations and times of the terrorists' choosing.[10]

High illiteracy rates and large concentrations of rootless and frustrated people in cities enhance opportunities for terrorist propaganda and recruitment. Of equal importance, in cities it is easier for terrorists to blend with the population; it is extremely difficult, particularly in a free society, to maintain an adequate check on transients who frequent urban neighborhoods. Because the insurgents "can work through so many thousands of people . . . the enemy is made to feel him as an impalpable presence, until every ordinary pedestrian seems like a guerrilla in disguise."[11]

This constant uncertainty has a profound psychological impact on the police officer. He is constantly open to harassment, and yet he can trust no one, for the most innocuous person or incident can deal him a fatal blow. Added to his constant anxiety is the extreme difficulty experienced in seeking to implement counterinsurgent techniques in the city. The police cannot hope to initiate a comprehensive counterterrorist operation without arousing the ire of people thus inconvenienced.[12]

In April 1974, for example, the residents of San Francisco were horrified by the the twelfth "ZEBRA" killing . . . a designation derived from the "Z" radio band used by the police, who where ordered by Police Chief Donald Scott to become involved in a manhunt, which included a massive stop-and-search sweep. As a consequence of the sweep, hundreds of young black men were halted, interrogated, and "frisked" for weapons. When cleared, the blacks were given identification cards. As the police dragnet continued, however, a cry of bitter protest came from San Francisco's black community. Lawsuits demanding an end to the searches were filed by the National Association for the Advancement of Colored People (N.A.A.C.P.) and the American Civil Liberties Union (A.C.L.U.). On April 25, 1974, a federal judge granted a preliminary injunction severely restricting police action.

Even before the ruling, police backed down, announcing that the controversial operation was being restricted in scope, because it was unproductive and ineffective. Some citizens, mostly blacks, even began to look on policemen with fear, not as protectors.[13]

[10] J. Hobsbaum, "Cities and Insurrection," *Eckistrics* (May 1969), p. 208.

[11] Momboisse, *Blueprint of Revolution*, p. 283.

[12] Robert Daley, *Target Blue: An Insider's View of the N.Y.P.D.* (New York: Delacorte Press, 1973), pp. 412–445.

[13] "Frightened People and Frustrated Police," *U.S. News & World Report*, May 4, 1974, pp. 37–38.

Urban terrorists' actions are also likely to attract mass publicity because they are more difficult for the government to cover up or rationalize away.[14] Thus, they often succeed in politicizing the established government. The terrorist hopes that his action will cause the people to realize that their time is now, and that by militant action they can mold their destiny. Through the demonstrated effects of sustained terror, the insurgents thus try to raise the revolutionary consciousness of an entire people. In Frantz Fanon's *The Wretched of the Earth*, this idea of political agitation and terrorism acting as the catalyst for the awakening of the masses and the subsequent forging of the revolutionary mentality through the carrying out of armed struggle received its most elaborate treatment.[15]

It is important to note the circumstances under which urban terrorist campaigns most readily occur. These activities generally take place in countries whose topography tends to be flat, or consists mainly of deserts or plains rather than mountains or heavy forests, as these conditions usually preclude a full scale rural insurgency because of insurmountable problems relating to logistics, escape, and concealment. The introduction of technical improvements, principally helicopters, and the development of sophisticated infrastructural networks also give the counterinsurgent force a speed and mobility which would be difficult to counter. If the terrain is unsuitable and the incumbent's forces can move with great rapidity, it usually proves most difficult to launch a large-scale rural insurgency. In view of these limitations, the urban environment thus presents the best opportunities for launching a terrorist campaign, which is very different from a rural guerrilla struggle.

URBAN TERRORIST STRATEGISTS

On the basis of personal experience, Mao states that a guerrilla war must evolve through three stages of ever-increasing peasant-based rural activity, culminating in conventional warfare.[16] Guevara felt that the urban environment was unfavorable to large-scale guerilla groups and their free activity.[17] Both these men, however, assumed that, to be suc-

---

[14] Debray, *Revolution in the Revolution*, p. 56; Carlos Marighella,"Handbook of Urban Guerrilla Warfare," in idem, *For the Liberation of Brazil* (Harmondsworth, England: Penguin Books, 1971), p. 89.

[15] Frantz Fanon, *The Wretched of the Earth* (New York: Grove Press, 1968).

[16] Mao Tse-tung, *On Guerrilla Warfare* (New York: Praeger Publishers, 1961).

[17] Albert Parry, *Terrorism: From Robespierre to Arafat* (New York: Vanguard Press, 1976), pp. 249–251.

cessful, the guerrilla forces must be composed of large numbers of men, which each of them had. But other insurgent movements have been just as successful with far smaller numbers of men, the most notable examples being the Cypriot E.O.K.A. insurgents and the Tupamaros.

The Tupamaros conducted their operations largely within the confines of Montevideo, Uruguay, a city of some 1.25 million people, and they displayed a remarkable capacity to survive under urban conditions. In the 3 years between August 1968, when they committed their first political kidnapping, and August 1971, the Uruguayan police were unable to locate a single hostage. A former police chief estimated that their membership increased from about fifty active terrorists in 1965 to about three thousand in 1970.

What is the reason for this wide incongruity in revolutionary experience? One explanation may be the nature of the enemy: Mao and Castro fought fellow nationals, whereas the Cypriots battled a colonial power. However, the Tupamaros also fight and kill their own people. Another reason may be that the objective of the insurgents varies in each situation. The Chinese and the Cubans sought to defeat their opponents militarily. The Cypriots and the Tupamaros merely sought to raise the costs of governing until their opponents saw that the situation had become untenable and withdrew. Because of these fundamental differences, the tactics that each utilized were very different, as were the numbers of men involved in the armed struggle.

Thus, urban insurgency arises when guerrilla operations in the countryside are believed to be impractical, primarily because of a lack of a political base which the city provides. Some theorists regard the death of Che Guevara in the hills around Vallegrande, Bolivia, on October 8, 1967 as symbolic of the failure of rural guerrilla movements and the Guevara-Debray strategy as a whole. However, due to the inherent limitations imposed on insurgents when operating within the urban environment, actively engaged personnel must be kept at a minimum; and the strategic objective must be that of raising the costs of governing for the incumbent, rather than his actual military defeat. These two factors make the nature of the struggle significantly different from that of rural guerrillas.[18] For example, the Tupamaro terrorists lived at home, and only met with their comrades for the planning and the execution of operations. Instead of subsisting on donations and requisitions, they usually were gainfully employed, or, more ironically, subsisted on welfare.

But these differences are at best only superficial, and the real dif-

[18] Marighella, *Liberation of Brazil*, p. 65.

ference between urban and rural insurgency lies in the strategic realm. Owing to their small numbers, urban-based terrorists at best can only hope to raise the cost of governing for the incumbent so that he abdicates; or, they may precipitate the seizure of power by a clique which they find more to their liking. For them, to go beyond these objectives in the hope of inflicting an actual military defeat on the incumbent is foolish adventurism. Because of the limits imposed on the size and scope of operations by the environment and the objectives which can realistically be pursued, the principal tactics employed by urban insurgents are those most often associated with terror. Although all guerrilla organizations use terror to some extent, the urban insurgent uses it as his primary mode of operation. The destruction of an enemy involves breaking either his ability or his will to resist; thus, the nature of violence is both physical and psychological.

This modern pattern of revolutionary warfare has been derived from a conceptualization of force and violence, each step of which is designed to have a calculated psychological impact.[19] In this context, force is employed to demoralize the enemy more than to defeat him, as the insurgent seeks to create an atmosphere of fear and tension by placing the enemy in almost constant danger of death. The use of terror is most appropriate for an insurgent movement which must operate within the narrow confines of the city; by necessity it can have but a few active participants, and is thereby peculiarly suited for the quick execution and rapid disengagement which are required for urban fighting.

"Terror is a symbolic act designed to influence political behavior by extranormal means."[20] It is symbolic because its impact is usually of much greater significance than the actual material deed: "The real target of terrorist intent is the group or person to be propagandized, not the victim who is beyond propaganda effect if the act is successful."[21] For this reason, terror produces results far in excess of the time and resources expended on it, for while "it kills individuals . . . it intimidates thousands."[22] Furthermore, by the use of terror the insurgents hope to create a certain atmosphere which will lend credibility to their threat to the incumbent regime.

Consequently, the use of terror entails more than the impairment of the enemy's will to fight. It seeks to build the morale both of the

---

[19] George Janos, "Communist Theory of the State and Revolution," in Black and Thornton, *Political Violence*, p. 39.

[20] Thomas P. Thornton, "Terror as a Weapon of Political Agitation," in *Internal War-Problems and Approaches*, ed. Harry Eckstein (New York: Free Press, 1974), p. 73.

[21] Ibid., p. 79.

[22] Leon Trotsky, *The Defense of Terrorism-Terrorism and Communism: A Reply to Karl Kautsky* (London, 1935), p. 55. (street pamphlet)

insurgent forces and of the wider masses, by demonstrating through daring acts that the incumbent is not unassailable, Terror, with the publicity that results from it, serves to advertise the existence of an organization which is actively contending the right and the ability of the incumbent to govern. By the suddenness and the unpredictability of his attacks, the terrorist thus seeks to disorient the society by eliminating the sense of stableness which surrounds daily life. Such action helps to isolate the individual, while demonstrating that the incumbent is unable to maintain order. Finally, by such acts of outrage the insurgent hopes to provoke countermeasures by the incumbent, which usually redound to his advantage. For example, to counter the terrorist the incumbent must inconvenience the entire population through searches, endless questioning, and, inevitably, some false arrests. These activities only serve to intensify existing social tensions.[23]

MODERN WARFARE

Although the actions which the terrorist could conceivably perform are as numerous as the diabolical thoughts of man, they can be categorized in a hierarchy of intensity. The first category is labeled "material terror," and contains all acts of sabotage and disruption. Although "no government can protect all potential targets, failure to protect any symbolically significant target can be used as a demonstration of weakness."[24] The second category, termed "personal terror," includes acts committed against individual members of the incumbent regime and its supporters and armed forces. Finally, this progression of violence culminates in "total terror," acts against the general public which demonstrate the inability of the present regime to maintain the public order that is necessary for normal life and business activity.[25] Total terror creates such extreme anxiety that the people hope for any settlement of hostilities, so long as it brings peace.[26] The objective of this spiraling violence is to sustain a state of confusion and destruction, whose effect is to induce "a state of panic and thus dislocate, if not completely stop, the normal process of life."[27]

The goal of modern warfare is to gain control of the population.

[23] Thornton, "Terror as a Weapon," pp. 82–86.
[24] Ibid., p. 88.
[25] Richard H. Sanger, *Insurgent Era: New Patterns of Political, Economic and Social Revolution* (Washington, D.C.: Potomac Books, 1967), p. 21.
[26] Carl Leiden and Karl M. Schmitt, *The Politics of Violence: Revolution in the Modern World* (Englewood Cliffs, N.J.: Prentice-Hall, 1968), p. 26.
[27] Momboisse, *Blueprint of Revolution*, p. 285.

Consequently, attacks on the political structure, bureaucracy, and police apparatus serve the twin function of breaking the government's control mechanism and destroying the necessary political supports for daily life. The police and the military forces are continually in action, yet do not achieve results which are consistent with their efforts and with the inconvenience which their operations impose on the population.[28] This state of affairs may precipitate a crisis of government, because the citizen living under a constant threat to his life comes to feel that he is an isolated and defenseless target. Thus, the state, failing to demonstrate that it can adequately ensure public safety, causes citizens to lose confidence in public authority, and to shift their allegiance to the insurgents, because they can, at least, better guarantee protection.[29]

One of the effects of terrorism is to force the incumbent into an ever-increasing expenditure on security. In this situation, the goal of the insurgent is not to achieve an actual military victory, but rather to precipitate a political situation which renders further military operations untenable. The principal task of terrorism, therefore, is to make repression so costly that the government will prefer to withdraw, rather than continue the struggle.[30] In such an event, the military forces are reduced to undertaking police-like operations to ferret out the insurgents in a reactive way, while desperately trying to maintain internal political stability. They cannot perform both tasks.

[28] Colonel de Rocquigny, "Urban Terrorism," in *Revue Militaire d'Information* (February, 1958), summarized in *Military Review* (February, 1959), p. 94.
[29] Roger Trinquier, *Modern Warfare* (New York: Praeger Publishing, 1964), p. 16.
[30] Thornton, *Terror as a Weapon*, p. 79.

ORGANIZATION AND MANAGEMENT PRACTICES OF URBAN TERRORIST GROUPS

A terrorist organization, existing for a specific purpose and mission, is a social unit (human grouping), deliberately constructed, which manages to achieve rational cooperation as it pursues specific goals. Consequently, ideological commitment by members of a terrorist group to the goals of their organization is necessary for organizational survival. For this purpose, results to be achieved by terrorist propaganda and armed actions are expressed in terms of goals.[1] Used in this broad sense, goals of a terrorist organization would include such things as objectives, purposes, missions, deadlines, targets, and quotas. Goals, therefore, are a vital link in the administration of a terrorist organization, as they aid in decentralization, provide a basis for voluntary coordination, become a focus for individual motivation, and also are essential elements in the process of control.[2]

ARTICULATING THE GOALS OF A TERRORIST ORGANIZATION

Bent on influencing human behavior by extranormal means (bombings, kidnappings, assassinations, etc.) through the use or threat of

---

[1] Peter F. Drucker, *Management: Tasks, Responsibilities, Practices* (New York: Harper & Row, 1974), pp. 40–41.
[2] William H. Newman, *Administrative Action: The Techniques of Organization and Management* (Englewood Cliffs, N.J.: Prentice-Hall, 1963), pp. 18–22.

25

violence, contemporary terrorist groups seek to camouflage themselves as zealous patriots whose only credible options are the "bullet or the bomb." A terrorist organization tries to avoid, therefore, undertaking any action which might fall beyond the ambit of a real or a contrived popular cause.

For example, a major political casualty of the collision between Boeing 747 "jumbo jets" on the congested, fogbound Los Rodeos airstrip at Tenerife, Canary Islands, in April 1977 was the Movement for the Self-Determination and Independence of the Canary Archipelago (M.P.A.I.A.C.). Until the crash, which took more than 570 lives, M.P.A.I.A.C. was considered little more than a somewhat violent nuisance—"an extreme expression of the grievances of the neglected, backward Spanish Canary provinces in the Atlantic."[3]

But M.P.A.I.A.C. and its leader Antonio Cubillo became figures in the aviation disaster after the explosion of a bomb placed by a terrorist cell in a florist shop at the Los Palmas airport exploded and wounded eight persons. The same explosion caused the diversion of the 747s to Tenerife, and thereby contributed to the conditions which led to the crash. The tragedy was followed by a powerful backlash against M.P.A.I.A.C., as expressed vocally a few days after the incident by a crowd gathered in the main square of Los Palmas to denounce violence, shouting, "autonomy yes, terrorism no."[4]

TARGET-ASSESSMENT TECHNIQUES

Terrorists are further aware that the indiscriminate use of terror is self-defeating. They try to assess beforehand the propaganda impact that an attack against a particular target will have on a specific audience, and avoid undertaking an armed attack until the preliminary operations of site reconnaissance and target analysis are completed. These operations are necessitated by the need for terrorists to be provided with assurances that the fatalities or injuries which might be caused by their attacks will be explainable in terms of their organizational goal, and not serve as a testament of their exceptional and uncivilized behavior.

An act of terror is designed to attract the mass media, and is undertaken to influence a predetermined target audience. Undertaken by a relatively obscure group, for example, the Hanafi Muslims or the Croatians, the terrorist act is intended to enhance the fearsome image of its

[3] James M. Markham, "Wreck of 747's Sets Back Cause of Insurgents on Canary Islands," *The New York Times*, April 2, 1977, p. 5.
[4] Ibid.

initiators. A formidable and well-publicized terrorist group, however, views a terrorist act as a means of further conditioning its target audience through the use of armed propaganda.

The primary target of a terrorist is always an aggregate of people who share certain predispositions which may assist the terrorist group in attaining its organizational goal. Consequently, the F.A.L.N. (Fuerzas Armadas de Liberacion Nacional Puertoriquenas, or, Armed Forces of Puerto Rican National Liberation) has undertaken a calculated campaign of nighttime pipe bombings of corporate and government structures in New York and Chicago, to emphasize their disdain for "*Yanki* Imperialism." Intended to influence extremist members of the "independentista" portion of the Puerto Rican community who live in these cities, the structures bombed must be symbolic in the eyes of the intended audience of "capitalist exploitation." The strategic purpose of F.A.L.N. terrorism, therefore, is to emphasize the viability of the cause of Puerto Rican independence to its advocates, and dissuade corporate investment in the island, thereby displacing the island's economy and creating related unhealthy conditions suitable for manipulation by trained agents.

Anti-Castro Cuban extremists, for another example, attack targets that enhance the power and prestige of the Havana government. On December 20, 1977, Omega–7, a Cuban exile terrorist group, claimed responsibility for the bombing of a Union City, New Jersey, warehouse where pharmaceuticals were packaged for shipment to Cuba. The warehouse was targeted as a consequence of its obvious pro-Castro significance, and the propaganda impact that its destruction would have on the Cuban exiles inhabiting the New York metropolitan area.

Both the F.A.L.N. and the anti-Castro terrorists target United States government facilities, calculating that sympathetic support from officials in Washington, D.C., will result in the eventual enactment of legislation and adoption of policies favorable to their ends. Fidel Castro's involvement in African affairs, for example, triggered a series of bombings by anti-Castro groups in the United States, intended to remind Congress of his threat to American national interests, and thereby to promote a modification of the Carter administration's policy of closer relations with Cuba.

THE CELL: BASIC BUILDING BLOCK OF A TERRORIST ORGANIZATION

Urban terrorists, waging a protracted program of armed actions, organize themselves in a cellular type of structure which has for its core a group of persons who know each other as a consequence of marriage, friendship, or employment. Traditionally, this core is enveloped by a circle of sympathizers, which includes associates who take part together in demonstrations, protest meetings, dissemination of propaganda pamphlets, and other related forms of "street-type" political activities. Terrorist cells, therefore, are initially homogeneous, with some social, professional, religious, or political basis for association, and are formed spontaneously from within. The organizing talent of the foreign agent, however, better provided with resources, training, direction, and orders, and acting as a recruiting agent, should not be discounted.

Cells, furthermore, are formed by terrorists for the purpose of assigning specific units to perform certain tasks, and thereby overcoming the inherent weakness usually associated with a popular-based movement or party—the lack of specialization. "Ill-defined in outline, uncertain in numbers, amorphous in structure, brittle and unstable, splitting more easily than they coalesced," parties and movements are subjected to penetration and disruption by individuals who are inimical to their policies and programs, and are therefore rejected by terrorists, who prefer a more clandestine type of organization.[5] Members of terrorist cells, therefore, should be regarded as being technically competent in their particular area of specialized assignments (i.e., assassination, sabotage, or hijacking), and skilled in communications, security, and weaponry. Contemporary terrorists are also knowledgeable in the tactics of escape and evasion, and many have acquired the discipline needed to live outwardly a normal life while actively involved in operations.

In Northern Ireland, the I.R.A. once issued a regulation which specifically stated that a member must not keep arms on his person, or in any place which could be associated with him. All I.R.A. arms were secreted in central places. Thus, as a prerequisite to arrest, the British army or police had to stake out the arms cache, and apprehend the terrorist as he withdrew a weapon from the cache for a specific operation. Aware of this British tactic, the I.R.A. began a practice of countersurveilling its arms caches with teenagers and women. Organizational discipline approximating this degree of harshness is not characteristic of popular-based movements and parties.[6]

THE CONCEPT OF COLUMNAR ORGANIZATION

An effective administrative and support structure is another prerequisite for a terrorist group which seeks to challenge the government

[5] Henri Michel, *The Shadow War: European Resistance 1939–1945* (New York: Harper & Row, 1972), pp. 102–107.
[6] "In the Shadow of the Gunmen," *Time*, January 10, 1972, pp. 30–40.

for control of an urban area. Consequently, terrorist leaders work to harmonize relations between support and operating units, establishing thereby services with staffs to manage such functions as recruitment, propaganda, and safe houses. The day-to-day existence of operational cells is dependent on these genuine services.

Supply is also a problem, as it forces terrorists to maintain an aboveground support unit for this purpose in a city; and money, always a vital commodity, is needed to purchase supplies and equipment, and to issue a minimum pay to colleagues who are heads of families. Terrorist organizations are often actively involved, therefore, in bank robberies, extortion, kidnappings for ransom, and other activities from which cash can be obtained to sustain their operations.

Since the cells of a large urban terrorist movement are unable to handle their own logistical tasks while simultaneously maintaining their clandestine style of operation, they rely on a columnar style of organization to offset this disadvantage. (The term "column" is derived from the designation used for the "fifth column" sabotage units which operated during the Spanish Civil War. It was also used as a name for the major subdivisions of Fidel Castro's Cuban guerrilla army, each of which was assigned to conduct operations in a specific geographical area. Tupamaro combat columns in Montevideo used numerical identifiers. Column 7 [also known as "collar"] formed a ring around the city through its suburbs. Column 10 operated in the downtown area, and Column 15 was responsible for the rest of the city. Two specialized columns, Column 45, which handled logistics, and Column 70, which was responsible for intelligence and political affairs, were also formed by the Tupamaros.)[7]

Urban terrorist columns, usually consisting of between 50 and 300 members, are assigned a specific military, support, or political task, and are divided into a number of sectors, which are in turn subdivided into cells of 3 to 10 members each. Generally, specialized columns are formed to handle logistics, recruitment and training, intelligence and political affairs; such was the task of a captured Tupamaro medical column in Montevideo that ran a complete underground medical center.[8]

Columns are not decisionmaking entities, but administrative units which facilitate and coordinate the actions of the individual cells contained within them. There is usually no column leader, and no hierarchical relationship within a column; information flows from the cell

---

[7] Jay Mallin, The Military vs. Urban Guerrillas, Exhibit No. 14, *Terrorism, Part 2, Hearings before the Committee on Internal Security House of Representatives 93rd Congress, Second Session,* U.S. Government Printing Office, Washington, 1974, pp. 3285–3286.

[8] Ibid.

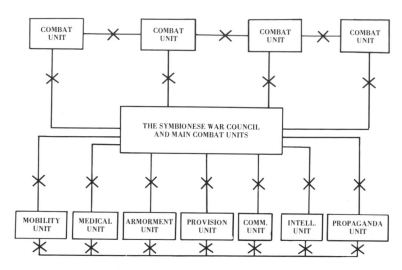

Figure 1. S.L.A. Urban Terrorist Organization Structure, X = Dead Drops and/or Cut Outs (modified from Exhibit No. 17 on page 4039 of *Terrorism Part 3*, Committee on Internal Security, U.S.G.P.O., Washington, 1974).

through its leader to the top level of a terrorist organization, and vice versa. Contact among cells within the same column is restricted in accordance with the principle of compartmentalization, which prohibits the supplying of information to any single terrorist beyond what is needed for him to be operational. Therefore, members of a column do not know each other, and communicate through a system of "dead drops," usually post-office boxes, airport lockers, or public telephones. Consequently, the lines diagramming a terrorist structure are marked at intervals with an X indicating a "dead drop" or a "cutout."

Often contact between the cells themselves is "cut out," and only the cell leader, if anyone, knows how to contact other cell leaders within the same column.[9] (A diagram of a terrorist organization with cutouts appears as Figure 1.)

The cell–column type of clandestine organization is particularly suited for use by a broadly based terrorist movement which, because of its size, has to be particularly cautious of infiltration by the police, and of the possibility that its captured colleagues would provide law-enforcement agencies with information that would lead to the arrest of

[9] "Terms of Military/Political Alliance and the Symbionese War Council" Exhibit No. 17, *Terrorism, Part 3*, Hearings before the Committee on Internal Security House of Representatives, 93rd Congress, Second Session, U.S. Government Printing Office, Washington, 1974, pp. 4037–4058.

other members of the organization. In addition, the "cutout" system insures that terrorists do not know each other's true identity, that communication from different cells is minimized to include only task assignments and operational orders, and that movement is relatively secure.

TERRORIST COMMAND COUNCILS

Urban terrorist organizations conducting citywide operations on a regular basis establish upper-level councils, to provide overall military and political direction for their programs, and to create and eliminate a cell, column, or any other unit, as they deem necessary. The National Liberation Front (F.L.N.), aware that a structure different from the one it used in rural areas was needed for its urban operations, established a separate command for its people in Algiers, which it called the Autonomous Zone of Algiers (Z.A.A.). This structure resembles the "National Direction" used by Fidel Castro to coordinate his struggle in Havana, and the "Executive Committee" established by the Tupamaros to direct their columns in Montevideo.

All three of these bodies included the national leader and the chief coordinators of the urban movements, but operated under a council whose decisions reflected the consensus of its members. Concerned with the overall military and political direction of an urban terrorist movement, but primarily involved with target selection, operational planning, and the establishment of priorities, members of these councils, whose names are held confidential, may or may not live underground, and need not work full-time for a terrorist movement. Figure 1 indicates that the Symbionese Liberation Army (S.L.A.) aspired to the use of an overall command structure to coordinate the activities of its secondary combat units and support columns. The S.L.A. unit was called the Symbionese War Council and Main Combat Units.[10]

ASPECTS OF TERRORIST RECRUITMENT AND DISCIPLINE

Although the internal organization of all urban terrorist groups is primarily designed to facilitate clandestine operations, it provides a se-

[10] For the F.L.N., see Roger Trinquier, *Modern Warfare* (New York: 1964), pp. 10–15; on the Tupamaros, see Arturo C. Porzecanski, *Uruguay's Tupamaros: The Urban Guerrilla* (New York: 1973), pp. 32–37; the Cuban model is described by Norman A. La Charité, *Case Studies in Insurgency and Revolutionary Warfare, Cuba 1953–1959* (Washington, D.C.: 1963), pp. 71–117. The S.L.A. organization is described in *Terrorism, Part 2* (Washington, 1974), pp. 4037–4058.

cure means of recruiting personnel. For a terrorist organization, selection of personnel is a rigorous and lengthy process, designed to screen out those who lack caution and prudence, and others who might serve the police as informers, or perhaps be undercover police officers. Liberal recruitment methods could cost the lives of comrades, and/or jeopardize the success of a future operation.

The most essential character traits needed by people engaged in terror operations are discipline, endurance, technical expertise, and willingness to work within a semimilitary command system. Tupamaro instruction sheets written for recruits contain the following remarks: "Remember that your worst enemies are boasting, the lack of discretion, the lack of discipline and gossiping. Don't ask, don't tell, and don't let anyone talk you into anything. If you are not discreet and feel swayed to talk about what you do, then all your other qualities become worthless."[11]

Preliminary to being assigned to a basic training program consisting of paramilitary skills, a terrorist recruit is usually subjected to an exhaustive background investigation, which includes a documented report prepared by his sponsor. During basic training, a recruit attends indoctrination sessions, and is assigned to a support column. Eventually he is given an opportunity for increased participation in activities that carry greater responsibility and increased risk.[12] Thus, the enforcement of internal discipline for the sake of organizational survival and efficiency within a terrorist group must be ruthlessly effective, and the life itself is harsh.

Safe houses, uncovered by the police, reveal that a terrorist lives a cloistered life which is characterized by lack of comfort, absence of expendable income, and denial of leisure activity and personal privacy. Food, weapons, clothing, and propaganda materials, however, are usually adequate. A terrorist who is unable or ill-equipped to cope with life in the underground is sometimes recruited. For that reason, terrorist organizations of the F.L.N. or Tupamaro variety have established specialized enforcement units and attached them to their command councils for the purpose of executing sentences pronounced by a "revolutionary judiciary" on those who attempt to leave the organization, or others who are found guilty of some other serious breach of discipline. Organized crime families in America, similarly specialized, include a person known as "The Enforcer," who reports directly to the Don or "Boss" for all matters related to internal family discipline.[13]

[11] Prozecanski, *Uruguay's Tupamaros*, p. 35.

[12] Ibid, p. 35.

[13] Frederick D. Homer, *Guns and Garlic: Myths and Realities of Organized Crime* (West Lafayette, Ind.: Purdue University Press, 1974) pp. 94–138.

However, a terrorist is not superhuman, and the very austerity of his life may cause even a committed one unwittingly to violate the basic security principles of clandestine operations. In the spring of 1976, two I.R.A. gunmen, their judgment apparently impaired by overimbibing at a pub, led British crime-squad officers to what they thought was a "safe" address in Liverpool. In seems, however, that another terrorist had ordered the displacement of a cache of arms and explosives from a house in Manchester to the same address. Shortly before the guns arrived by hired car, the Special Branch of the British police had "staked out" the Liverpool residence. Intemperance on the part of the Liverpool-based I.R.A. gunmen, therefore, resulted not only in their own apprehension by the police, but also in the arrest of the terrorist from Manchester, and the seizure of a stock of arms and explosives as well.[14] Thus, the size and scope of an urban terrorist movement is often dependent on its ability to enforce internal security measures and to prevent sheer size from exposing its organization to infiltration by police informers or undercover operatives.

Communist-controlled terrorist groups utilize a "triangular system" of internal controls to guard against this menace. This system contains three appointed commissars, one for personnel, one for operations, and one for miscellaneous services, who oversee the activities of the cells, and thereby prevent them from becoming gangs bent on undertaking independent activity to satisfy the taste of a particular group of members for action or revenge. It is anticipated, therefore, that the commissars of the triangular system have contacts, as needed, with members of specialized enforcement squads.[15]

For minor infractions of disciplinary codes, some terrorist organizations impose punishments, such as the deprivation of tobacco, food, sex, or a weapon. An S.L.A. pamphlet entitled *Terms of Military/Political Alliance* contains a section entitled "Penalty By Disciplinary Action," which prescribes the denial of these very items. It is most difficult, however, for terrorists to enforce these sanctions which they impose on their associates, and thus they may regard them more as penance than penalty.[16]

THE 26TH-OF-JULY MOVEMENT IN HAVANA

The 26th-of-July Movement, the urban arm of Fidel Castro's rural-based guerrillas which dealt primarily in sabotage and other forms of

[14] Malcomb Pithers, "Wine Argument Uncorks a Bloody IRA Terror Trail," from the *Manchester Guardian* as reprinted in *The Star Ledger* (Newark, N.J.), June 1, 1976, p. 26.
[15] Michel, *The Shadow War*, pp. 102–118.
[16] *Terrorism, Part 3*, p. 4034.

subversive and disruptive operations in Cuban cities, is an excellent example of the cellular/columnar form of organization. Its operations were planned by a combined staff composed of the chief coordinators of the urban columns situated in all Cuba's principal cities. This staff was responsible for the organization and control of urban terrorist sections composed of three cells, of three persons each, and a section leader. All sections were attached to columns, and task-oriented and trained for specialized operations (i.e., destruction of industrial plants, communications systems, and public utilities). Eventually, the 26th-of-July Movement embraced the overwhelming majority of all who actively participated in the Cuban revolution, and its efficacy forced Batista to maintain the bulk of his security forces n the cities, thereby forfeiting the countryside, and finally the entire island, to Castro.

Important logistic functions for this movement were performed by a separate column, known as the Civic Resistance Movement (C.R.M.). Composed of three major sections, propaganda, fundraising, and supply, all of which were subdivided into cells of approximately ten persons each, the C.R.M. acted as a conduit for funneling support to urban and rural assault units.

The Cubans used an overseas underground network, composed of exiles living in the United States, Puerto Rico, and several Latin American countries, to distribute propaganda, gather information, solicit funds, and smuggle arms.[17] Miami once contained an important Fidelist network, and perhaps still does, although various anti-Castro groups also operate out of Florida.[18]

THE F.L.N. AND THE CITY OF ALGIERS

The Algerian F.L.N. emphasized urban terrorism, and for this purpose it split the city of Algiers into regions, divided into sectors that were further subdivided into districts. Responsible for a specific number of city blocks, and supported by supply and service columns, each district became the F.L.N.'s basic unit for urban attack in a specific locale, and was analogous, therefore, both in structure and in mission, to similar organizations within the Cuban 26th-of-July Movement.[19]

---

[17] La Charité, *Case Studies*, pp. 4037–4058.
[18] "Castro Threatens Pact with U.S. on Hijackings," *The New York Times*, April 20, 1976, p. 3, and "Castro Foes Set Off Blast," *The Star Ledger* (Newark, N.J.), June 7, 1976, p. 2.
[19] Trinquier, *Modern Warfare*, pp. 10–15.

THE TUPAMARO ORGANIZATION IN MONTEVIDEO

"Combatants," working full-time as terrorists and living clandestinely, were organized in cells and used for armed military actions by the Tupamaros in Montevideo. Cell members did not know each other's true identity, and they were given nicknames and false identification papers from the very beginning of the recruiting process. Noncombatant columns were organized and used to support the "combatant" network with consumable supplies: food, clothing, arms and ammunition, and specialized requirements. Vehicle repair, explosives manufacture, medical assistance, and the resolution of transportation and communication problems were handled by units organized for these specific tasks. The terrorist organizations in Havana, Algiers, and Montevideo were markedly similar.

One unique aspect of the Tupamaro organization, however, was its reliance on "peripherics" and "sympathizers" for various critical tasks. "Peripherics," living aboveground and working part-time for the terrorist organization, distributed propaganda, recruited new members, developed sources of information, and served as links between full-time members of the terrorist organization and "sympathizers." The Tupamaros counted on their "sympathizers" for arms, ammunition, information, and medical and legal aid. Each cell, whether commando-type or service-oriented, established contacts with its own particular group of "peripherics" and "sympathizers," and utilized information obtained from these sources to make suggestions to the Tupamaro Executive Committee regarding operations.[20]

SAN FRANCISCO BAY AREA TERRORISTS

Groups that once conducted terrorist operations in the San Francisco Bay area of the United States were aware of the traditional techniques of terrorist organization, and aspired therefore to the establishment of cells and columns. Among the terrorist groups once identified with the American west coast are the Symbionese Liberation Army (S.L.A.), now defunct, and the New World Liberation Front (N.W.L.F.), which unleashed attacks against corporate targets, International Telephone and Telegraph and the Pacific Gas and Electric Company bearing the brunt of their assaults.

[20] Porzecanski, *Uruguay's Tupamaros*, pp. 34–35.

N.W.L.F. worked hard at image building, and utilized its aboveground propaganda publication *The Urban Guerrilla (T.U.G.)* to explain why it selected certain corporate facilities for destruction. For example, an article in an issue of *T.U.G.* compiled by the N.W.L.F.'s "Intelligence Unit" contained a strategic intelligence summary of Pacific Gas and Electric, its history and corporate connections, the business interests of its board of directors, and "its crimes against the people."[21]

Additional evidence of the N.W.L.F.'s calculated effort to attract sympathizers was the naming of its cell, which claimed responsibility for the bombing of a Pacific Gas and Electric facility near San Jose, California, during January 1977, after a cold-weather victim in Ohio. The N.W.L.F. cell said that it called itself the Eugene Kuhn Unit in memory of an old man who lived on social-security payments, and who froze to death in his home because his utilities had been turned off for nonpayment of an $18 monthly bill.[22]

According to Figure 1, the S.L.A. leaders aspired to develop a broadly based popular insurgent movement, and planned to have their combat units supported by seven aboveground service units or columns, and its column commanders subservient to the United Symbionese War Council. The degree of specialization outlined on the S.L.A.'s organizational chart indicates that this terrorist group planned to expand the size and sophistication of its clandestine network, as evidenced both by the number of special units created, and the extent to which each unit had exclusive responsibility for the performance of tasks within a special field.

For example, the S.L.A. envisaged that expansion of its operations would require the support of a mobility column responsible as follows:

1. Movement of Supplies:

   It is the responsibility of The Mobility Unit for the movement of supplies and military personnel and the necessary equipment needed to safely move said personnel and supplies.

2. Providing Cover and Concealment:

   It is responsible for the safe movement of supplies between other units and to and from the combat units, and providing needed hiding places and disguises necessary in the movement of combat elements, and supplies and equipment.

---

[21] "Underground Documents: Corporate Bloodsuckers," *Counterforce*, March 1977, pp. 15–16.

[22] "Memorandum," *Counterforce*, March 1977, p. 9–10.

3. Storage of Supplies:

It is also responsible for the receiving and decentralized stocking of those supplies and equipment under its authority and which combat forces have found to be in excess of their supplies after expropriation operations.

4. Safe houses:

The building of hideouts for hiding personnel and supplies, the acquiring of apartments and houses that will serve from time to time the needs of combat units in operations in different areas of the state and other states as actions allow.

5. Vehicles:

a. The acquiring, building and camouflaging of vans, buses, and other means to allow safe movement of supplies and personnel.

b. Arming and armor plating of said type autos and the building of means of concealment for supplies and personnel, to also build defense systems into said autos, such as oil, smoke, and nail release systems.

c. Maintaining of autos in top condition and giving them top speed and drive ability at the same time bulletproofing and tires, etc.

6. Credentials and Disguises:

Acquiring, decentralized stocking and receiving and providing of phony and real I.D. papers, uniforms of movement, such as disguises for mailmen, priest, gas man, policemen, nun, army, navy, air force, wigs, shoes, and type said equipment, parts to repair autos, gas and oil facilities, tires, and power generating equipment for tools.[23]

A CRITIQUE OF THE TERRORIST STYLE OF ORGANIZATION

Essentially, the complex organizational structures used by terrorists are designed to facilitate the undertaking of an effective and efficient program of specialized armed actions in urban areas by clandestine armed cells. These structures contain a hierarchical command system, "dead drops" and "cutouts" to ensure a terrorist's physical survival, and specialized columns which fulfill basic organizational needs: recruits, weapons, vehicles, supplies, information, propaganda, and other necessities. A terrorist organization also contains an enforcement apparatus, to ensure internal discipline, and to establish evaluation tech-

---

[23] *Terrorism, Part 3*, p. 4055.

niques to identify individual talent and commitment, and thereby make possible an elaborate division of labor among individuals involved in full-time and part-time work.

But a compartmentalized structure has disadvantages. Once an armed cell is involved with other cells in an operation which is temporarily disrupted by a sudden climatic change, a police action, or a missed rendezvous, it is most difficult to reestablish control, since terrorists from different cells do not know each other. A terrorist must have an ego which permits him to render great obedience to an unknown leader, and plan for operations which he is not permitted to undertake without permission from a higher authority. Consequently, a terrorist organization cannot move without the absolute and unswerving cooperation of all its members. Thus, compartmentalization, which facilitates the survival of a terrorist organization on the one hand, is its major operational liability on the other.

ABRAHAM GUILLEN'S RECOMMENDATIONS

Abraham Guillen, a Latin American authority on the strategy and tactics of the urban guerrilla, is highly critical of any organizational structure which fixes a terrorist group to a terrain. He explains that the terrorists can best survive "not by establishing fixed urban bases, but by living apart and fighting together." Apparently accepting Guillen's remark, the I.R.A. adopted the organizational strategy of insisting that its gunmen either be gainfully employed or live on welfare, thus preventing their presence in a neighborhood from being regarded by police patrols as suspicious.

Concerning safe-house networks, Guillen mentions that guerrillas must spread out among a favorable population, and not rely on concealment in rented houses or in those of sympathizers.[24] Guillen also cautions terrorists about the dangers of relying on columns for housing, food, medical supplies, transport, and ammunition. He remarks:

> If the guerrillas are regularly employed, they should live as everybody else does and come together only at designated times and places. Houses that serve as barracks or hideouts tend to immobilize the guerrillas and to expose them to the possibility of encirclement and annihilation.[25]

[24] Donald C. Hodges, *Philosophy of the Urban Guerrilla: The Revolutionary Writings of Abraham Guillen* (New York: William Morrow & Co., 1973), pp. 229–277.
[25] Ibid.

CARLOS MARIGHELLA'S CAUTIONS

Carlos Marighella, in his *Minimanual of the Urban Guerrilla*, also recognized that the mobility-column personnel are particularly visible to police surveillance:

> One must avoid rescue or transfer of prisoners with children present, or anything to attract the attention of people in casual transit through the area. The best thing is to make the rescue as natural as possible, always winding through, or using different routes on narrow streets that scarcely permit passage on foot, to avoid an encounter of two cars.[26]

Perhaps aware of Marighella's caution, the West German Baader–Meinhof gang used the BMW automobile as their favorite getaway car because it was fast and maneuverable, and not because of its acronymic coincidence as the "Baader-Meinhof Wagen."[27]

To reduce further exposure of the Mobility Column personnel, Marighella mentions that the urban guerrilla must either expropriate the type of vehicle he needs, or utilize other methods of acquisition, if he has monetary resources. He cautions the guerrilla about the dangers related to permanent ownership of vehicles, although he does mention that experienced drivers are "not made in one day and the apprenticeship must begin early."[28]

CONSIDERATIONS RELATIVE TO THE USE OF VEHICLES

Unlike the S.L.A., who were fascinated by the notion of owning a number of camouflaged and armored vans with built-in defense systems, the Baader–Meinhof organization usually stole an automobile, preferably a BMW, preliminary to the execution of each operation for which a vehicle is needed, and disposed of it when the "job" was completed.

Other terrorist groups use rental cars for operations, particularly for bomb placements. During the night of March 6–7, 1973, two explosive devices were recovered from vehicles in the New York City Police Department's automobile impoundment lot. Each of the devices was in the trunk of a rental car, one of which had been parked illegally in front of

---

[26] Carlos Marighella, *Minimanual of the Urban Guerrilla* (no publisher listed but dated June 1969), pp. 26–27.

[27] Melvin J. Lasky, "Ulrike and Andreas," *The New York Times Magazine*, May 11, 1975, pp. 73–79.

[28] Marighella, *Minimanual*, p. 9.

the Israel Discount Bank, and the other in the vicinity of the First Israel Bank and Trust. During the same night, police discovered a third explosive device in the trunk of another rental car, parked adjacent to the El Al Airlines warehouse facility at John F. Kennedy International Airport, situated on the edge of New York City. Printed literature of the Black September Arab Terrorist Organization was found in all three automobiles.[29]

RECENT TRENDS IN THE ORGANIZATION OF TERRORIST GROUPS IN THE UNITED STATES

Currently, the F.A.L.N.—Fuerzas Armadas de Liberacion Nacional Puertoriquenas, or, Armed Forces of Puerto Rican National Liberation—and an array of anti-Castro Cuban groups are the organizations most actively engaged in conducting terrorist operations in the United States. Perhaps aware of Abraham Guillen's and Carlos Marighella's recommendations regarding clandestine organizations, both Cuban and Puerto Rican groups emphasize security, and simply do not accept as a member anyone whose identity cannot be verified. Consequently, it is reasonable to assume that the infrastructure of these groups is composed of only the required number of cells necessary to conduct operations.

However, the F.A.L.N.'s operational capability once was quite effective and efficient, regardless of the allegedly small number of "hardcore" members which it contains. For example, on October 27, 1975, between the hours of midnight and 3 A.M., ten F.A.L.N. devices exploded in three American cities: Chicago, New York, and Washington, D.C.[30] Furthermore, on April 9, 1977, seven incendiary devices claimed by or attributed to the F.A.L.N., went off in a space of sixteen minutes in three New York City department stores.[31]

American terrorists also abandoned certain criminal practices as a consequence of their high public visibility and in some cases harmful impact on operations designed to achieve organizational objectives. These activities were once part of the "game plan" executed by groups such as the Black Liberation Army (B.L.A.) in the late 1960s and early 1970s. For example, B.L.A. conducted a program of "stickup" operations

---

[29] Sharon Edens, *Airport News*, March 30, 1973, pp. 1 & 6.
[30] "F.A.L.N. Tied to 49 Blasts Since Aug. '74," *The New York Times*, February 20, 1977, p. 33.
[31] "F.A.L.N. Claims It Set Bombs on Saturday," *The New York Times*, April 12, 1977, p. 23.

of taverns and social clubs frequented by working-class black people, regardless of a barrage of severe criticism by individuals whom they hoped to convert to their cause. Consequently, B.L.A. "stickups" eventually alienated people in black neighborhoods, and prompted some of them to cooperate with the police. The B.L.A., however, mistakenly dismissed this criticism as irrelevant, "unless the critics can offer an alternative."[32]

During the past decade the American police, gaining increased sophistication in the areas of communication, mobility, and information gathering, have caused terrorists to refrain from B.L.A.-style expropriation operations and other visible criminal activity not directly related to the attainment of their organizational objectives. Thus, American terrorists today are more likely to be gainfully employed or living on welfare, a style recently adopted by I.R.A. gunmen in Northern Ireland for similar reasons. They have become smaller and more clandestine, and refrain from organizing broad-front movements, such as the Revolutionary Action Movement, the Minutemen, or the Black Liberation Front, all of which were penetrated by police undercover operatives.

Programs funded by the Law Enforcement Assistance Administration (L.E.A.A.) and designed to train selected police officers to handle the interpretation function of the intelligence process have enabled police intelligence units to become skilled in target analysis. In July, 1977, for example, New York City police officers "staked out" the Academy of Music in Manhattan, which was scheduled to host a musical and dance program sponsored by a pro-Castro group, and arrested three Cubans from a militant anti-Castro group just as they were attempting to light the fuse of a pipe bomb near the box office of the Academy.[33]

The primary organizational requirement for urban terrorist groups now operating in the United States is the development of a structure that is impervious to penetration by the police, yet sufficiently flexible to enable them to exploit opportunities for surprise. Their slogan must be, "Maximum damage to the enemy—Minimum damage to us."[34] Thus, it is anticipated that terrorism, providing the current state of socioeconomic conditions in the United States remains relatively stable, will

---

[32] Shakur, Zayd Malik, and members of the Black Liberation Army, "Spring Came Early This Year," in Break de Chains (New York: Community Press, 1973), pp. 10–12.

[33] Robert D. McFadden, "3 Cubans Seized with a Pipe Bomb," The New York Times, July 25, 1976, p. 1.

[34] Field Marshal D.C. Cox, On Organizing Urban Guerrilla Units (no publisher listed but dated October 8, 1970), pp. 8–14.

continue to be perpetrated in this country by groups knowledgeable in the techniques of terrorist organization and management, although they will be forced by police pressure to regulate and restrict their membership with care. Terrorist operations, however, are likely to be conducted with increased efficiency, and a high degree of technological sophistication designed to balance the increased effectiveness of the American police in the area of counterterrorist operations.

TERRORIST MANIPULATION OF THE DEMOCRATIC PROCESS

The political process is often conceived of as a bargaining, whereby an assortment of goals and values is maximized relative to the amount of power that can be marshaled in their behalf. Competition within this process is not often free; it is subject to manipulation by special-interest groups, which, by virtue of particular qualities, are able to maximize their ends at the expense of other, less fortunate groups. Occasionally these disadvantaged groups become dissatisfied with their subordinate position, and seek to tilt the political process to create a political climate which is more receptive to their demands. Often they accomplish this objective by introducing new methods of political action, which enhance their ability to compete. These new political methods are frequently quite violent.

These groups see violence, not as the repudiation of the political process, but rather as an indication that their involvement in the bargaining process is being intensified and carried on by other means. Consequently, the introduction of violence into the political process is regarded by some as an indication that the values at stake have come to be perceived as so fundamental that the existing political process no longer suffices. The central issue of their struggle is indeed viewed by a disadvantaged group as involving no less than the last chance for their political survival.

This widened political struggle sometimes assumes an especially intense form, and the urban environment, in which it is most frequently conducted, becomes the arena for a series of terrorist acts. Cities are the setting for many of these acts because they have features which facilitate political organization and cast into sharp contrast positions of disparate power. Metropolitan areas are thus apt to become the scene of violence, once a disadvantaged group of people seek to aggrandize themselves by altering the present allocation of power through the use of force or other extralegal means. Almost without exception, however, these attempts have ended in failure when the power of an urban police force has been fully brought to bear.

Although it is true that most urban political violence is caused by crowds running amok, some of it is the highly organized material type of terror which is directed against railway bridges, power lines, or public buildings. Personal terror is also frequently employed by urban insurgents. This involves the assassination of their opponents—people such as police officers, dignitaries, public officials, popular figures, and businessmen. Urban insurgents will, on occasion, indiscriminately employ personal terror against the general public for the purpose of undermining morale. Primarily, though, the intent of terrorism is not to kill or to injure people, but to advertise the fact that a group with a real potential for revolutionary violence exists. Even a token bomb set off somewhere in a capital city each night for a week, a terrorist calculates, will keep the police on the run, and let the populace know that his cause is alive.

TERRORISM AND REVOLUTION

Terrorism by itself will not win a revolution; nor is it likely even to lead to negotiations for the settling of grievances. Most frequently, it is stifled by the strict discipline and technical superiority of the police forces, which are supplemented by military units in critical situations. Friedrich Engels, Karl Marx's collaborator, seemed convinced of this point when speaking about certain of his unpleasant experiences in the mid-nineteenth century. He remarked that the era of the barricade and of street corner revolution had passed. He came to this conclusion because he felt that improved technology and military techniques had rendered street fighting ineffective, while urban redevelopment in the form of broad boulevards and gridlike patterns of streets facilitated the employment of these new techniques.

Regardless of Engels's observation, many contemporary terrorist groups insist that terror is a weapon which, when intelligently employed, can circumvent the technological capabilities of their opponents and bring final victory. They continue to refine and adapt the techniques of their trade. They regularly attack targets whose destruction or abduction is calculated to gain for them the international publicity which will force the government they anathematize to concentrate on the repression of terror for a long period of time. The obvious purpose of their strategy is to make the government neglect all its other duties in the interests of public security; which, when continued over an extended period, might lead to a popular revolution of the masses with the terrorists as the vanguard.

This contemporary notion of terrorism is tied somewhat to the ideas of Sergius Stepniak, a nineteenth-century Russian terrorist, who believed that terrorism was employed, not to overthrow a government, but to compel it to neglect everything else. It does not, however, embrace the ideas of Ernesto "Che" Guevara, who called terrorism a "negative weapon" because it often produces results that are detrimental to the revolutionary cause, including indiscriminate bombings of public places and assassinations of public officials. Modern terrorists, however, claim that the efficacy of the terrorist should never be evaluated in terms of his tactical targets, as Guevara attempted to do, but rather in some measurable reduction in the political flexibility and morale of his opponent as a consequence of an extended terrorist campaign. A trained terrorist never selects a target on the basis of its intrinsic value, but primarily for the political and psychological impact which it will have on people once it is seized or destroyed.

STRATEGIC CONSIDERATIONS

Strategically, terrorism when employed on an international scale is used simply to convince major world powers that there is a real, immediate, and urgent need for them to correct the conditions responsible for its existence. Terrorist campaigns of this type need a publicity campaign which emphasizes that moderation over an extended period is not capable of bringing about the required political change—be it the termination of a colonial situation, or the achievement of social equality. Furthermore, the press accounts must emphasize that the employment of terror is clearly a response to the denial of the basic freedoms of a politically identifiable and deprived people, whom the major powers, in the interests of their own national security, should "liberate." Without a credible publicity campaign skewed to this consideration, the terrorist risks not having his activities accepted as logical and tolerable. Therefore, terrorist targeting practices are linked to a propaganda campaign intended to convince an audience that a particular group is composed of zealots who are grimly determined to end the injustice to and humiliation of their people.

In the pursuit of this objective, the terrorist must also demonstrate to the international community his ability to be militant and to withstand prolonged suffering. Consequently, he seeks an environment dominated, not by terrain and physical factors, but mostly by human beings and political and psychological factors. It is this emphasis on personal terror which lends credence to the terrorist threat, since its employment makes sense only when its advocates understand that terrorism is not so much a military technique as the creation of a political condition. The international terrorist knows that he must predicate his strategy on his ability to convince the major world powers that his plight must be resolved in the interests of world peace. He also knows that he must somehow alienate most people everywhere from his enemy.

A public-relations assessment would be a prerequisite for any terrorist plan, and the controlling factor relative to its intensity, direction, and duration. The periodic release of unharmed hostages by various terrorist organizations usually indicates that their captors realize that there is nothing further to be gained, and much to be lost, by their continued retention or their death.

For example, Geoffrey Jackson was a British diplomat who was once held captive for a sustained period by Uruguay's Tupamaros. Since the media had already widely publicized the activity of that group, the British government would not give anything in return for his life. By the time the Tupamaros kidnapped him, their Robin Hood image was impressed on the minds of Uruguayans.

Although a few terrorist groups conduct operations which are international in scope, most contemporary extremist groups advocate a cause which is related to a rather isolated domestic political situation which in no immediate way has ramifications which require them to attempt manipulation of the existing international balance of power. The I.R.A. is an example of a group of this type. The Arab terrorists, however, are typical of terrorists whose organization and operations closely conform to the theoretical aspects previously mentioned which pertain to the worldwide utilization of terror as a weapon. These groups realize that all their actions and inactions have a dramatic impact on the Middle East, where the United States and the Soviet Union have vital, but divergent, national interests.

Arab terrorist strategy is to claim that their people are unable to redeem their lost lands inside Israel through diplomacy, conventional warfare, or a Maoist-type guerrilla struggle. Thus, they present themselves as people who are free to employ the tactics of terror against Israeli people and their international supporters everywhere. They also use terror to intimidate the world community into believing that the cost of maintaining the status quo in the Middle East will be an eventual nuclear confrontation between the United States and the Soviet Union. Consequently, Arab terrorism supplements those aspects of conventional Arab diplomacy and propaganda which emphasize that a lasting peace in the Middle East is dependent on a resolution of the "Palestinian Question."

LAW-ENFORCEMENT LIAISON SHORTCOMINGS

Although aware of the threat posed by terrorist groups, the urban police departments, particularly of the United States, lack the resources and training required to control it. To control terrorism it is necessary for municipal American police departments to cooperate with every federal investigative agency, in a pooled effort against this menace. The federal agencies, however, find it most difficult to effect cooperation among themselves, and they are consequently unable to develop any lasting and mutually beneficial liaison with local police departments.

Evidence of this shortcoming in American law enforcement is plainly visible. Eighteen federal strike forces have been established to combat Mafia-dominated organized crime throughout the United States. The record of these forces has been mixed, and, until recently, the United States attorneys had been urging their dissolution because the various federal agencies pooled in the strike forces tend to compete with and be distrustful of each other. Included among the federal agencies normally grouped in the strike forces are the Federal Bureau of Investigation (F.B.I.), the Drug Enforcement Administration (D.E.A.), the United States Immigration and Naturalization Service (U.S.I.N.S.), and the Alcohol, Tobacco and Firearms Division of the United States Treasury Department (A.T.F.).

There is some justification for the competition and distrust which exists among the various American federal agencies. One strike-force attorney, for example, who had been asked whether he could show a reporter F.B.I. charts on the Mafia, said cynically, "They'll hardly show them to us." "Why is that?" he was asked. "Well, the bureau has the attitude that one day you're a prosecutor, and the next day you're a defense attorney," he said. That is frequently true of the young attorneys who work in the federal strike forces and the United States Attorney's offices, where a prosecutor's term averages three years.

INTELLIGENCE NETWORKS

Fettered both politically and economically, most American police departments are unable to construct the top-level operational intelligence network which is required to keep records on extremist groups. Yet these same intelligence networks are an effective counter to terrorism, since they consist of components which will allow rapid acquisition, analysis, and dissemination of current data from a specially constituted and specially skilled group. Even when convinced of the need for sophisticated intelligence networks, most American police departments would still find it very difficult to conduct any intelligence operation on a prolonged basis, unless the performance statistics could justify the support of budgetary appropriations and thereby provide additional financing. Thus, the drive of the American police for statistics tends to divert investigative energy to a succession of low-level arrests, most of which have little or no impact on any organized criminal group. Furthermore, most urban American police commanders also realize that intelligence operations normally yield a low number of arrests; consequently, they often are reluctant to undertake them, as the size of their budget is often related to the total number of arrests made during the previous 12-month period.

Yet it is absolutely necessary for a free society to build into its structure the safeguards which it needs to protect basic freedoms. It is judgmental, however, whether intelligence systems should be included in or omitted from any list of necessary safeguards. Aware of this situation, the terrorist is often able, sometimes openly, to manipulate the democratic process to create a climate favorable to himself. This is evidenced by the following recent example. More than 25 years ago, fearful of the designs of the Soviet Union, Congress authorized the creation of the Central Intelligence Agency (C.I.A.). But Congress was also concerned about the designs of the agency itself, and the National Security Act of 1947 specifically provided that the C.I.A. "shall have no police, subpoena, law enforcement or internal security functions."[1] But, in February 1973, the C.I.A. acknowledged training policemen from about a dozen domestic police departments, including 14 men from the New York City Police Department, in the storage, processing, filing, and retrieval of intelligence data, and in security devices and procedures. This acknowledgment came in response to an inquiry from a New York congressman pertaining to press accounts about such training sessions.[2]

---

[1] Lyman B. Kirkpatrick, Jr., *The U.S. Intelligence Community* (New York: Hill & Wang; 1973), pp. 25–27.

[2] "Why Did CIA Train Police?" in *The New York Times*, February 11, 1973, p. 3.

Meanwhile, a suit was brought in a federal court which challenged the constitutionality of many New York City police intelligence activities. Police Commissioner Patrick V. Murphy subsequently announced that the names of more than a million persons and organizations had been purged from the files, and new restrictions were established to regulate the collection and dissemination of such material in the future. The Commissioner stated, further, that there was legitimate and absolute need for his department to gather intelligence.

> However, there is always the possibility that some police practices may infringe on individual rights. The line between public and private interest is so fine that any system which is required to collect information about individuals and groups is susceptible to such infringement.[3]

As previously indicated, most American municipal police departments are not equipped to conduct a counterterrorist effort in the area of intelligence gathering of the kind which could serve as the basis for a nationwide program of preventive countermeasures. The national government is thus placed in the position of having to assess situations without the extensive hard intelligence data which could be readily supplied by municipal police forces, once they had been trained, financed, and equipped for this mission.[4]

If a nationwide counterterrorist intelligence system is implemented, its managers must be extremely careful that its operations do not include activities which, in the words of former Attorney General William B. Saxbe, are "abhorrent in a free society." The American attorney general used this expression to condemn some of the practices used in COINTELPRO (Counter Intelligence Program). COINTELPRO was used by the Federal Bureau of Investigation to spy on and disrupt extremist groups. Its tactics included the spreading of information to create dissension and cause disruptions in militant organizations. For example, F.B.I. informers planted false information identifying prominent members of the extremist organizations as federal agents, and distributed false or unsubstantiated damaging information about prominent leaders to friendly members of the press, employers, business associates, credit agencies, family members, and local law-enforcement agencies. Although COINTELPRO was disbanded in 1971, former F.B.I. Director Clarence M. Kelley saw some future applications for its use. But he also recognized that a policy decision is involved which would have to come from the attorney general.[5]

---

[3] Ibid.
[4] President's Commission on Law Enforcement and Administration of Justice, *Task Force Report: Organized Crime* (Washington, D.C.: 1967), pp. 16–24.
[5] *The New York Times*, November 24, 1974, p. 3.

The C.I.A., meanwhile, maintains a computerized file in its headquarters in Langley, Virginia, which it calls "Octopus." "Octopus" has the capability of matching television pictures of known terrorists and their associates against profiles contained in its system. These television pictures are taken in various overseas airports, bus terminals, and other transportation centers. Within microseconds, "Octopus" can analyze a picture, along with information already in its file on targets in the area, and the equipment and talents required to attack them. Within a few minutes after this computerized analysis takes place, a radio alarm is transmitted to a counterterrorist team, who apprehend the terrorist. When terrorists are picked up and accused in this manner, "they often are flabbergasted at being presented with plans they hadn't yet made."[6] The use of television surveillance in a free society, however, must be carefully controlled and tightly monitored, and all people who are within view of the camera's lens should be aware of its presence.

NATURE OF THE DEMOCRATIC RESPONSE

A democracy, even when confronted with a serious terrorist threat, is still reluctant to suspend basic freedoms as a countermeasure, in the belief that this action is a greater danger to the legitimacy of the democratic state and the mass consensus vital to its preservation than a terrorist challenge itself. It is exactly this hesitancy, which the terrorist group seizes for the prime input into its strategic plan. This plan is a strategy for eventual conquest, which makes sense only when it is understood that terrorism is not so much a military technique as a political condition. Always, the strategic aim of the terrorist is not the military defeat of the forces of the incumbent regime—this is an impossible tactic—but the moral alienation of the masses from the existing government, until such alienation has become total and irreversible.

The Brazilian guerrilla leader, Carlos Marighella, mapped out part of that strategy when he wrote:

> It is necessary to turn political crisis into armed conflict by performing violent actions that will force those in power to transform the political situation of the country into a military situation. That action will alienate the masses, who, from then on, will revolt against the army and the police and blame them for this state of things.[7]

[6] Miles Copeland, *Without Cloak or Dagger: The Truth about the New Espionage* (New York: Simon & Schuster, 1970), pp. 96–97.
[7] Carlos Marighella, *Minimanual of the Urban Guerrilla* (no publisher listed but dated June 1969), p. 3.

Consequently, democratic states, confronted with an outbreak of insurgency are truly "damned if they do and doomed if they don't."

The citizens of a free society must be prepared to accept restrictions of their basic freedoms, once terrorists gain a foothold in regions where they live. For example, on November 22, 1974, the British government, following a bombing of two pubs in Birmingham, announced that it would quickly introduce legislation to give emergency powers to the police to help combat terrorism by the Irish Republican Army (I.R.A.). One of the major questions was whether to introduce identity cards, as was done during World War II. There were strong objections, on the ground that identity cards would give the British government too much control over the individual. Yet, regardless of their misgivings and the evidence of recent abuses, citizens of democratic states should insist that selected municipal police officers receive intelligence training for the single purpose of containing terrorism in its incipient stage. Otherwise, the use of the identity cards, and a broader interpretation of the existing laws of arrest, search, and seizure, may one day become commonplace in every democratic state.

There always remains the temptation for the military forces of a democratic state to act outside the law while confronting terrorists. There are two excuses for this action: (1) that the normal safeguards in the law for the individual are not designed for a terrorist, and (2) that a terrorist deserves to be treated as an outlaw anyway. Sir Robert Thompson, British expert on counterinsurgency, in his book *Defeating Communist Insurgency* comments that action outside the law

> not only is morally wrong, but, over a period, it will create more practical difficulties for a government than it solves. A government which does not act in accordance with the law forfeits the right to be called a government and cannot then expect its people to obey the law. Functioning in accordance with the law is a very small price to pay in return for the advantage of being the government.

But, unless the municipal forces of a free society have a real and reliable intelligence capability which can be used to nip insurgency before it constitutes a real threat, the bringing in of the army, regardless of its grave consequences, is the only option left.[8]

To avoid the consequences resulting from the use of military force to quell domestic insurrections, the United States has adopted a policy of "gradualism," its sole remaining alternative to autocracy to meet the insurgent challenge. This policy, which seeks to correct the political,

---

[8] Sir Robert Thompson, *Defeating Communist Insurgency* (New York: Praeger Publishers, 1970), pp. 52–55.

social, and economic conditions responsible for the violence, is designed to administer a long-range cure, when an immediate action response is required. Such a policy has the potential to hinder the government's cause, as its pronouncements are usually interpreted by the insurgents as mere sops, and twisted by their propagandists to indicate the efficacy of their own movement.[9]

BRITISH APPROACH TO SMALL-SCALE TERRORISM

It is evident that American law-enforcement agencies lack a well-developed and coordinated program to meet the challenge posed by terrorism, while simultaneously maintaining the fabric of a free society. They should, perhaps, adopt the British solution to this threat. Once confronted with insurgency, the British strengthen the social sanctions, and thereby act on the supposition that counterinsurgency is normal police work and not social engineering. The British approach seems more sensible than the American because if an insurgency explodes in the streets, it is foolish to undertake preventive measures that contain the potential of being manipulated by the insurgents to serve their cause.[10] A prerequisite for the implementation of the British approach is the establishment of statewide and uniform penal codes, which many of the fifty American states presently lack.

Another conspicious feature of the British approach is that military units are not committed against the insurgents until the police operations have been given a reasonable opportunity to quell the insurrection. Police operations, therefore, are intended by the British to "buy the time" they need to evaluate and contain a situation. Meanwhile, they try to devise a strategy which will not alienate the civilian population and shatter the national image, as might result if military force were used indiscriminately.

A demonstration of this sort of British police response took place on the island of Bermuda in March 1973. It was triggered as a consequence of the murder on the island of the governor general and his aide. Although the media reported the possible implication in the affair of a politically motivated insurgent group called the Black Cadre, the British felt that a team of detectives from Scotland Yard should investigate the

[9] Lucian W. Pye, *Aspects of Political Development* (Boston: Little, Brown & Co., 1966), pp. 129–31.
[10] Ibid., pp. 131–34.

matter and prepare the normal report. The police reports were then used by the British to assess the parameters of the situation and shape their future response, if, indeed, any should be required. Meanwhile, the Black Cadre group did not become the beneficiary of publicity which it might be seeking, nor were its activities considered by the media as a formidable factor in Bermudan affairs.

DEMOCRATIC STATES AND REPRESSION

But what of the tremendous repressive capability of American police departments? Is it not possible for them to use this capacity to seize the initiative from the terrorists? If terror is such a powerful tactic in the hands of the insurgent, can it not be equally efficacious when employed by the police? The answer to these questions is not so obvious as it would at first glance appear to be. There seems to be little doubt that counterterror by the police can be just as effective as the terror employed by the insurgents. However, whether it is an alternative which is open to the government of a free society is an entirely different matter. The problematic nature of the decision to resort to the employment of counterterror is a function of the political culture of the incumbent, as well as of the international environment.

Pure repression has, in fact, become virtually impossible for American police departments, exposed as they are to the shifts of governmental debate and an unfettered press.[11] This, however, may be an oversimplification, unless one takes account of the political culture within which these police organizations function. In American life, for example, there are certain preconceptions as to what the government may legitimately do, and an exact definition of the fundamental rights of man. Its democratic system is both a necessary and a sufficient limitation on the employment of repressive force.

Yet, for American police departments to cope with the terrorist challenge, they must eventually request that certain constitutional safeguards be suspended. This action, however, places the rights of the entire population in jeopardy, and there is great reluctance, therefore, to give the police the extraordinary powers needed to uncover evidence of terrorist activity. Public opinion aside, it may not be farfetched to say that, in certain cases, the socialization process by which these values are

---

[11] Brian Crozier, *The Rebels: A Study of Post War Insurrections* (London: Scribner, 1960), p. 12.

inculcated into American life may be so intense as to render the government officials and police officers themselves reluctant to contravene cultural norms.

As long as this is the case, the police are at a decided disadvantage, by reason of the public opposition which forceful measures might invoke. Thus American police agencies are unable to respond early enough and in a strong enough way to catch a terrorist scheme in the incipient stages, at the time when it is most vulnerable. Later, the suppression of the terrorists requires a much more intense application of force, the application of which becomes ever more open and more costly, thereby increasing the obstacles to the government's freedom of action.

American police organizations are in a difficult situation. Whether from political pressure or through personal dislike, they are unable to employ the measures that they must employ in order to detect and to crush a terrorist threat. Yet, failure to deal with this threat may lead citizens to question the ability of the police to act as a sovereign authority. When in this quandary, the police are forced to deploy their forces in accordance with regular operating principles. This kind of strategy is really a compromise, by which they seek to stay within what are considered constitutional limits of force, while at the same time endeavoring to give the impression that they are actively engaged in combating the terrorist menace. Thus, the American cities contain conditions which are conducive to the establishment of terrorist cells, since it is difficult for the police to implement the intelligence system, or the courts to grant the suspensions of civil liberties, necessary for the uncovering of these minuscule, clandestine networks.

5

PRISONS, COURTS, AND TERRORISM

The corrections component of the American criminal justice system has experienced considerable difficulty in its efforts to control terrorist conspiracies spawned among confined offenders who view themselves as "political prisoners" being held for "revolutionary crimes." Compounding this situation is the composition of the American prison population, whose average age is lower than that of the 1970 population, and the fact that the offenses for which people are incarcerated include more crimes against persons —murder, rape, robbery, assault. An inmate recruited into a terrorist group is likely to be a young man or woman with a previous history of violent crime who utilizes a prison-taught revolutionary ideology as justification for continuing to perpetrate crimes against humanity upon release.

THE ISLAMIC GUERRILLAS IN AMERICA

According to a Muslim chaplain affiliated with the jails in the Washington, D.C., area, a majority of the black converts to Islam in the United States still make their conversion in jail, as they have since the Nation of Islam, popularly referred to as the Black Muslims, was founded in the 1930s. Some of these converts became enamored of the religious inspiration and leadership qualities of the pro-Ayatollah Khomeini

Muslim volunteers who explained the Koran to them during their period of incarceration. When released from prison they joined with their teachers to form the Islamic Guerrillas in America.

Consisting of approximately 50 men, this group came to the attention of law-enforcement officials in November 1979, when its members distributed a leaflet in front of the Islamic Center on Massachusetts Avenue N.W.—a street flanked by diplomatic facilities, and known as "Embassy Row"—which carried the name of their organization. Outlining a general strategy for Islamic guerrilla warfare in the United States, this handout concluded with a statement that "the Muslim population of America applauds the Islamic struggle in Iran and would be most receptive to a request from our devout brother the Honorable Ayatollah Khomeini for Holy War."[1]

The nature of the tie between the Black Muslim element and the pro-Khomeini faction was evident on April 1, 1980, the first anniversary of the Islamic Revolution in Iran, when 40 men, introduced as American Muslims, provided a security force for the Iranian Embassy in Washington. According to an embassy spokesman, the security unit was assigned the mission of protecting the facility from attacks by off-duty United States Marines. "The American black brothers are being used as muscle," charges an official of Washington's Islamic Center.[2]

The alleged leader of the group, Bahran Nahidian, is an Iranian-born naturalized United States citizen, and a longtime anti-Shah activist. He owns a dwelling in northwest Washington, D.C., known as the Islamic House, that serves as a nationwide mecca for revolutionary and anti-Shah students. Also, Mr. Nahidian was an active participant in the prison volunteers program, and his lectures were geared to communicate the Ayatollah Khomeini's opinions regarding the rights of the oppressed. Daoud Salahuddin, formerly David Belfield, is a close associate of Mr. Nahidian, and shares his disdain for the deceased Shah of Iran.[3]

On November 4, 1979, Mr. Nahidian and Mr. Salahuddin were part of the "muscle" used to invade the Statue of Liberty on Liberty Island in lower New York harbor, and unfurl a 140-foot banner that proclaimed "Shah must be tried and punished." Approximately a thousand visitors were on the island when the extremists chained themselves to railings in the crown of the statue and near its base.[4]

[1] Marc Kaufman and Michael Isikoff, "Islamic Guerrillas in America: Muslims Linked to Militant Iranians Here," *The Washington Star*, July 24, 1980, p. B1.
[2] Ibid.
[3] Michael Isikoff, "Khomeini Backer Happy about Murder," *The Washington Star*, July 24, 1980, p. B1.
[4] "Chief Suspects in Assassination Probe Profiled," ibid.

On the morning of July 22, 1980, a mailman wearing a white pith helmet arrived at the doorstep of Ali Akbar Tabatabai, the last press secretary of the Iranian Embassy in Washington during the rule of the Shah, in Bethesda, Maryland. The caller said that he wanted a signature for two special delivery letters. But when Mr. Tabatabai came to the door, the "mailman" pulled out a 9-mm handgun and fired three shots into his abdomen. A friend of the victim, who was with him when he was shot, picked Mr. Salahuddin's photograph out of a pack of pictures shown to him by police.[5]

Regardless of the probable link between a few persons involved in rendering volunteer services in prisons, politicized inmates, and terrorism, however, existing constitutional guarantees inhibit the implementation of the restrictions needed to prevent this tie.

Officials associated with the management of American prisons also must cope with laws defining potentially dangerous inmates, which have in many cases changed little in the past century. Reluctance to change antiquated laws is owing largely to the people's adherence to questionable assumptions: that dangerousness can be clearly defined, and that psychiatrists can accurately predict who is dangerous. There are virtually as many definitions of dangerousness as there are psychiatrists and judges pondering the question. But, since prison classification officers use "dangerousness" as a criterion for giving an inmate minimum or maximum security status, it should be possible for these officers, and paroling authorities as well, to estimate accurately, within defined ranges, the probability that a particular inmate will inflict harm on someone if confinement and isolation are not continued. The American criminal justice system has not demonstrated that such predictions can be made accurately.[6]

STATEWIDE CORRECTIONAL ALLIANCE FOR REFORM

On July 15, 1976, for example, grand juries in Boston, Massachusetts, and Portland, Maine, indicted four former inmates of the Maine State Prison, who were allegedly tied to a radical prison-reform group called the Statewide Correctional Alliance for Reform (SCAR), in connection with the bombing of an Eastern Airliner jet, two National Guard trucks, and a suburban courthouse in Boston, on the beginning of the

---

[5] Maureen Dowd, "D.C. Man Sought as Killer of Former Iranian Attaché," ibid., p. A 1.
[6] "Cannot Predict Who Is Dangerous," Ross Laboratories Bulletin, 23, no. 1 (January-February, 1976) : 1.

Fourth of July weekend. In July 1976, these terrorists formed a group known as the Sam Melville–Jonathan Jackson Unit, and tried to dynamite a state-police barracks. Authorities, however, prevented the attack by arresting a member of the bombing network who was using his car to transport a charge of 46 sticks of dynamite to the blast location. The group's name references were to Sam Melville, a bomber, killed in the 1971 uprising at Attica State Prison in New York, and Jonathan Jackson, killed in a 1970 California shoot-out while attempting to kidnap a judge from a San Rafael courtroom during the trial of the black militant, Angela Davis.[7]

ARREST AND ESCAPE OF JOANNE CHESIMARD

Meanwhile, at New Jersey's Trenton State Prison, black leaders of various Muslim groups, utilizing weapons which may have been forged in prison workshops, struggled for dominance. In October 1975, some of these prisoners participated in an armed struggle for black leadership which injured 10 persons before it was suppressed. A few months later, in January 1976, another outbreak occurred, which prison officials regarded as part of a comprehensive plan to liberate Clark Squire. A Black Liberation Army (B.L.A.) leader, Mr. Squire is serving a life sentence for killing a state trooper on the New Jersey Turnpike during the early morning hours of May 2, 1973. Outside Trenton State Prison, a rental van was discovered stocked with New England road maps, guns, food, blankets, a first-aid kit, spare gas, and phony identification cards. State police traced the van back to Newark, New Jersey.[8]

Joanne Chesimard, also known as Assata Shakur and the "soul" of the B.L.A., was in the car with Clark Squire when the New Jersey state trooper, Werner Foerster, was murdered. Shot in the arms and left shoulder during the incident, Miss Chesimard was immediately placed under heavy guard in a Middlesex County, New Jersey, hospital. Shunted to various county jails, she eventually went to New York City in late 1973 to stand trial for bank robbery.[9]

However, an embarrassing security breach came to light while she was in custody; she became pregnant. According to befuddled officials,

[7] John Kifner, "Four Are Indicted in Boston Blasts," *The New York Times,* July 16, 1976, p. 17.
[8] "Jailbreak Probe Fails to Uncover Additional Guns," *The Star Ledger* (Newark, N.J.), February 11, 1976, p. 5.
[9] Stuart Marques, "Chesimard Escapes from Clinton," *The Star Ledger* (Newark, N.J.), November 3, 1979, p. 1.

Miss Chesimard and Fred Hilton, also a member of the B.L.A., had a rendezvous in a security cell during the trial. Although this episode delayed her murder trial in New Jersey (a judge postponed the proceedings while she had her child), and served to reinforce security around her, police and prison officials were afraid that, somehow and somewhere, someone would make an attempt to help Miss Chesimard escape from jail.

Convicted of Trooper Foerster's murder in March 1977, she was immediately sentenced to life imprisonment. She was transferred from the Middlesex County Courthouse, where she was being held in a basement cell away from other inmates, to New Jersey's state reformatory for women at Clinton. Since it was surrounded only by a fence and situated in a rural county, state corrections officials did not regard this institution as tight enough to hold her, and so moved her to the all-male facility at Yardville.[10]

Her lawyers tried to get her sent back to Clinton, but an official of the New Jersey Department of Corrections told a judge that Miss Chesimard was a poor security risk, and a revolutionary with contacts that other inmates did not have. The judge agreed, and she stayed in Yardville.[11]

In April 1978, Miss Chesimard was transferred to a federal prison for women in Alderson, West Virginia, where she stayed for 10 months, until prison officials closed the maximum-security unit at this location. Returning to Clinton in November 1979, she was detained with six other female inmates in the prison's only maximum-security section, a one-story brick building surrounded by a 15-foot chain-link fence topped with 2 feet of barbed wire. On November 2, 1979, three men armed with .45-caliber handguns burst into Clinton reformatory, briefly held two guards hostage, and freed Miss Chesimard in a bold daylight escape.

Because of the ease of the escape, penal officials began reexamining the visitation policies at Clinton. According to James V. Stabile, a spokesman for the Department of Corrections, "the whole procedure is under review."

The prison, he said, maintains lists of all visitors, their addresses, Social Security numbers, and physical descriptions. That information is provided by the inmates. When visitors arrive at the registration gate, they must produce identification papers that match information on the visitation list. Although Miss Chesimard's three visitors all produced

[10] Stuart Marques, "Weak Security Aided Chesimard Escape," ibid.; November 4, 1979, p. 1.

[11] Stuart Marques, "Lawmen Never Felt Secure," ibid., November 3, 1979, p. 1.

identification documents that matched information that she had provided earlier, Mr. Stabile said that he did not know whether authorities had previously verified the validity of her information.[12]

A fugitive warrant for Miss Chesimard was granted by a federal district court in Newark after state-police investigators told federal authorities that they believed "that she's out of the state." On November 3, 1979, the F.B.I. joined the search for Joanne Chesimard, who was still a fugitive as of September 1, 1980.[13]

ESCAPE OF KEY TERRORIST PERSONALITIES

The escape on May 22, 1979, of William Morales from a prison ward at Bellevue Hospital in New York City is also indicative of the great difficulty experienced by prison officials when attempting to detain dangerous terrorist offenders while simultaneously protecting their civil rights. Mr. Morales was sentenced on April 1979 to 29 to 89 years in prison for possession of explosives and other offenses. At his sentencing, the terrorist, who lost most of both hands in an explosion and is suspected of being a member of the Armed Forces of National Liberation of Puerto Rico (F.A.L.N.), exclaimed in court, "They're not going to hold me forever."

Using a pair of 14-inch wire cutters smuggled into his hospital cell, Mr. Morales cut open a metal window gate, and escaped by using an elastic bandage as a makeshift rope to climb down from a 40-foot-high window. A pair of "deeply indented" shoe prints in a grassy patch beneath Mr. Morales's cell, noticed by investigators, suggested that an accomplice had caught or otherwise aided the bomber as he dropped from a window three floors above the ground.

The main criticism leveled against the New York City Department of Corrections was lodged by the investigators and the Correction Officers Benevolent Association. This group complained that the department had ended round-the-clock surveillance of Mr. Morales to save money because of rising overtime costs for guards. The end of the 24-hour watch may have contributed to the escape, investigators said.[14]

---

[12] Ibid.

[13] Robert Hanley, "F.B.I. to Aid Search for Miss Chesimard," *The New York Times*, November 4, 1979, p. 31.

[14] Selwyn Raab, "A Maimed Terrorist Flees Cell at Bellevue," *The New York Times*, May 22, 1979, p. 1, and idem, "Wife of Morales Sought by Police for Questioning," ibid., May 23, 1979, p. B1.

Additional escapes of key extremist personalities include the April 24, 1979, disappearance of John William Sherman from the Federal Correctional Institute at Lompoc, California, and the July 21, 1979, escape of Leonard Peltier from the same facility. As a member of the George Jackson Brigade, named after a militant black San Quentin inmate who was killed in prison, Mr. Sherman participated in 14 robberies and 11 bombings or bombing attempts in Oregon and Washington. He is included on the F.B.I.'s list of ten most wanted persons.[15]

Leonard Peltier, American Indian Movement (A.I.M.) activist, was captured without incident 5 days after his escape. He was serving two consecutive life terms for the killing of two F.B.I. agents who were gunned down while trying to serve a warrant on the Pine Ridge Indian Reservation in South Dakota in 1975.[16]

NEW WORLD OF ISLAM

The New World of Islam, a fanatical but compact and well-disciplined religious sect, is known to use terror to enforce internal discipline and recruit inmates who take part in crimes immediately on their release from prison. Responsible for dozens of armed robberies and at least 15 murders since its formation in late 1971, the New World founders were a group of young members of the Nation of Islam's (N.O.I.) Mosque #25 in Newark, New Jersey. They became disenchanted with the work of Minister James Shabazz, whom they regarded as not militant enough in his efforts to take over business in Newark. When, on September 4, 1973, Minister Shabazz was murdered in front of his Newark home, the New World of Islam was charged with the crime.[17]

Alvin Dickens, currently serving a 38 to 51 year sentence on a number of charges, is regarded as the leader of the New World Sect. Some observers regard it as highly probable that he coordinates its activities from prison by passing out instructions through associates. Membership in the New World of Islam is said to be approximately 300 people, many of whom were once inmates at the Rahway and Trenton State prisons in New Jersey.

Incarcerated terrorists at times become the victims of terror, rather

---

[15] "F.B.I. Adds Terrorist to Most Wanted List," *The Star Ledger* (Newark, N.J.), August 5, 1979, p. 2.

[16] "Indian Activist Is Recaptured in Tree Grove," ibid., July 26, 1979, p. 59.

[17] Brian Smith, "New World of Islam is Linked to Rash of Killings, Robberies," *The Daily News* (New York), January 26, 1976, p. JL7.

than its purveyors. On October 16, 1975, for example, one New World member was killed and seven others injured in a battle with other Black Muslims at Trenton State Prison. After this incident, inmates incarcerated in New Jersey prisons at Trenton, Rahway, and Leesburg, and identified as New World members, were isolated by prison authorities.[18]

HOLMESBURG PRISON AND "BUBBLES" PRICE

On January 18, 1973, eight Black Muslims from Philadelphia stormed the Washington home of Hamaas Abdul Khaalis, patriarch of the Sunni (Orthodox) Hanafi Muslim sect, who had written a letter accusing Elijah Muhammad, leader of the Nation of Islam, N.O.I., of heresy. In an episode marked by intense violence and shouts accusing Khaalis of heresy, the attackers shot three persons repeatedly with shotguns and pistols, and drowned four babies in a bathtub. Haamas Khaalis, however, was away from home when this incident took place.

In 1974, five of the Muslims responsible for the Washington incident were convicted of first-degree murder (two others were dead, charges were dismissed against another). But one of the surviving Muslims, James ("Bubbles") Price, who gave federal investigators a minutely detailed statement regarding the Washington killings, was incarcerated in Pennsylvania's Holmesburg Prison and housed in "D–block." Virtually all the prisoners housed in "D–block" were Black Muslims, including four of the five men convicted in the Hanafi case, partly on the basis of Price's statement. Consequently, it was not surprising when prison guards one day discovered Mr. Price dangling by a knotted shoelace in a vacant cell with stab wounds in his body. A non-Muslim prisoner named Calvin Hunter, who was also held in "D–block" and who talked to police following the Price murder, was found dead on February 21, 1975, shortly after his release from prison.[19]

SYMBIONESE LIBERATION ARMY

Associations which first developed among inmate members of a black cultural association in California's Vacaville prison, 45 miles northeast of San Francisco, were later translated into affiliations which gave birth to the Symbionese Liberation Army (S.L.A.). It seems that prison

[18] Ibid.
[19] Mike Leary, "Trail of Death Leads to a Hollow Verdict," *The Philadelphia Inquirer*, July 27, 1975, p. 1.

officials permitted inmates to engage in "rap sessions" with college students, as these sessions were intended to prepare the prisoner to handle conditions "outside the walls." However, radical students bent on harnessing a participating inmate's zeal to their concept of revolution eventually penetrated the program, and were assigned to work with inmates, some of whom had long records of arrests on charges including possession of explosives and shoot-outs with the police.

Donald DeFreeze, later known as Field Marshal Cinque of the S.L.A., was one of these inmates. After escaping from custody while being transferred from Vacaville to Soledad prison, Mr. DeFreeze went underground, and joined with some student acquaintances from the prison volunteer program to form the S.L.A.[20]

NEW WORLD LIBERATION FRONT

Other California-based terrorist groups which included former inmates are the New World Liberation Front (N.W.L.F.), the Black Guerrilla Family, and the militant Tribal Thumb group. The S.L.A. issued several communications supporting the N.W.L.F. Its two most significant releases were its defense of the N.W.L.F. in the "Popeye" Jackson case in 1975, and its support for the N.W.L.F.'s demand from the Hearst family that $250,000 be raised for the S.L.A. defense of William and Emily Harris. The N.W.L.F. originally claimed credit for the assassination of Wilbert "Popeye" Jackson, head of the United Prisoner's Union, whom it accused of being a police informant. It has also taken credit for 30 bombings on the Pacific coast. General Motors, the Pacific Gas and Electric Company, the Bureau of Indian Affairs, the Hearst mansion at San Simeon, and two sheriff's cars bombed in August, 1975, outside the San Rafael, California, courthouse were among the targets attacked by the N.W.L.F.

In 1970, the N.W.L.F. published Brazilian revolutionary Carlos Marighella's *Minimanual of the Urban Guerrilla*. Also, the N.W.L.F. is believed by some authorities to have evolved from a group called Americans for Justice, and to have absorbed two smaller underground groups, known as the Chicano Liberation Front and the Red Guerrilla Family.[21]

---

[20] Nathan M. Adams, "The Rise and Fall of the S.L.A.," *The Reader's Digest* (September 1974) : 64–69.

[21] Leslie Gehrke and Anita Szemes, "The New World Liberation Front," unpublished paper, May, 1976. (Prepared for Special Police Operation Course, Union College, Cranford, N.J., U.S.A.)

TRIAL OF THE "SAN QUENTIN SIX"

In the San Rafael Courthouse at the time of the N.W.L.F. bombing the trial of the "San Quentin Six" was being conducted. These six men were being tried on murder and conspiracy charges which stemmed from a "breakout attempt" at San Quentin Prison on August 21, 1971, during the course of which black revolutionary George Jackson, two other prisoners, and three guards were killed. Conducted under extraordinary security, the trial of the "San Quentin Six" took place with the defendants chained and shackled, and separated from jurors by a thick sheet of plexiglass. Jury selection took $3\frac{1}{2}$ months.[22]

The defense said that the violence was provoked by authorities as an excuse to kill Mr. Jackson.

BAADER–MEINHOF "ANNEX"

In May 1975, the rigid courthouse security measures devised by the West German government for the trial of the terrorist Red Army Faction, also known as the Baader–Meinhof gang, were completed, and the trial of Andreas Baader, Ulrike Meinhof, Gudrun Ensslin, and Carl Raspe, all leaders of the gang, opened as scheduled. The four terrorists were charged with murder, bank robbery, bombing, and the forming of a criminal association.

The combination prison-and-court edifice, constructed at Stammheim outside Stuttgart for the trial, is a fortress which is sealed off from the surrounding area by rows of barbed wire. It is protected also by shields canted to deflect missiles fired from hand-held launchers which terrorist groups are believed to possess, and encircled by hundreds of heavily armed police. With German practicality, the "Baader–Meinhof Annex," where the prisoners are kept during the proceedings, is designed to be converted subsequently into a modern workshop for prisoner rehabilitation.[23]

Although the Stammheim complex may be the most secure penitentary yet devised and its adjacent courtroom fortified against surprise assaults, the most careful precautions are not always protection against the kind of resourcefulness and fervor that unite terrorists inside the walls with their comrades at liberty. The scenario which follows is evidence of the cunning and determination of terrorist groups.

---

[22] Ibid.
[23] "Trial of Germans for Terrorism Begins," *The New York Times*, May 21, 1975, p. 3.

PRISON ESCAPE SCHEMES

In 1968, Ulrike Meinhof, a columnist for a Hamburg magazine called *Konkret*, which attracted a wide following of agitators, students, anarchists, and terrorists, met Andreas Baader, who was imprisoned with his "revolutionary bride" Gudrun Ensslin for arson attacks on two Frankfurt department stores. Meinhof was able to obtain a series of prison interviews with Baader, and subsequently reported in her *Konkret* column that his acts of arson were "politically progressive because they represented audacious defiance of the law." In 1970, Meinhof was herself a terrorist, and consequently joined in a plot to free Baader from jail. "We needed Baader," Ulrike later testified, "to set up the urban guerrillas."

Securing Baader's release from custody was a relatively simple test of terrorist ingenuity, as prison authorities permitted him to visit local libraries, under guard, to pursue his sociological research. Baader had convinced authorities that his book for a radical Berlin publisher on youth problems was serious. Thus, on May 14, 1970, while he was in a reading room of the Free University, Meinhof and four accomplices appeared, exchanged pistol shots with guards, and discharged tear gas. Several guards and librarians were wounded in the "fire fight," but all the terrorists got away unharmed. Baader and Meinhof escaped by jumping out a first-floor window and driving off in a stolen car. In 1972, Baader was recaptured, along with Meinhof and thirty-odd additional members of the gang.[24]

However, in March 1975, resurgent members of the Baader–Meinhof gang kidnapped Peter Lorenz, the Christian Democratic candidate for mayor of West Berlin, and demanded the release of five of their imprisoned comrades who had already been tried and convicted. Within 72 hours, all the terrorists demands were satisfied. Mr. Lorenz was released, and the five convicted terrorists, with $10,000 apiece in their pockets, were set free, and flown first-class by Lufthansa to South Yemen.

Baader–Meinhof terrorists, however, did not relax. In April 1975, six of them made a forced entry into the West German embassy building in Stockholm, killing the military attaché and seizing a group of hostages. The terrorists threatened to execute their hostages one by one unless the Bonn government released the 26 Baader–Meinhof members still in jail, gave them $250,000, and flew them from Frankfurt to freedom. This time, however, Bonn refused to deal. Consequently, the terrorists killed

[24] Melvin J. Lasky, "Ulrike and Andreas," *The New York Times Magazine*, May 11, 1975, pp. 73–79.

the commercial attaché, and set off an explosive charge which demolished a portion of the embassy. Six terrorists were captured after a brief gun battle with police, and charged with murder.[25]

INMATE COMMUNICATION SYSTEMS

The Baader–Meinhof terrorists were placed in a dozen jails, both in West Germany and West Berlin, but they developed an extraordinary communication system which enabled them to transmit and receive messages, and thereby keep in touch with each other. Meinhof continued to write and circulate her manifestos. Baader's memorandums on escape plans were distributed regularly among incarcerated gang members and their accomplices on the outside. Other gang strategies were also all coordinated: when to begin a hunger strike, when to end it, how to put pressure on comrades who talked to the police. One prisoner was kept fictitiously on a medical "danger list" by prison authorities because her life was thought to be in jeopardy when she stopped fasting without "official approval."

Another incident concerns a young militant who was still at large and had talked secretly to the West Berlin police. Shortly after his conversation with the authorities, copies of the police report on his testimony were located in the Baader–Meinhof cells. The informer was found dead in a West Berlin park, with a bullet in his head.[26]

All this terrorist activity inside the West German prison system was possible because the Baader–Meinhof gang understood how to circumvent and manipulate the liberal West German prison regulations. There can be no doubt, for instance, that a few of the Baader–Meinhof lawyers smuggled documents into and out of prisons. One West German police antiterrorist operation terminated with the arrest of 24 terrorists, some of whom were lawyers. Furthermore, one accused terrorist once had 22 lawyers representing him, and another had 18. Surprise searches of the Baader–Meinhof cells by guards continued to turn up escape plans, research assignments, leaflets, and lists of target assignments, which included the names of West German politicians.[27]

On May 9, 1976, the Stuttgart prosecutor's office reported that Ulrike Meinhof had been found hanging from the window rails of her maximum

[25] "Four Terrorists Charged with Murder," *The New York Times*, April 26, 1975, p. 11.
[26] Lasky, "Ulrike and Andreas," pp. 78–79.
[27] "New Laws Proposed in West Germany," *The New York Times*, November 28, 1974, p. 11.

security cell by a piece of her prison toweling. An official spokesmen said that the former journalist had last been seen alive on the night of May 8 by a guard, and that she was heard typewriting in her cell until 10:30 P.M. Supporters of the 41-year-old Mrs. Meinhof said that she was murdered, and did not commit suicide.

After news of her death, West German police and special antiterrorist squads braced for a possible resurgence of terrorist activity by other West German radicals. As anticipated, another outbreak of terror occurred 6 months after her burial.[28] On December 2, 1976, an organization which called itself "Revolutionary Cells" bombed the officers' club at a United States Air Force base at Rhein–Main, West Germany. The terrorist group, in letters sent to Western news agencies, said that it had attacked the base because the United States stored atomic bombs there, and because it was used as a staging area for operations by the Central Intelligence Agency.[29]

FUTURE CONSIDERATIONS

This review of violent events associated with the courtroom trials and prison behavior of terrorists and their comrades indicates that institutions housing an inmate population derived largely from urban areas and courts which hear cases involving extremists are prime targets for terrorists seeking to gain the release of their fellows or searching for recruits. West German and American experience alike indicates that imprisoned terrorists are able to establish both internal and external communication channels, which they use to maintain, extend, and control their organization, both inside and outside prison walls. Furthermore, connections between prisoners and terrorist groups are available. According to the Italian police, the gunmen of the "Armed Proletarian Nuclei," a leftist extremist group which emerged in 1973, say they would involve the "subproletariat," including prisoners and criminals, in an armed battle for communism and against the state.

Prison custodial staffs should be prepared to handle organized group activity, rather than just single individuals serving their sentences as in the past, and an increased amount of protective security coverage should be provided for courthouses when extremists or terrorists are

[28] "Ulrike Meinhof, an Anarchist Leader in Germany, Is Found Hanged in Cell," *The New York Times*, May 10, 1976, p. 6.
[29] "West German Terrorists Assert They Bombed U.S. Officers Club," *The New York Times*, December 13, 1976, p. 9.

tried. New courthouse and courtroom construction should reflect the need for a more secure structure to withstand any terrorist threat.

In California's San Quentin Prison during the period 1971–1975, approximately 500 stabbings occurred which were responsible for the deaths of about 80 convicts and 10 guards. Most of this violence was traced to black and Chicano gangs who were at war with the guards or with each other. Thus, the social structure of the American prison, which once could be considered as an armed bureaucracy controlling an unorganized population, can no longer be viewed in this manner, as large segments of the population of some prisons have coalesced into unified groups organized for terror, both "inside and outside the walls."

Yet, on February 2, 1976, the former United States attorney general Edward H. Levi suggested the abolition of the federal parole system, and the jailing of convicted criminals for their full sentences, with time off only for good behavior. He said that consideration of such a plan "is an important and necessary first step" toward reform that could deter crime and provide greater fairness in the criminal justice system. At the time, such a plan appeared to be consistent with President Ford's call for legislation establishing mandatory minimum prison sentences for certain violent crimes and for repeat offenders.[30] Implementation of these recommendations will require many states to construct new correctional facilities to accomodate the increase in the inmate population occurring as a result of more strict sentencing and speedier trials.[31]

Continued citizen reluctance in approving public questions on construction of new prison facilities, in states where they are warranted, has dire consequences. Opportunities for terrorist recruitment are certainly enhanced by the overcrowded prison. However, the vagaries of human behavior and the limitations which a free society imposes on prison control also contribute to the formation of situations which have facilitated the escape of an assortment of American terrorists from custody.

RECOMMENDATIONS FOR PRISONS

Recommendations which should be included in prison-reform programs devised by administrators who are aware of the trend of terrorism

---

[30] "Levi Suggests Abolishing Parole, Jailing Criminals for Full Term," *The New York Times*, February 3, 1976, p. 7.

[31] County Board of Elections, Hall of Records, Morristown, New Jersey, U.S.A., *Official General Election Sample Ballot*, November 2, 1976.

in American and West German prisons and are simultaneously confronted with the demand to house an increased inmate population are among the following:

1. Complete background investigations by state police agencies on all corrections employees, members of prison volunteer groups, and all other persons seeking access to prisons or prisoners.

2. Increased use of magnetometer and other security devices to inspect all persons and parcels entering prisons, and manual disassembly of any item which could conceal a weapon.

3. Additional education of correction guards and other prison employees in the area of political ideology, sociology, and psychology for the purpose of understanding and countering the spread of revolutionary propaganda among inmates.

4. The development and delivery of courses in the Islamic religion and culture to prison employees to facilitate their understanding of Muslim inmates and to serve as an input into decisions relative to the classification and isolation of factions engaged in open warfare or having the propensity for such conduct.

5. The development of additional safeguards to protect the lives and persons of inmates and their associates who provide information to the police and corrections officers.

6. Utilization of a computerized inmate-transaction system to serve as a general management tool and to provide the additional capability of monitoring the development and extension of prison-based criminal conspiracies and other illegal activity.

7. Establishment of a computerized correctional intelligence information system operated by a state police agency or another law enforcement agency not included in a state department of corrections, to control prison abuses (e.g. drug trafficking, payoffs for privilege, criminal conspiracies, and other irregularities).

8. Increased supervision of all inmates participating in work release and furlough programs to assure society that they are not being used by terrorist groups as couriers between cells implanted both "outside and inside" prison walls.

9. Development of a definition of "dangerousness" which will permit prison and paroling authorities to make meaningful estimates relative to continued confinement or release.

It is anticipated that the adoption of these recommendations will greatly reduce acts of terror perpetrated by organized groups of inmates.

PART II
CONTROLS

CONTROLLING POLITICAL TERRORISM
IN A FREE SOCIETY

Skyjackings, abductions, bombings, slayings, and the seizure of hostages and government buildings are the tactics usually employed by political terrorists, whose victims range from helpless school children, religious pilgrims, vacationing travelers, and business executives to diplomats, officers of government, and dignitaries. During the 1970s, acts of terrorist brutality were commonplace, as leftist terrorists, who, according to the Italian prime minister Francesco Cossiga, "strike at the heart of the state" by murdering magistrates, businessmen, and police officers, competed with neo-Fascist or black gangs for notoriety. Right-wing extremists, preferring the massacre because it promotes panic and impulsive reactions, do not receive as much publicity as such leftist organizations as the Italian Red Brigades, but they are equally dangerous. On August 2, 1980, one of Italy's neo-Fascist terrorist gangs is believed to have been responsible for an explosion at a Bologna railroad station that killed 76 people.

STRATEGIC CONSIDERATIONS

Political terrorism may be defined as the threat or the use of calculated violence, indiscriminately or selectively, against either enemies or allies, to achieve a political end. Terrorist acts are always intended to make a predetermined impact on a particular target for the purpose of altering an existing state of affairs in such a way that it will come to favor the perpetrators. Terrorists' actions directed against democratic states, particularly those containing many minority groups, or others which contain historically antagonistic people—Israel, Northern Ireland, Cyprus, Zaire—are intended to discredit existing governments by causing them to concentrate their coercive powers on a particular segment of the population with which the terrorists try to identify. Thus, the terrorists strive to implement a protracted campaign of violence which is designed to make life unendurable for a democratic government until their demands are satisfied. Unfortunately, some of these governments submit to terrorists' demands, and thereby obtain a temporary respite, rather than risk undertaking a counterterrorist campaign which might serve only further to isolate them from segments of their population. However, many of these same governments are at a later date again confronted by terrorists with additional demands. Although it is expensive in terms of human life and property, it seems that the most effective counterstrategy for a liberal democratic society to adopt is one which ignores terrorist demands, particularly since submission to terrorists only serves to reinforce their behavior.

TUPAMARO TACTICS AND THE POLICE OFFICER

The urban guerrilla tactics of Uruguay's Tupamaros and the massive publicity generated by some of their more spectacular propaganda actions have made them the most popular and imitated revolutionary group in the world. The Weathermen, the West German Baader–Meinhof gang, the Symbionese Liberation Army (S.L.A.) and other groups all duplicate Tupamaro tactics and actions. The established Tupamaro propaganda tactic of hijacking trucks from food stores and dispensing their contents to slum dwellers, for example, was used by the S.L.A. when it demanded that a multimillion-dollar food handout be undertaken in selected California cities in exchange for the release of their captive, Patricia Hearst.[1]

Most terrorists select targets similar to those chosen by the Tupamaros. The most favored targets are large international corporations with facilities in "Third World" countries, diplomats and other representatives of North American and Western European states, and police

---

[1] Martha Crenshaw Hutchinson, "The Concept of Revolutionary Terrorism," *Journal of Conflict Resolution*, XVI, no. 3 (September, 1972):383–396.

officers, whom they regard as the tool of the "capitalist forces of repression." Techniques of operating in urban areas have been demonstrated by the Tupamaros to other terrorists, who now realize that in a city one "can work through so many thousands of people . . . the enemy is made to feel him as an impalpable presence, until every ordinary pedestrian seems like a guerrilla in disguise."[2]

Terrorists know that this constant uncertainty has a profound psychological impact on the police officer, who is constantly open to harassment. Yet he can trust no one, for the most innocuous person or incident can deal him a fatal blow. Added to the police officer's constant anxiety is the extreme frustration he experiences when trying to implement terrorist-control measures in a city without arousing the ire of the people he inconveniences.

Consequently, the police agencies of democratic states should anticipate an escalation in the number of direct terrorist actions such as attempts to disarm, kidnappings, and assassinations, taken against members of police forces. These same agencies must, nevertheless, train police officers to react rationally and objectively, even in those most trying situations when a member of their profession is slain by a terrorist. When doing otherwise, they risk becoming the dupe of a terrorist who aims at breaking their morale and discipline, particularly when the media are present. The Black Liberation Army (B.L.A.), who killed police officers "because of their color, which was neither black nor white, but blue," tried but failed to employ these tactics successfully against members of the New York City Police Department in 1972.[3]

POLICE EDUCATION AND INTEGRITY

Although terrorists avoid contacts with the police, except when trying to obtain information on plans and events from individual policemen or police informants working as double agents, they do actively seek to identify and exploit the police's "contradictions, weaknesses, and fissures." Police commanders should anticipate that acts of police intimidation and reprisals, genuine or fabricated, will be manipulated by terrorists, such as the B.L.A., who were known to practice acts of "revolutionary justice" by executing selected police officers. The Tupamaros, particularly, were convinced that this "vigilante approach to po-

---

[2] Raymond M. Momboisse, *Blueprint of Revolution: The Rebel, the Party, the Techniques of Revolt* (Springfield, Ill.: Charles C Thomas Co., 1967), p. 282.
[3] Robert Daley, *Target Blue* (New York: Delacorte Press, 1973), pp. 402–445.

lice brutality gives excellent fruits and must not be abandoned."[4] Police agencies, therefore, should develop and implement a comprehensive program of in-service training geared to provide individual police officers with the skills in interpersonal relations and survival techniques which are needed for coping with this aspect of terrorist tactics. Furthermore, "since the policing service in a free society is almost entirely a personal service, every condition in a police organization and its environment is traceable in a large measure to the acts of policemen and to the success or failure of their operations."[5] Consequently, internal investigation units must be established or extended within police agencies to monitor the integrity of a department and thereby identify and correct failures and errors through a process of periodic inspections before they assume serious proportions and/or can be manipulated by terrorists who are consistently trying to discredit the police.

SPECIAL POLICE OPERATIONS PROGRAMS

It is recommended that colleges and universities, particularly those with criminal justice programs, develop courses which emphasize the challenge presented to a free society by political terrorism, and the difficulties involved in controlling activity of a criminal conspiratorial nature while simultaneously operating within the framework of constitutional provisions. Such courses should familiarize students with the important distinction between terrorism and other forms of violence (i.e. guerrilla warfare, partisan actions, etc.), how each is employed, and the countermeasures, both proactive and reactive, utilized by law-enforcement agencies to reduce the menace of terrorism.

Appropriately entitled "Special Police Operations," these courses should also emphasize intelligence as the focus for police action intended to counter terrorism. Intelligence is the critical element in such operations, as it is only a properly organized intelligence unit which contains the components required to collect, evaluate, collate, interpret, report, record, and disseminate analysed information relative to the infrastructure, modus operandi, membership, operations, etc., of covertly organized criminal groups.

Students enrolled in a special police operations course should be given information to enable them to understand the process by which

---

[4] Arturo C. Porzecanski, *Uruguay's Tupamaros: The Urban Guerrilla* (New York: Praeger Press 1973), p. 21.
[5] O. W. Wilson, *Police Administration* (New York: McGraw-Hill, 1972), p. 197.

intelligence operations provide an agency with the data necessary for making the informed judgements and preparations required to combat clandestine organizations and to police adequately the disorders, meetings, rallies, parades, strikes, and other events which take place within an agency's jurisdiction. Information relative to legal principles, and to public policy with respect to intelligence operations, should be included in the course. In a few other areas, it is as important to be especially sensitive to constitutional rights and community values as it is in the operation of a domestic intelligence system.

It is quite possible that the role of the F.B.I. in domestic surveillance might never have reached the proportions it has if municipal law-enforcement officers were better trained in the use of intelligence to control organized conspiracies. Their inability to cope with these problems on the local level has made it necessary for federal agencies to enter the vacuum thus created. Consequently, there is a current unsatisfied need for qualified analytical personnel to staff police and other intelligence agencies.

In January 1975, Union College, situated in Cranford, New Jersey, offered what is thought to be the nation's first special police operations course. This instruction consists of three sections: terrorism, organized crime, and police countermeasures. Approximately six hundred students, consisting of current law-enforcement personnel and nonpractitioners, have already been enrolled in this course which emphasizes the organization of a police intelligence unit, information flow, and modern analytical techniques. Additional information included in the course is material relative to the characteristics, history, and philosophical aspects of terrorism, urban terrorist operations, disinformation and deception operations, hostage situations, extremist groups (domestic and international), political corruption, and the organization and operations of police internal-affairs units.

During the week of August 8, 1976, the content of the Union College Special Police Operations Course was presented to selected personnel of the New Jersey Division of State Police at their "Sea Girt" training center. The objective of this training was to provide police administrators with the necessary knowledge to review and revamp existing policies in order to improve the capabilities of the police officers in dealing more efficiently and effectively with civil disorder and terrorist acts.

The material presented at "Sea Girt" was modified by the training staff of the New Jersey State Police, and used by them as the foundation for the construction of a series of 30 management seminars on terrorism, which were funded by the Law Enforcement Assistance Administration (L.E.A.A.). These meetings featured guest lectures with expertise in areas related to terrorist groups, hostage situations, and other subjects. Similar programs conducted by the Illinois State Police at their Academy in Springfield, Illinois, and the Texas Department of Law Enforcement at their facility at Austin, Texas, were derived from the "Sea Girt" program.

A program entitled "Counter-Terrorism: Techniques for Practitioners," a refinement of the L.E.A.A. programs, which emphasized the application of intelligence to the combatting of terrorism, was conducted at John Jay College of Criminal Justice, City University of New York, during the week of June 4, 1978.

Law-enforcement agencies affiliated with the states of Georgia and Massachusetts and the United States Air Force, the United States Park Police, the International Association of Chiefs of Police, and the Provincial Police of Ontario have also conducted antiterrorism training for police and security personnel. Another innovative program entitled "Anti-terrorism Skills For the Practitioner," emphasizing communication theory and its application to antiterrorism, has been conducted at John Jay College's Criminal Justice Center.

DISCRETIONARY DEATH PENALTY

On August 5, 1975, the United States moved toward a type of legal uniformity when it enacted Public Law 93–366, which reimposed the death penalty in hijacking cases involving the death of individuals, subject to a special hearing and assurance by a jury that mitigating circumstances were not present. This law could be extended to cover other areas of terrorism, and no longer be restricted exclusively to hijacking, which has decreased. Although no one knows the exact deterrent value of capital punishment, a discretionary death penalty is well worth having if it will save the life of one person.

The discretionary death penalty also has certain other advantages which are worthy of consideration. Factual information pertaining to a terrorist infrastructure of membership is not often obtained from a terrorist who has received an unequivocal and irrevocable death sentence. Whereas a mandatory death penalty stops the flow of information, the discretionary death penalty might actually encourge it. Furthermore, a terrorist would have very little to lose by killing all the people aboard an aircraft if the penalty for a crime of airline hijacking was a mandatory death penalty. Yet capital punishment is not a deterrent for some suicidal terrorists, the totally fanatic, who are prepared and intend to die as martyrs for their cause.[6] However, the proposed criminal code revision seeks to restore the death penalty for certain federal crimes by amending federal law to comply with the Supreme Court's 1972 decision, which held that the death penalty was unconstitutional because it was capriciously imposed.

IMPROVED COURT-MANAGEMENT PROCEDURES AND POLICIES

It is important for terrorists to be brought to trial within 45 to 60 days after their apprehension, so that maximum benefit is obtained from the imposition of the discretionary death penalty. Court-management procedures and policies must be devised to reduce the delay of between 18 and 24 months which now takes place between the apprehension and trial of those few terrorists who finally stand before a jury. Terrorists are particularly aware that only a few of the Arabs responsible for hijackings, kidnappings, and the seizure and execution of hostages over the last few years, when captured, have suffered meaningful punishment. Many of them, who were incarcerated for extended periods pending prosecution, were freed in compliance with the demands of their compatriots, who held innocent people as hostages. It was this sort of extortion which forced the West Germans to release the three surviving members of the Munich team of killers.

West Germany has also been subjected to a variety of terrorist demands and onslaughts by resurgent members of the Baader–Meinhof gang who seek the release of their leaders, and about 30 other members of their gang, who were captured in 1972.[7] Obviously, terrorists must be made to realize that, if found guilty, they will be swiftly punished, and that, therefore, any sort of demonstration, petitions, or violence on their behalf by compatriots or supporters would be futile.

RECOMMENDED LAWS REGARDING PAYMENT OR RECEIPT OF RANSOM

The passage by the United States Congress of a law which made illegal the payment of ransom could serve as another deterrent to ter-

---

[6] Committee on Internal Security, *Terrorism, Part 2* (Washington, D.C.: Government Printing Office, 1974), pp. 3222–3223.

[7] Melvin J. Lasky, "Ulrike and Andreas," *The New York Times Magazine*, May 11, 1975, pp. 73–79.

rorism. It would be most difficult, and perhaps counterproductive, however, to prevent people from paying ransom to obtain the release of loved ones. But, as a minimum, income-tax laws could be revised for the purpose of denying American corporations the opportunity to deduct ransom payments as business expenses. If this measure proves impracticable, perhaps American corporations themselves could recognize that they are living in a different world, and decide on their own not to pay ransom.

Although it would perhaps be impossible to enforce, Congress might consider formulating additional legislation which would make it a crime for a third party to receive the benefits of ransom payments. This law could eliminate the "Robin Hood" aspects of terrorist propaganda actions, since it is aimed specifically at the general public, who receive, for example, a distribution of food by reason of demands, such as in the Hearst case.[8]

THE OFFICIAL HOSTAGE POLICY OF
THE UNITED STATES GOVERNMENT

For law-enforcement officials, terrorism and its implications have thus become a universal nightmare, particularly when "nonnegotiable" demands are issued for the release of prisoners, for money, or for passage to another country. Is the safety of the hostages to be secured at any cost? Or must their lives be risked to discourage other terrorists and save future victims? Forced to confront the problem through a heavy overlay of politics, emotion, and history, different countries have found different answers. Israelis argue that hijackings and other extortion attempts would escalate if they complied with terrorists' threats to release hostages. However, Israel is also interested in the well-being of the hostages as its primary concern. But when the murderers of the Israeli athletes at Munich are freed after a plane is hijacked, or when a young terrorist is given a safe-conduct flight to Kuwait after his attack on an airline office is thwarted and he holds 17 people hostage for 4 hours, it becomes obvious that terrorists thrive on taking advantage of the common decency of peoples and governments.

The official United States Government hostage policy closely resembles Israel's policy of "no deal" with the terrorists. This policy was formulated in 1973 when an American diplomat was slain in the Sudan

[8] Committee on Foreign Affairs, *International Terrorism* (Washington, D.C.: Government Printing Office, 1974), pp. 68–69.

by Arab terrorists. At the time, President Nixon declared that the United States would not meet any demands for the release of hostages, saying that such action would encourage political kidnapping and terrorism. Thus, the federal government of the United States will not yield in any way to extortion or blackmail for the release of any of its citizens anywhere in the world; rather, it is the responsibility of the host country to take every step possible to assure the well-being of American diplomats and other citizens.[9]

The argument against acquiescence is persuasive. Still, there is little evidence that the tough approach is the best. Psychiatrists have found that political terrorists are often paranoid schizophrenics with overt suicidal tendencies—a deadly species. To this kind of mentality, death is not the ultimate punishment; it is the ultimate reward. Law-enforcement agencies should realize that a terrorist often does not take his victims in order to achieve some goal; rather, he dreams up a goal in order to take hostages.[10] It may be true in certain cases that a terrorist is merely using a pretext in order to take his hostages and stage a production for all the world to see.

"THE HOSTAGE MUST LIVE" CONCEPT

One big gap in the existing American public security system which should be narrowed if terrorists are to be discouraged from undertaking actions in this country is the lack of a nationwide and uniform hostage policy. Presently, the hostage policy adhered to by the New York City Police Department, for example, in substance is that "the hostage must live." This policy is in direct opposition to the official federal policy, but in practice it seems unlikely that the two policies would apply simultaneously. If, for example, Arab terrorists hijacked an airliner at John F. Kennedy International Airport and demanded the release of Sirhan Sirhan in exchange for the lives of hostages whom they held, the entire event would be within the jurisdiction of the federal government. The F.B.I. would handle enforcement aspects within the F.A.A. jurisdiction, and a federal official would most probably reject the terrorists demand to free Sirhan, who is held in San Quentin Federal Prison.[11]

If, as another example, a terrorist group seized a hostage within the

---

[9] Committee on Internal Security, *Terrorism, Part 2*, pp. 3133–3138.
[10] Gerald Arenberg, *Hostage* (Washington, D.C.: American Police Academy, 1974), pp. 22–26.
[11] Ibid.

limits of New York City and demanded safe passage to the nearest international airport, the New York police would comply with the city's hostage policy and submit to the terrorist demand, assuming, of course, that the only alternative would be "death for the hostages." Once the terrorists and their hostages reached the outer limit of F.A.A. jurisdiction at the airport, what would happen next, however, is not clear. Would federal authorities take over jurisdiction and deal with the terrorists, or would they refuse to deal? It is assumed that they would not deal, and thus New York City's hostage policy would be, in practice, negated.

It is recommended that discussions be held between federal and state officials and those of some large cities to resolve all possible points of conflict and confusion involving the handling of terrorists who hold hostages.

RESPONSIBILITY OF THE PRESS AND MEDIA

A political terrorist depends on a publicity campaign to assist him in his effort to convince an audience of the immediate and urgent need for society to adjust the conditions responsible for his demands. A public-relations assessment would be a prerequisite for any terrorist plan, and the controlling factor relative to its intensity, direction, and duration. In the rhetoric of the Spanish-speaking Tupamaros, this evaluation process is called a diagnosis of the *coyuntura*, that is, an assessment of "the political, economic, military and organizational conditions of both the society and the social movement."[12]

Freedom of the press, however, is basic to the concept of a free society, and, as a consequence, it is extremely difficult to devise any restraints that would be accepted voluntarily by the media. The media have, on occasion, reported the news of terrorist activities in a manner that encourages its practitioners to believe that they are extremely important persons. It is anticipated that a greater degree of cooperation between federal intelligence agencies and the media in the form of an educational approach might encourage all concerned to appreciate the contagious nature of terrorism, and thereby come to realize that terrorists are not just reformers or idealists, but criminals who should be treated as such in news releases.[13]

---

[12] Porzecanski, *Uruguay's Tupamaros*, p. 11.

[13] Less than 90 minutes after the Eastern Airlines jet crash in New York last June, NBC went live with electronic cameras (minicams) from the site. Within 30 minutes, the NBC audience was almost triple its usual size at 6:00 P.M.—1.5 million viewers versus a half million. (Source: *New York Magazine*, July 7, 1975, p. 67.)

In a crisis situation, television crews should practice objective reporting, free of embellishment, so as not to exacerbate a situation that the police are attempting to control. They might voluntarily agree not to provide their audience with specific locations of violence, until it has been contained by the police. The adoption of this practice would reduce the large numbers of people who are drawn to a place of excitement by radio and television news releases, and who thereby cause a diversion of scarce police manpower to the additional problem of crowd control, or serve the terrorists themselves by attracting "fillers" for a mob under their control.[14]

The media might also strive to strip terrorists of their self-delusions, rather than providing them with several million dollars worth of free publicity, since this type of inadvertent cooperation plays precisely into the terrorists' hands. The British solution to this matter is to subject its newspapers to a D–notice system, under which the press is notified prior to publication that a particular news item could violate security laws.[15] Voluntary restraints by the American media themselves, rather than the institution of censorship, seems to be the best approach for this country to take, providing that its national security needs are regarded as sacrosanct by all persons who do not have a need or a right to know any or all details.

POLICE TASK-FORCE APPROACH

Although pressured by news publicity to respond dramatically to a terrorist situation, the police of a free society must be careful not to overact, and thereby gain public sympathy for the terrorist. The task force has many advantages for the police in this respect.

Essentially, the value of the task-force approach is in concentrating trained manpower on a single case. In May 1975, the West German government created a terrorism branch of their national police, the Federal Criminal Office, to search for members of the Baader–Meinhof Gang who were still at large. A few years earlier, the New York City Police Department used this task-force approach to counter and eliminate attacks by the Black Liberation Army (B.L.A.) on its personnel. The New York police detailed a team of detectives to collect information on individuals associated with the B.L.A. and coordinate the activities of police officers working undercover within the terrorist group. Only de-

[14] Ibid.
[15] Alvin Shuster, "Secrecy Veils British Intelligence Service," *The New York Times*, October 28, 1974, p. 7.

tectives actively involved in the investigation were privy to all field reports, and consequently sensitive information was not "leaked" to the press.[16]

A few members of American police vice-control units have gained considerable expertise in charting the relationships between organized-crime figures on whom syndicated crime relies to extend its criminal conspiracy. Many of these organized crime structures and networks are akin to those maintained by political terrorists. It might appear that the police methods used in control of organized crime might also be used effectively against terrorists. But police have tried for years to eliminate the Mafia, and have failed, not because their methods are ineffective, but because they find it very difficult to conduct any intelligence operation on a prolonged basis which cannot be justified by the performance statistics required to support budgetary appropriations for additional financing. Thus, only a few detectives in a handful of large urban American police departments have the training and experience required to control organized conspiracies or handle public security aspects of municipal police intelligence operations.

CABINET COMMITTEE WORKING GROUP

Following the tragedy at Munich, which illustrated that international terrorism had reached the point where innocent people anywhere can be victimized, the president of the United States directed his secretary of state to chair a cabinet committee for the purpose of identifying the most effective ways to prevent both domestic and international terrorism. Responding to the president's request, the secretary of state called a meeting which resulted in the formation of the committee and the establishment of a working group composed of senior representatives or agency heads of the groups represented on the committee. Although members of the working group are in close contact as issues arise and incidents occur, the cabinet committee itself rarely meets.[17]

[16] Albert A. Seedman and Peter Hellman, *Chief* (New York: Avon, 1975), pp. 419–498.
[17] Members and participants are as follows. Cabinet Committee: the secretary of state, the attorney general, the secretary of defense, the director of the F.B.I., the director of the C.I.A., the secretary of the treasury, the secretary of transportation, the president's assistants for national security and domestic affairs, and the United States ambassador to the United Nations; Working Group: Senior representatives of cabinet committee members listed above, and nineteen other agencies. Other participants are included on an ad hoc basis. (Source: Committee on Foreign Affairs, *International Terrorism*, pp. 13–14).

The Working Group has an interest in global terrorist matters for the purpose of ensuring the collaboration of agencies and departments with domestic and foreign responsibilities, and in recommending countermeasures which may close gaps in the security screen around Americans abroad and foreigners in this country whom agencies represented by the Working Group help to protect. With respect to the protection of Americans at home from terrorists, the Working Group relies on the customary agencies, local and federal, to continue with their usual responsibilities. For example, the Working Group is informed by the F.B.I. of the international potentialities or implications of domestic terrorist groups, and it uses the C.I.A. in matters beyond the frontiers of the United States.

The Cabinet Committee Working Group's main effort is the collection of information on terrorism, which it uses as a basis to improve procedures in this country and abroad to deter terrorists. In this area it performs quite well, as it is active in pressing for ratification of important multilateral conventions dealing with hijacking and the adoption of security standards by the International Civil Aviation Organization (I.C.A.O.) designed to, improve further security of airports abroad. It also works with the United Nations. Its discussions with groups of members of that organization, however, usually get bogged down in debate over the issue of justifiable, as opposed to illegal, violence. Unfortunately, members assigned to the Working Group do not handle terrorist matters on a continuous basis, but rather provide input into the group from their respective agencies, and obtain information in return only as incidents occur. Thus, task forces have been established by the Working Group to observe some incidents after they take place, such as the unsolved murder of an Israeli attaché in Washington and the murder of two Turkish consuls in Santa Barbara, California. However, some cases occur so quickly that the Working Group does not respond. In those cases where it is involved, its task forces are disbanded once the incident is over.[18]

ANTITERRORIST ASSESSMENT AND RESPONSE GROUP

Although the American public today is against surveillance, data banks, dossiers, or any other aspect of a continuous intelligence operation, intelligence is the only available process which is capable of ren-

[18] Committee on Foreign Affairs, *International Terrorism*, pp. 13–30.

dering assessments relative to the future actions of terrorists. Consequently, there is a definite need for legislation to establish an antiterrorist assessment and response group at a high level in the national government. The activities of this group would supplement the work of the Cabinet Committee Working Group, and serve as an immediate information resource for other authorized agencies. It would not duplicate the work of the C.I.A., which is restricted by law from performing internal security functions, or that of the F.B.I., which does not collect intelligence abroad or employ analysts with the requisite skills in international politics and economics to function in strategic public-security-intelligence modules. The new group could be staffed with people who know how to gather and analyze public-security information from both domestic and foreign sources, for dissemination on a regular "need-to-know" basis to law-enforcement agencies. [19]

Once established, it is recommended that the Counterterrorist Assessment and Response Group contain three primary units: an assessment unit, a teaching unit, and a response unit. The assessment unit could receive terrorist information from members of the Cabinet Committee Working Group, municipal law-enforcement agencies, and the response unit. It would then process this information for its own use and for dissemination in the form of strategic reports to other agencies. The teaching unit could provide training for local law-enforcement agencies in subjects relating to terrorism which are not currently taught by the F.B.I.

Initially, the teaching team would concentrate on further developing the expertise of persons assigned to existing police public-security-intelligence units which were established by a number of large urban police departments once they realized that their detective bureaus were unable to handle the work. The response team, composed of qualified experts from various disciplines such as management, law enforcement, psychology, and public relations, would travel to the site of terrorist actions at home or abroad where American citizens or corporations were involved. Although fully respectful of the sovereignty and limits of power of other nations, the jurisdictions of other agencies, and the wishes of the victim as well, the response team could be used to urge another government to accept all American resources which would be put at its disposal, including intelligence and communications. The response team could collect specific field information for the assessment team on those foreign terrorist groups which have the capability to infiltrate highly-trained teams of persons into the United States without detection.

---

[19] Committee on Internal Security, *Terrorism, Part 2*, pp. 3086–3190.

AN EYE ON THE FUTURE

Confronted with a continuing spiral of increasingly more sophisticated terrorist activity at home and abroad on the one hand, and the absolute necessity to maintain the basic constitutional freedoms and safeguards which collectively add up to democracy on the other, the United States must develop the programs and policies needed to control and combat political terrorism within the framework of a free society. The government of the United States should undertake an educational program designed to inform its citizens about all aspects of political terrorism, including the difficulties of combating it within the framework of a free society. Once apprised of these matters by their government, many Americans might support the institution of uniform penal codes, a discretionary death penalty, improved court-management programs, laws regarding payment or receipt of ransom, and other measures necessary for controlling terrorism.

A program such as this would help Americans understand the rationale of their government's official hostage policy, and thus comprehend its intent and purpose. The press would benefit from this education, since a portion of it could be designed to enlighten reporters about aspects of terrorism which are especially intended to obtain mass-media exposure. Individual police officers, too, would profit from such a program, as it would help them guard against being manipulated by a terrorist into undertaking an action which violates their code of conduct.

The United States Government should expand the scope of its cabinet committee and its working group to combat terrorism and advocate the passage of legislation which would establish a full-time and highly specialized antiterrorist assessment and response group with defined duties at a high level in the national government. Subunits of this new group would perform the vital tasks of educating police public-security analysts, assessing both domestic and international aspects of terrorism, developing a consolidated and uniform terrorist information system, observing significant worldwide incidents of terrorism, and supporting the cabinet committee and its working group.

Once this group is established it is mandatory that properly safeguarded and constitutionally authorized procedures be implemented to regulate the operation of its computerized intelligence system, and that it exchange its information with federal and local law-enforcement agencies in accordance with guidelines promulgated to regulate such exchanges.

It is imperative that police public-security operations be continued, but made responsive to the legal principles and public polices that are developing with respect to them. Police intelligence units should be upgraded in the areas of personnel selection and training, information-handling techniques, and unit organization. Meanwhile, the individuals involved in the several continuing probes of the American intelligence community should recognize that the defense of the United States requires a certain amount of unpleasantness, and, therefore, be careful not to destroy the effectiveness of the C.I.A. as global collector of information relative to terrorist matters, or of the F.B.I. as the nation's primary guardian of internal security.

In our highly politicized age, it would appear that the dangers of political terrorism are likely to confront the world more often in the immediate future. Americans must be prepared to cope with terrorist acts which occur in their cities, although some may assume that there is just no way to guard against the unknown and the unseen, and thus fail to support the expenditure of tax dollars for preventive measures. Such a passive attitude might be responsible for a terrorist incident that would be not only costly, but also internationally embarrassing.

It would be foolish to pretend that the tide of airline sabotage, extortion, bombings, and hijackings can be totally turned back; but efforts to control terrorism must be continued and expanded, to make it less attractive to extremist elements, and more expensive for them to employ.

7

APPROACHES TO ANTITERRORISM

A democratic society, although dedicated to the peaceful settlement of dissent and disagreement, must devise and implement legislation which permits its police to conduct antiterror operations, otherwise it may one day come to realize that it has ceased to govern a free people. Some Latin American countries, for example, unable to control the extension and development of a terrorist organization through the use of traditional police methods, have devised and implemented state-of-siege legislation which prohibits all public dissent, and utilizes military courts martial to handle a wide range of offenses, from kidnapping to guerrilla ambushes of police personnel. Although a generally successful counterterrorist technique, a state-of-siege decree often results in a shift of power to the armed forces who use it to overturn or control most civilian institutions, arguing that a terrorist movement is only a manifestation of the decay of a nation's political and social structure. Democracy as a viable institution, therefore, ceases to exist.

In 1972, the Uruguayan military, utilizing state-of-siege powers to detain approximately ten thousand terrorist suspects and other leftists, wiped out the Tupamaro organization. However, 5 years later, the military, confident of their ability to conduct counterterrorist operations, only began to talk about an eventual return of the government to civilian politicians.[1]

[1] Jonathan Kandell, "Uruguay Awaits Form of Democracy Army Says It Will Eventually Restore," *The New York Times*, June 15, 1976, p. 2.

Canadians have experienced the use of broad-based legislation to control terrorism. In October 1970, Canada, for the first time in its history, used war measures to control an internal emergency, and thereby raised a group of Front de Libération du Québec (F.L.Q.) terrorists to the status of belligerents against the realm. Implementing the provisions of the War Measures Act, Prime Minister Pierre Trudeau stated on nationwide television, "I think a society must take every means at its disposal to defend itself against the emergency of a parallel power which defies the elected power in this country." Shortly after the Prime Minister made his remark, two events happened in rapid succession: first, the Canadian police detained about 250 people in Montreal, and second, the terrorists released James Cross, the senior British trade commissioner in Montreal, whom they held captive.[2]

ANTITERRORISM AND AMERICAN SOCIETY

At a May 1976 meeting in Princeton, New Jersey, the National Advisory Committee on Criminal Justice Standards and Goals approved language in a report prepared by its Task Force on Disorders and Terrorism. The report outlined a variety of legislation intended to authorize counterterrorist measures designed to help American society defend itself against terrorists. Among these recommended measures are police tactics designed to cause havoc and chaos within a terrorist organization. For example, under the control of a policy-review board supervised by the United States or a state's attorney general, police officers would be permitted to infiltrate a terrorist group, not merely to gather information, but to inhibit or provoke hostile activity among individual terrorists or groups. The task force also advocates legislation, similar to the Canadian War Measures Act, which would provide for emergency measures such as curfews following "acts of extraordinary violence of a politically inspired character which cannot be controlled or contained by ordinary means."[3]

It is unlikely that the recommendations of the Task Force on Civil Disorder and Terrorism will be acceptable to the American people. Elected representatives are currently involved in investigations and debates relative to the limitation of police power, and not the extension called for by the Task Force, even though the F.B.I. has for years been

---

[2] Robert Moss, *The War for the Cities* (New York: Coward, McCann & Geoghegan, Inc., 1972), pp. 121.

[3] Daniel Hays, "Terror and the Law," *The Star Ledger* (Newark, N.J.), May 3, 1976, p. 1.

successfully engaged in programs of disruptive techniques against racist organizations and leftist political groups. Of the 14 different Ku Klux Klan organizations existing in the South, the F.B.I. penetrated every one through informants, and, between 1942 and 1968, was involved in 238 surreptitious entries in connection with investigations of "domestic security targets." "Black-bag jobs," jargon for this break-in technique, are necessary, according to F.B.I. officials, "because they represent an invaluable technique in combating subversive activities of a clandestine nature aimed directly at undermining and destroying our nation."[4] The F.B.I. was studied by the Senate Select Committee on Intelligence Operations, and its countersubversive activities have, as a consequence, been reduced.

OPERATION "PHOENIX"

It seems that American law-enforcement agencies must first involve themselves in programs designed to educate a free people about the hazards to a democratic society posed by terrorism before they become involved in antiterrorist operations specifically designed to dismember a terrorist organization. "Phoenix," a joint American military and Central Intelligence Agency (C.I.A.) antiterrorist venture in South Vietnam, which was defamed by the media, is a case in point. Founded in 1965, "Phoenix" used Counter Terror (C.T.) teams as its main operating units. The C.T.'s were later renamed Provincial Reconnaissance Units (P.R.U.'s) as a consequence of the adverse publicity which surrounds the use of the word "terror."[5] Markedly successful in identifying and neutralizing members of Viet Cong cells, in 1969 alone the C.T.'s identified twenty thousand Viet Cong members, and their precision cost fewer lives than the shotgun methods used by the South Vietnamese police and security authorities before "Phoenix got into the picture."[6] But Americans are unable to accept on the basis of faith alone that the personnel of its security services are honorable men devoted to their protection and service. Thus, their law-enforcement agencies must develop techniques which permit them to control terrorism within the limits of tolerance imposed by the people whom they serve.

[4] "FBI Burglarized Leftist Offices Here 92 Times in 1960–66, Official Files Show," *The New York Times*, March 29, 1976, p. 1.
[5] Victor Marchetti and John D. Marks, *The CIA and the Cult of Intelligence* (New York: Knopf, 1974), p. 245.
[6] Miles Copeland, *Without Cloak or Dagger* (New York: Simon & Schuster, 1974), pp. 218–220.

"LOW-INTENSITY OPERATIONS"

Brigadier Frank Kitson, author of a book entitled *Low Intensity Operations* and a person with considerable field experience with British security forces in Malaya, Kenya, Cyprus, and Northern Ireland, regards counterterrorist operations as "a sort of game based on intense mental activity allied to a determination to find things out and an ability to regard everything on its merits without regard to customs, doctrine or drill." Frank Kitson's style is further notable for its intense, almost fanatical attention to detail, total lack of the standard gentlemanly thoughts about the cowardly or despicable nature of the terrorists, and a low police and/or military profile; hence the name "low intensity operations."[7] Designed for maintaining law and order while conducting counterterrorist operations within the United Kingdom (in Ulster specifically) and a reflection of two hundred years of British experience with the techniques of social control within the framework of a free society, low-intensity operations appear to be based on the notion that acts outside the law are morally wrong, and therefore, as Sir Robert Thompson said, "create more practical difficulties for a government than they solve."[8]

The "pseudo gang" is a particularly effective counterterrorist technique utilized by the practitioner of low-intensity warfare. Composed of British soldiers all of whom are natives of Northern Ireland, these gangs are trained for undercover operations, and assigned the task of penetrating and surveying I.R.A.-controlled urban areas under the cover of a legitimate service industry—vending-machine replenishment, food and beverage delivery, laundry pickup and return. Other soldiers, in civilian clothes, are used by the British to launch an attack on a city block suspected of harboring terrorists. The intent of this tactic is to upset the people of the area under attack, and have them attribute the sudden burst of gunfire to a rump faction of the I.R.A. which have unwittingly been granted sanctuary in their homes. Often I.R.A. gunmen are forced into the open, or people inform the police of their whereabouts, when these tactics are used. However, shortly after the I.R.A. penetrated one British laundry-van surveillance unit in Belfast, killing five undercover agents, the public outcry in England caused by the exposing of police and soldiers to these out-of-uniform dangers allegedly led to the issuance of a government directive prohibiting infiltration of I.R.A. areas by military personnel in plain clothes. Consequently, in Ulster, the plainclothes effort on the part of the police Special Branch

---

[7] James Kelly, *The Genesis of Revolution* (Dublin: Kelly Cane, Ltd., 1976), pp. 24–31.
[8] Sir Robert Thompson, *Defeating Communist Insurgency: The Lessons of Malaya and Vietnam* (New York: Praeger Publishers, 1966), pp. 52–53.

was stepped up, and an increased supply of money was allocated to the police for the purpose of buying information from informers in the Catholic community.[9]

UNDERCOVER OPERATIONS

Police undercover work, designed to obtain information on terrorist groups, is extremely dangerous to the police officer, as there is a constant risk that he will face torture and death if discovered. Police undercover operatives nevertheless must often be used to supplement routine police counterterrorist operations. The police undercover agent must be a person who blends in with the surroundings of the target area, and, in so doing, leaves the public totally oblivious as to what he is doing. Counterterrorist undercover operatives should be experienced police officers with a proven track record of success in deep-cover operations, since they will not be controlled by any onsite intelligence or undercover groups. Many of these onsite units are not so "tight" as some police officers believe them to be, and, therefore, undercover operatives are usually on their own, insofar as looking after themselves is concerned. A task assignment for undercover agents must be specific, and generally should be directed at the top-level leadership of a terrorist organization.

It is best that all other police officers operating in an area where a deep-penetration undercover operation is being conducted should not be aware of the operation. Information should be transmitted by the undercover operative to his control from one public telephone to another. Numbers and locations of these telephones should be varied on a daily basis. Furthermore, undercover operatives should be completely familiar with their prospective area of operation—street locations, escape routes, ambush positions, back entries, cul-de-sacs, and strategic crossroads. Also, all this geographical information should be made available to the undercover operative in the form of maps or other printed literature which he is asked to commit to memory during the course of an intensive briefing period of substantial duration.

COMPUTER-BASED TACTICAL POLICE
INFORMATION SYSTEMS

The main problem confronting a free society engaged in counterterrorist operations is the development of politically acceptable and le-

[9] Kelly, *Genesis of Revolution*, pp. 218–220.

gally permissible police tactics to gain reliable information about terrorist organizations and to act on this information while the "tips are still hot." Exceptionally hazardous police tactics, such as pseudo gang, are to be avoided. Increased emphasis could be placed, however, on the further development and cost reduction of recently introduced computer-based tactical police information systems. These systems, containing information on dangerous persons, stolen vehicles and property, and driver licensing and vehicle registration data, are important to police patrol operations, because they can accomplish in minutes a series of record checks that once required hours or days to complete. Computerization eliminates the time-consuming telephone inquiries, and the manual searches of cumbersome filing systems, which currently preclude a patrol officer from routinely checking all vehicles within the confines of his beat, or identifying a stolen vehicle before he stops it. Computerized police-patrol operations, engaged in a regular and routine check of all motor vehicles, would seriously impede if not eliminate the aboveground operations of terrorist support columns, particularly mobility units, and thereby force the terrorists to place increased reliance on the general population for services and support.[10]

CRIME-PREVENTION PROGRAMS

To counter the efforts of a terrorist cell blending with the daily routine of an urban area, or relying on sympathizers for its basic necessities, a police department should establish ties with the community which preclude the possibility of this ever happening. Community-based crime-prevention programs—blockwatchers, neighborhood watch, etc.—are intended to encourage people to become alert to suspicious criminal activity and to report it to the police, thereby facilitating a police department's effort to control crime generally, and terrorism specifically, in all areas of a city. Participants in crime-prevention programs are taught to look for such activity as "salesmen" attempting to force entrance into a home, anyone walking down the street peering into each parked car, or anyone loitering in a parked car with the motor running.

New York City, subdivided into 73 police precincts, has a particularly effective crime-prevention program. Its auxiliary police number over ten thousand citywide, and its civilian patrol force contains about fifteen thousand people. New York City also has a civilian taxi patrol

[10]National Advisory Commission on Criminal Justice Standards and Goals, *POLICE* (Washington, D.C.: U.S. Government Printing Office 1973), pp. 578–582.

which serves as the eyes and ears of the police, a blockwatchers program, a police–clergy conference, and a program of police–youth dialogues.[11] Because of the latent effectiveness of community-based crime-prevention programs to control and prevent terrorism and other crimes, police officers should attend recruit and in-service training programs designed to help them to appreciate the role played by the citizen in police antiterrorist operations. Most of all, the foot-patrol officers should be trained to function as the primary link between a community-based crime-prevention program and a police department, as it is their specific assignment to know what is happening on their beat, (i.e., who knows whom, who can be trusted to be discreet, who are the blabbermouths, who are the "window detectives").

Most citizens, although willing to participate in crime-prevention programs, are reluctant to become involved as witnesses. Sometimes, because of human frailty, money is used by the police to purchase information from a citizen whose confidentiality is guaranteed. Although project funding for "tipster programs" of this type cannot usually be obtained from a city or county treasury, a local chamber of commerce or other business association might be willing to finance a project as its part of a community endeavor. The city of Racine, Wisconsin, an industrial community situated on the shores of Lake Michigan, used a "tipster program." Since the program has been initiated, payments have been made to informants for information regarding burglary, homicide, armed robbery, attempted homicide and auto theft. Approximately 42 arrests were made by the Racine police as a consequence of information received from "tipsters" during the course of a 12 month period.[12] Tipster programs, blockwatchers, taxi patrol, and other community-based crime-prevention programs are, thus, particularly useful ways to isolate the terrorist from the community which he must penetrate if he intends to survive.

INVESTIGATIVE TECHNIQUES

Standard police investigative techniques, if applied in a regularized and routine manner and not simply used as a consequence of the oc-

---

[11] Thomas P. Mitchelson, "Decentralization of Authority: Field Services Bureau," American Academy for Professional Law Enforcement, New York Chapter, *Proceedings, 1, no. 1* (circa 1978), pp. 1–2.

[12] Lawrence C. Hagman, "The Tipster Program: A Community Program to Increase Apprehensions," *The Police Chief* (September 1975) p. 34.

currence of a terrorist act, are most effective in detecting a terrorist cell. Among the sources of information to be routinely checked by detectives or plainclothes personnel are car-rental agencies, taxi driver records, airline reservations, and hotel and motel registration cards. Regular liaison should be established with agencies which maintain information on stolen vehicles, and with city clerks, building inspectors, and tax collectors. In a free society, a terrorist organization is best countered and effectively controlled by the systematic application of routine police patrol, investigative, and crime-prevention techniques, provided that the police themselves are aware of the effective antiterrorist capability of a democratic policing service, and strive to utilize their policing powers to protect the communities which they have been sworn to serve.

PROPAGANDA OPERATIONS AND CONTROLS

A favorable press is needed by the police to help them enlist the aid of the public in crime-prevention programs, and in countering the sophisticated blend of truths and half-truths used by terrorists and other groups to distort the image of the police. The police are unable to counter this variety of grey propaganda with similar propaganda of their own, as they are not permitted in a free society to utilize the press for purposes of deception and disinformation. Law-enforcement agencies, assisted by the press and the community, must, therefore, develop procedures to classify and evaluate all community-based and other sources of information for the explicit purpose of countering information planted in a neighborhood for the purpose of defaming the police or inciting violence.[13]

In 1973, American journalists demanded that the media print and broadcast the full texts of various S.L.A. communiqués, although it was evident to the police that mass publicity is exactly the kind of exposure that terrorist groups seek to obtain. The Black Panther Party (B.P.P.) announced itself to the world, seizing the front page of newspapers throughout the country, by walking onto the floor of the California legislature bearing guns. Terrorists are often provided by the press with exactly the type of coverage they need to dramatize their cause, particularly if the terrorist group seeks to effect a "Robin Hood" image. Both the S.L.A. and the Tupamaros are involved in food giveaway programs,

[13] O.W. Wilson and Roy Clinton McLaren, *Police Administration*, 3rd ed. (New York: McGraw-Hill 1972), pp. 222–228.

the Emiliano Zapata Brigade bombs Safeway stores in California to force a lowering of food prices, an Italian food executive is kidnapped because the price of poultry is too high in Rome, and the Save Our Israel Land (SOIL)group destroys New York City banks whose policies are allegedly anti-Israel.

Carlos Marighella describes, in his *Minimanual of the Urban Guerrilla*, the benefits accruing to a terrorist group which undertakes a planned program of kidnappings, bombings, and assassinations. He claims that these programs, which he calls "terrorist action models," have a remote cuing effect via the mass media, which inspires "all malcontents to follow our example and fight with urban guerrilla tactics."[14]

THE MEDIA AND TERRORISM

The perils of publicizing political terrorism should be fully recognized by the media of the democracies, which must report its occurrence honestly, soberly, and in perspective. They should avoid the type of program which might assist the criminal elements. Bronx, New York, youth gangs, for example, are reportedly intrigued by television programs from which they may learn something such as how to build a homemade bomb, or a new way to break into a building. It is evident that there is an unfortunate tendency in certain sectors of the media to serve unknowingly as a tool for a terrorist group by presenting them and their tactics in a romantic light. The criminal Tupamaros, despite their murders of the innocent and their shootings of police officers, were presented as modern Robin Hoods. Reports pertaining to the S.L.A. in the United States also contain a romantic aura. But murder is murder, and criminals are criminals, and a free press has an obligation to report the facts, and not become a tool of alienated and confused misfits who are bent on destroying the structures of justice and peaceful change built with pain over the centuries.

Terrorist actions are designed primarily for the purpose of having a propaganda message, but frequently they are intended to disrupt and discredit the government in power in other ways. Listed among the usual terrorist targets in the advanced democracies are large corporations with international affiliates, and the alleged tool of the "forces of repression," the police. Thus, terrorists undertake armed actions against police

---

[14] Carlos Marighella, *Minimanual of the Urban Guerrilla* (no publisher listed but dated June 1979), pp. 39–40.

officers on a regular basis, particularly in Northern Ireland, Spain, and Italy.[15]

To gain headlines, and thereby increase public awareness of their cause, terrorists use tactics which involve the assassination of government leaders, the sabotage of critical facilities, the bombing of embassies and foreign corporations, assaults on military installations, skyjackings, kidnappings of diplomats and businessmen, and seizures of embassies to hold their staffs for ransom.[16] The latter three situations involve the taking of hostages.

Usually, police officers who respond to hostage situations are decisive, but their actions are often uncoordinated, as a consequence of the extremely difficult, if not impossible, task of developing standardized police procedures which are applicable to every case involving a hostage seized by a terrorist. Often the hostage taken and the cause he represents are unknown to the police. A successful culmination of a hostage situation, which takes place when all participants walk out alive, is often dependent on the receipt of information by the police negotiator regarding the terrorist's motivation for the abduction of the people whom he holds captive.[17]

ROLE OF NATIONAL INTELLIGENCE SERVICES

Intelligence is a vital prerequisite for the correct handling of hostage situations involving terrorist groups. The information-gathering and analytical capabilities of the intelligence units of the world's major metropolitan police organizations must be upgraded to an extent which facilitates their ability to cooperate systematically with each other in pooling information about the organization, motivations, and tactics of terrorists. MI–5, a British counterespionage agency, for example, needs information which could be supplied by the American C.I.A. regarding clandestine shipments of Armalite AR–15 rifles to the I.R.A. and the Ulster Defense Forces (U.D.F.). MI–5 most certainly has information which the Spanish could use regarding alleged connections between the

---

[15] Robert D. McFadden, "Liberation Unit Is Rated as Murderous by Police," *The New York Times*, January 29, 1973, p. 57, and Emanuel Perlmutter, "Extra Duty Tours for Police Set Up After 2nd Ambush," ibid., p. 1.

[16] Edward F. Mickolus, "Negotiating for Hostages: A Policy Dilemma," *ORBIS, A Journal of World Affairs*, XIX, no. 4 (Winter 1976): 1309–14.

[17] Gerald Astor, "Cops with an Alternative to the Shootout," *The New York Times*, January 1, 1975, p. 18, and Conrad V. Hassel, "The Hostage Situation: Exploring the Motivation and the Cause," *The Police Chief* (September 1975): 55–58.

I.R.A. and Basque terrorist groups (E.T.A.), whereas the French Territorial Surveillance Bureau might profit from MI–5's information on Breton separatist groups. The C.I.A. undoubtedly could use any information supplied by foreign intelligence services which links domestic American extremist groups with foreign terrorist organizations.

The West German Bundesnachrichtendent (B.N.D.), the equivalent of the American C.I.A., might want to exchange information on terrorist groups, since it serves as the central depository for information gathered by the special German police commando task force which tracked down and captured the leaders of the Baader–Meinhof urban terrorist group. American intelligence organizations are interested in the activities of German terrorists; many of their operations involve the use of explosives stolen from N.A.T.O. organizations, among which is the American Arms Depot in Meisau, West Germany.

INTERPOL, the global police network and an international intelligence exchange, has come under heavy fire by officials of the International Association of Chiefs of Police (I.A.C.P.) for its current affiliations with both communist and terrorist nations. One I.A.C.P. official once remarked that he was disturbed over Syria's membership in INTERPOL, because of that country's sanction of terrorist activities, and felt that the idea of any INTERPOL–I.A.C.P. link needed further study. Similar misgivings were voiced by several police chiefs from American cities, who regarded INTERPOL's information-collection activity as an infringement on their local departments.[18] Instead, it is recommended that liaison between national intelligence agencies be conducted on a direct agency-to-agency or "one-to-one" basis, rather than through a "third agency" acting as a global intelligence exchange.

THE SIEGE TECHNIQUE

Each new kidnapping by terrorists seems to present fresh obstacles and varying responses by the police. Hostage negotiation by the police of the free world is characterized by prudence, relentless psychological pressure, patience, and the establishment of a personal relationship between hostages, terrorists, and policemen which the psychologist calls transference. When transference occurs, the police officer develops a relationship with the terrorist which makes it most difficult for him to kill his captive.

Sir Robert Mark, formerly chief of London's police force, devised

---

[18] Steven R. Heard, "Interpol Bids for Police Group Favor," *Freedom* (November 30, 1975):1.

a "siege formula" that has worked well in England. Sir Robert believes that the best way to deal with kidnappers is to let them know that, whatever they do, there is no exit. Thus, in September 1974, after a siege of 5 days, both gunman and hostages walked out of the basement of the Spaghetti House restaurant in London, and in December 1975 the same approach was used successfully when a cell of I.R.A. terrorists barricaded themselves in the apartment of a middle-aged British couple in London's West End. The police wanted to ensure the safety of the couple who were held captive by the gunmen, but they wanted no less to capture the terrorists.[19] Both their objectives were realized as a consequence of their application of Sir Robert's "siege formula."

POLICE SPECIAL WEAPONS AND TACTICS UNITS (S.W.A.T.)

The possibility of taking direct action against a barricaded terrorist, particularly when an opportunity arises to conclude an operation successfully with minimal damage to the hostages or when hostages are not involved, should not be precluded. In May 1974, the Los Angeles police engaged in a fiery shoot-out with members of the S.L.A. The police unit which distinguished itself by bearing the brunt of the action was the Special Weapons and Tactics Unit (S.W.A.T.). Although Americans nationwide watched the contest between S.W.A.T. and the S.L.A. on television, few of them were familiar with the S.W.A.T. organization. Although most Americans now regard S.W.A.T. as a "cure all" for violent crime, others denounce the units as "shock troops" or "execution squads."[20] A S.W.A.T. unit's training closely parallels that of a military unit. Consequently, the reasons behind the lack of complete public support for S.W.A.T. may be its military posture. Some hostage barricade situations, however, can be controlled only by a military action undertaken by specially trained police or soldiers.

ANTITERRORIST MILITARY UNITS

The people of free societies have long demanded that military forces be wedded to the concept of minimum force in dealing with urban

---

[19] Robert B. Semple, Jr., "Police Toughening Antiterrorist Tactics," *The New York Times*, February 25, 1975, p. 1.

[20] G.N. Beck, "SWAT: The Los Angeles Police Special Weapons and Tactics Teams," *FBI Law Enforcement Bulletin* (April 1972):8, and "Fiery End for Six of Patty's Captors," *Time* (May 27, 1974):19.

conflict. They regard the commitment of federal military forces as a drastic last resort, to be used only after the police and National Guard have employed all their own available force and are unable to cope with an insurgency. Democratic states should carefully consider the development and utilization of specially skilled units of both their police and armed forces to suppress terrorist actions in progress. The Dutch, Italian, and British governments have already trained and used elite military units.

On December 2, 1975, a 30-man tactical force of the Royal Dutch Marine Corps, specially trained to handle terrorist incidents, surrounded a train which had been seized by five armed extremists, who were holding 50 hostages at gunpoint. The extremists eventually surrendered to the marines, after a siege of 16 days. About a year earlier, this same Dutch antiterrorist group overcame four terrorists, including a Palestinian, who had taken 25 hostages in a prison in The Hague.[21] In September 1973, the Italians used a specially trained military police unit to raid a beach-front apartment rented by Arab terrorists, who planned to use Soviet-made portable launchers and missiles to attack an airliner of El Al after a takeoff from Rome's Fiumicino International Airport, or during a landing approach.

Great Britain, as well, has successfully deployed elements of its 900 man Special Air Service Regiment (S.A.S.) to contain terrorists in Northern Ireland. Primarily operating in rural portions of County Armagh, S.A.S. units were previously used against General Rommel's Afrika Korps in the Libyan desert during World War II, and against Mau Mau insurgents in Kenya. In 1973, forty Royal Marine commandos were trained at the United States Marine Corps base at Camp Lejeune, North Carolina, and then reassigned to operations in Northern Ireland. On May 6, 1980, after two hostages were killed, a crack S.A.S. unit stormed the besieged Iranian embassy in London rescuing 14 others during a gunfight that turned the city's Hyde Park area into a flaming combat zone. S.A.S. personnel have also attended United States Army programs at Fort Hood, Texas.[22]

France has utilized specially trained military personnel as antiterrorist squads to combat small groups of terrorists. On February 3, 1976, four armed terrorists claiming to be members of the Front for the Liberation of the Somali Coast (F.L.S.C.) seized in a suburb of Djibouti 30 children from 6 to 12 years of age who were on board a school bus, and forced the driver to take the bus across the frontier. Fortunately, the bus

---

[21] "Terrorists Kill 2, Hold 50 on Dutch Train," *The New York Times*, December 3, 1975, p. 3.

[22] "Uncle Sam versus Irish Freedom," *The Irish People*, January 10, 1976, p. 4.

was forced to stop about 10 meters from the Somali barrier, whereupon it was immediately surrounded by French soldiers brought in by helicopter. Meanwhile, the terrorists specified that the French government had 24 hours in which to comply with their political demands. On February 4, the French authorities decided to take action. Troops were ordered to take up appropriate positions, and sharpshooters, brought in specially from France, were positioned under palm trees in front of the French post, about 180 meters from the bus. At exactly 3:45 P.M., five marksmen fired simultaneously, and killed four terrorists whose silhouettes were visible in the bus, and a fifth who was on the ground behind the bus. A sixth terrorist, who rushed from the Somali border to the bus, was killed by a French soldier, but before he died he managed to fire a burst from an automatic weapon at the children, who had instinctively lain down inside the bus; he killed one, and wounded five others.[23]

On November 23, 1979, because of a close relationship between the Saudi minister of internal affairs and Alexander de Marenches, the head of French counterintelligence, the French were called in for the purpose of ousting several hundred ultraconservative Muslims who had seized the Grand Mosque in Mecca 3 days earlier.[24] On December 3, 1979, Saudi Arabian assault teams, organized, trained, and equipped by an elite French antiterrorist unit, retook the mosque. The Gardes Mobiles, an elite group of policemen, has also been used by the French to quell civil disorders. In March 1980, a 225-man unit of this organization was airlifted to Martinique, an overseas department of metropolitan France, to suppress a strike by members of a proindependence movement that was allegedly receiving financial and political support from Cuba.[25]

Israel's General Intelligence and Reconnaissance Unit Number 269, listing the 1972 rescue at Lod Airport of 90 hostages aboard a Sabena Jetliner and the spectacular rescue operation at Entebbe, Uganda, during the first hour of Sunday, July 4, 1976, among its accomplishments, is another example of a unit trained for the purpose of hostage extraction. West Germany's Border Group 9, consisting of 178 men, including specialists in explosives, weaponry, and other essential skills, is experienced in hostage-rescue operations. Formed in 1972, after Arab terrorists at-

[23] "Council Discusses Somali Border Incident Arising from Kidnapping of French Children," *U.N. Chronicle*, March, 1976, p. 15.
[24] "French Said to Play Role in Retaking Grand Mosque," *The New York Times*, January 29, 1980, p. 4.
[25] Tad Szulc, "Radical Winds in the Caribbean," *The New York Times Magazine*, May 25, 1980, p. 17.

tacked and murdered members of the Israeli team at the Olympics in Munich, Border Group 9 rescued 86 hostages aboard a hijacked Lufthansa jetliner in a daring and perfectly executed surprise attack at Somalia's Mogadishu Airport on October 18, 1977. A police commando unit, this group is organized in squads of 30 persons and a few smaller specialized teams.[26]

"BLUE LIGHT" ANTITERRORISTS

Events like those prompting West Germany's and Israel's rescue of hostages from aircraft hijacked by terrorists also prompted the United States to construct a small commando force equipped and trained to conduct strikes against groups who perpetrate terroristic crimes outside its borders. The decision to develop this force was revealed in March 1978 by President Carter. Given the code name "Project Blue Light," this antiterrorist unit, actually formed around November, 1977, consists of approximately 200 men, and has a nucleus of Green Berets from the Army's Special Forces. Housed in a converted military prison at Fort Bragg, North Carolina, the "Blue Light" group is a military unit responsible to the National Security Council, and it functions through the Department of Defense as a program of the Joint Chiefs of Staff.[27]

After February 1978, the unit attracted volunteers from all the American armed forces, but continued to depend heavily on Army Special Forces troops and training methods. Said to have an unlimited budget (approximately $2.5 million was spent in converting the Fort Bragg stockade into an antiterrorist training center) and access to sophisticated equipment and chemical agents, "Blue Light" commandos are all "super-patriotic and have a liking for action." According to a military source at Fort Bragg, "they picked people who are highly intelligent, in good physical condition and who could keep their mouths shut."[28]

Operating with "Blue Light" is the United States Air Force's 8th Special Operations Squadron, based at Hurlburt Field at Fort Walton Beach, Florida. This squadron, previously involved in the conduct of

---

[26] "For Tough West German Force, Feat Capped Years of Training," *The New York Times*, October 19, 1977, p. 4.

[27] Howell Raines, "Secrecy Shrouds Elite Antiterrorist Force," *The New York Times*, April 27, 1980, p. 18.

[28] "Angels Ready to Fight Forces of Evil," *The Star Ledger* (Newark, N.J.), April 27, 1980, p. 24.

air-commando rescue missions in Vietnam, is designed to conduct counterinsurgency psychological operations and unconventional warfare. Project Delta, a team that conducted long-range raids into North Vietnam during the war in Southeast Asia to rescue prisoners, is linked both to the Special Operations Squadron and to Fort Bragg's "Blue Light" unit. "Blue Light" has also been known as the Delta Team, because its missions are similar.[29]

A 90-member commando team from "Blue Light" was the primary component in an operation unleashed in April 1980 for the purpose of freeing the 50 American hostages held captive in the United States embassy building in Teheran, Iran. This group was viewed by operational planners as ideal for this difficult mission, as their most important planning goal was to avoid detection by using a minimum number of troops, helicopters, and transport aircraft.

Adverse weather conditions and mechanical troubles with a special-purpose variant of the Sikorsky H–53 Sea Stallion helicopter caused the rescue attempt to be aborted.[30] However, there is some evidence that the Americans did not apply the basic rules of combined operations formulated by Vice Admiral Lord Louis Mountbatten and other British commando leaders during World War II. These rules are (1) overwhelming force at the point of attack, (2) unusual mechanical backup, and (3) the mission commander on the scene empowered to make decisions without intrusion from headquarters.[31]

Although used successfully by the Israelis at Entebbe, the Lockheed C–130 Hercules, a fixed-wing aircraft, deployed for this operation was designed in 1951 for the Air Force's Tactical Air Command. In 1978, the Air Transport Command realized that the C–130 should be replaced by a faster plane, of greater range, that could accommodate bulky equipment. A Department of Defense annual report for fiscal year 1980, however, said that a program for a new tactical transport was not justified, when weighed against other programs. As a result of its failure in Iran, the United States is now learning "a depressing amount about the inadequacies in the combat readiness of American forces," and the complexity of antiterrorist operations.[32] On July 30, 1980, the United States armed forces were involved in an exercise conducted on Vieques, a small

[29] Ibid.
[30] Malcolm W. Browne, "RH–53 Probably Best Craft for Mission," *The New York Times,* April 26, 1980, p. 9.
[31] *Combined Operations: The Official Story of the Commandos,* Foreword by Vice Admiral Lord Louis Mountbatten, Chief of Combined Operations (New York: The Macmillan Company 1943), pp. 1–15.
[32] Drew Middleton, "Failed Rescue Attempt Raises Doubts about U.S. Maintenance and Planning," *The New York Times,* April 26, 1980, p. 9.

island about 9 miles east of Puerto Rico, that involved twenty-five hundred soldiers, sailors, and marines. The purpose of the operation was to gain field experience in a simulation exercise regarding regaining control of seized U.S. facilities.

NUCLEAR TERRORISM

Another recent capability of terrorist organizations which should be closely monitored by law-enforcement agencies relates to the gradual adoption of plutonium as a fuel for the present generation of nuclear reactors, replacing uranium, which is becoming scarce. It seems that the spent fuels from these reactors can be processed into pure plutonium, which can be made into bombs. This development caused a small group of experts, including Dr. Theodore Taylor, a former Atomic Energy Commission (A.E.C.) scientist, to suggest that the planned conversion to plutonium as the basic fuel of the atomic age is highly dangerous. Persons with little or no training could fashion homemade weapons if they were successful in seizing small amounts of plutonium.

Apparently similarly fearful, Senator Abraham A. Ribicoff has remarked:

> A thorough review of international nuclear safeguards is long overdue. It is essential that tough measures be taken to prevent the conversion of peaceful nuclear materials and technology to weapons by any nation or subnational group.[33]

Senator Ribicoff was chairman of the United States Senate subcommittee which subdivided the A.E.C. into two groups, the Energy Research and Development Administration (E.R.D.A.) and the Nuclear Regulatory Commission (N.R.C.).

On March 9, 1975, public television stations across the country presented a documentary on the dangers of plutonium which featured a 20-year-old undergraduate student at Massachusetts Institute of Technology, who was asked to test Dr. Taylor's thesis. Without talking to any experts, and using only publicly available reference works, the student designed a nuclear bomb in his spare time. His design was reviewed by a nuclear scientist on the staff of the Swedish minister of defense, who concluded that there was a "fair chance" that it could produce an explosion which might have been made by from a hundred thousand to two million pounds of T.N.T. As pointed out in the television documentary, the 1947 destruction of Texas City, Texas, was the result of

---

[33] David Burnham, "Nuclear Agency Suspends Export–Import of Reactors," *The New York Times*, March 27, 1975, p. 34. See also other remarks regarding this matter made by Senator Abraham Ribicoff in the *Congressional Record*, May 28, 1974.

the explosion of a shipload of ammonium nitrate equal to about one thousand tons of T.N.T. The student said that all the bomb parts except the plutonium could be obtained from available commercial suppliers, and that "If you had $30,000 you could do it very easily; if you had $10,000 you would be skimping but you could do it." Furthermore, the bomb would require "more than 10 pounds but less than 20 pounds of plutonium and could be moved easily in a pickup van." The student does not want to be identified. "I'm frankly worried that some nut might get the idea of kidnapping me—not that I really have any special knowledge."[34]

Thus, the dangers presented by the plutonium waste of nuclear reactors have forced the United States government to adopt scores of tough new regulations aimed at greatly tightening the control over its production and transportation. Despite the stringency of these controls, however, some scientists maintain that governmental and privately owned factories already are unable to account for thousands of pounds of what are known as "special nuclear materials."[35]

Although the N.R.C. and the E.R.D.A. insist that such reports are exaggerated, the United States Government has declined to answer a series of detailed questions from the *New York Times* concerning exactly how much plutonium cannot be accounted for. Remarked a spokesman for the N.R.C.:

> Obviously plutonium is a material that we don't want to fall into the hands of the wrong people. That's why we have all the protective systems in place; that's why the systems are constantly being expanded. But in our view, it would not be an easy job to design or fabricate an explosive device.[36]

If, as some experts believe, small terrorist groups could learn to fashion a nuclear weapon with a small amount of plutonium, it is im-

---

[34] David Burnham, "Bill Asks Curb on Plutonium Use to Prevent Building of Homemade Bomb," *The New York Times*, February 27, 1975, p. 12, *Congressional Record*, daily edition, 121, no. 39 (March 1, 1975), p. 3620, and an unpublished paper prepared for delivery to the XVII Annual Convention of the International Studies Association, Toronto, Canada, February 25–29, 1976 by Martha Crenshaw Hutchinson, entitled "Terrorism and the Diffusion of Nuclear Power."

[35] David Burnham, "Thousands of Pounds of Materials Used in Nuclear Bombs Are Unaccounted for," *The New York Times*, December 29, 1974. Note: Allegedly the nuclear material unaccounted for is missing from Kerr McGee, a plutonium factory situated near Crescent, Oklahoma. The Justice Department began investigating Kerr-McGee in November 1974, after the Washington representative of the Oil Chemical and Atomic Workers International Union contended that Karen Silkwood, a plant employee who was killed in a car crash, might not have died from natural causes. (See David Burnham, "Hearing on Plutonium Plant Is Told of a Conflict over Health Reports," *The New York Times*, April 27, 1976, p. 2.)

[36] David Burnham, *The New York Times*, February 27, 1975, p. 12.

perative that legislation be enacted that would prohibit the commercial use of the material, pending a major new scientific assessment of its risk. "We could do the terrorists and criminals of this world no greater favor than to make this element (plutonium) an article of commerce transported across the country in quantities measured in tons," Representative Les Aspin, Democrat from Wisconsin, said in a statement as he introduced a bill that would prohibit the N.R.C. from licensing the widespread use of plutonium as a reactor fuel until expressly authorized by Congress.[37]

On March 26, 1975, Representative Aspin disclosed an unannounced decision of the N.R.C. to put at least a temporary halt on the shipment of reactors and nuclear fuels into and out of the United States, pending a review of the commission's regulations and procedures in this area. The decision by the N.R.C. appears to have coincided with the publication of reports that two 100-pound shipments of plutonium were flown into New York's Kennedy International Airport, one in August 1974 and another in February 1975. The plutonium was then moved by truck to a Westinghouse Electric Corporation plant in Pennsylvania, where it was to be fashioned into fuel rods for a reactor in Italy.[38]

The prospect of terrorists becoming capable of nuclear blackmail, as was Doctor No, the infamous character from the James Bond novel, is surely not a happy one, but the warning signs are out, including the possibility of individuals, as distinct from governments, using and exploiting atomic weapons. Concerned nations of the international community should carefully examine the provisions of existing treaties designed to control the spread of nuclear energy, to ensure that the safeguards contained in these treaties relative to the imposition of international accounting requirements of those nations with reactors will prevent the pilferage of small amounts of plutonium by either terrorists, their sympathizers, or others whom they are able to extort or blackmail. It is imperative that agencies similar to the United States Arms Control and Disarmament Agency cooperate with the International Atomic Energy Agency in Vienna, which is the center for the world program to prevent the diversion of nuclear material from peaceful uses to weapons.

Verification, however, of worldwide developments in nuclear energy, particularly those which relate to unaccountable losses of plutonium, is an intelligence function. It is most important that the several developing probes of the Central Intelligence Agency do not destroy its effectiveness as a global collector of information relative to this.

---

[37] Ibid.
[38] David Burnham, "Nuclear Agency Suspends Export–Import of Reactors," *The New York Times*, March 27, 1975, p. 34.

ANTITERRORISM IN WESTERN EUROPE

Antiterrorist measures employed by the governments of western European nations include the enactment of legislation limiting constitutional guarantees in the areas of arrest, search and seizure, and lawyer–client communications, legalization of improved methods to gather covert information, computerized investigative networks, and the formation and utilization of specialized police squads. Intended to be hostile to the terrorists by impacting directly on their organization and operations, all these antiterrorist measures have been legitimately derived from established legislatures.

Unlike cases of counterterrorism or government-sponsored enforcement terrorism, which is intended to smother subversion in any form and which is applied against an entire populace, or any civilian, police, or military target that could be identified with a terrorist opponent, the targets of the antiterrorism are the terrorists themselves.

Adoption of these measures by western European governments has curtailed the proliferation of nongovernmental counterterrorist organizations for the purpose of self-defense, whether real, imagined, or contrived. However, a few counterterrorist organizations continue to plague the police of western Europe. A group known as Service d'Action Civique (S.A.C.) acted as a commando group, and exacerbated the May 1968 student and worker uprisings in France. A police official stated that, one night, all the shop windows along the Boulevard St. Michel in the Latin Quarter of Paris were smashed. "Everyone blamed the students," he said, "but it was not the students."[1] The Ulster Defense Association (U.D.A.), the central Protestant paramilitary group in Northern Ireland and the focus for counterterrorist actions against the Irish Republican Army (I.R.A.), continues to siphon off investigative resources which the British Special Branch might direct elsewhere.

The Spanish police are engaged in combating counter-terrorism, particularly the activities of an extreme ultraright group which calls itself the Guerrillas of Christ the King; and the Italians are attempting to cope with neo-Fascist terrorist groups, of which the Armed Revolutionary Nuclei is the most significant. Right-wing groups have been blamed for a number of Italy's worst terrorist acts: a bombing of a Milan bank in 1968 that took 16 lives, an explosion in a tunnel between Bologna and Florence on August 4, 1974, that killed 12 passengers on an express train, and an explosion in the Bologna railroad station on August 2, 1980, that snuffed out the lives of 79 persons.[2]

SUPPRESSING THE IRISH REPUBLICAN ARMY

In the Autumn of 1978, British troops in Northern Ireland started to relinquish security duties, including riot control, to the police, as the violence which had erupted in Ulster in 1969 began to level off. During the same period, Belfast experienced an upturn in business activity, and Londonderry became an open city for the first time in nearly a decade. A major factor in the reduction of the violence was the sheer emotional exhaustion of the people, weary after years of inconclusive violence, which served to counterbalance the fear that the I.R.A. and the U.D.A. were once able to instill in the populace.

The development and implementation of a comprehensive antiterrorist program known as the "Way Ahead Policy" by the British army and police also contributed to a reduction in terrorist attacks. Intended to tighten police security throughout Ulster, this policy specified that the police officer, and not the soldier, would do all the arresting and questioning of suspected terrorists, and therefore be responsible for law and order in the same way as any other regular police force. "Way Ahead" thus provided the means by which the army was able to channel

---

[1] Andreas Freund, "Paris Is Concerned by Right-Wing Militia," *The New York Times*, October 11, 1977, p. 8.
[2] "Bologna Station Blast Kills at Least 80 and Hurts 200." *The New York Times*, August 3, 1980, p. 1.

more of its energy into antiterrorist operations in the countryside and intelligence-gathering activities.[3]

Intelligence methods and techniques also were perfected by the British which permitted them to get tips on the hideouts and identities of terrorists. Each police officer and soldier was exposed to improved antiterrorist surveillance training that taught them to notice the unusual: a different number of milk bottles on the front doorsteps of a house; a different car parked in a certain street; different people coming out of the local pub. Also helpful was the use of improved technological devices of the army, including a vehicle-mounted unit known as "Caribel" which pinpoints the origin of a sniper's bullet, and "Twiggy," a night-vision device issued to troops in the security forces. Sensors of the type that once monitored the Ho Chi Minh Trail in Vietnam are another device, that the British have found helpful in detecting border crossers. Other useful devices include gadgets that distinguish human bodies or occupied rooms in houses as bright targets against a dark background.

Royal Air Force (R.A.F.) photoreconnaissance aircraft, operating from a base in Wyton, England, support the army's surveillance effort by providing it with aerial pictures of Ulster on a monthly basis, and special photographs—ordinary color, "false" color, and infrared—on request. Infrared, for example, penetrates cloud cover, and operates as well at night as during the day. On a cold night, the warm spots left by someone crossing a field will stand out as clearly as "though they had lit a bonfire." The film taken during R.A.F. overflights is taken to the Joint Air Reconnaissance Center at an airfield in Brampton for processing, and then passed on to the security forces. Additional surveillance devices include a network of computer-controlled and remotely piloted helicopters that are equipped with television cameras. Westland Aircraft Company, which makes one of these units, calls it the "Wisp," and says that it was originally intended for "urban surveillance in Northern Ireland."[4]

Additional training for British security forces in the area of antiterrorist psychological warfare skills has been helpful. "We've got to be behaved better than the I.R.A. and be more concerned about people," a British platoon leader in Belfast once remarked. This training is intended to enable the soldier to perform like a police officer, and not to contribute to an increase in violence by displacing his ire upon innocent

---

[3] Jan Bennett, "The Deadly Job of Keeping Order in Northern Ireland," *The Newsworld* (New York), January 17, 1979, p. 9.
[4] Duncan Campbell, "Terrorist Surveillance," *International Intelligence Report* (April 1980): 12–16.

bystanders as a consequence of astute manipulation of civil unrest by terrorists. Recognizing the need for self-restraint and "evenhandedness" when combating insurgents in a war for the hearts and minds of the people, the British police are always prepared to charge members of the security forces with crimes when committed, and bring them before the criminal court in Ulster. On February 1, 1979, two soldiers of the Special Air Services (S.A.S.) Regiment were arrested by police for murdering a 16-year-old youth who walked into an army stakeout. An autopsy found that he had been hit in the back by three high-velocity bullets.[5]

This willingness of the British to try all offenders in court, including those who undertake bombings and torture on behalf of Northern Ireland's counterterrorist Protestant paramilitary groups, has contributed to the success of its antiterrorist campaign in Northern Ireland. Furthermore, London's insistence that the Royal Ulster Constabulary, accused of brutality against the Catholic population, use more appropriate methods when performing its policing duties was a useful adjunct to the anti-I.R.A. propaganda campaign waged by the security forces.

Recognizing the need for troops to get to know the local population on a more intimate level than they were able to in the past, the British Army extended a soldier's tour of duty in Northern Ireland to 18 months. Previously a soldier completed a 4-month tour of duty in Ulster before being rotated to regular assignments in Britain or West Germany. This revised manpower-allocation scheme, based on the realities of antiterrorist operations, permitted the British to deploy a larger number of plainclothesmen in undercover operations. Most of these operatives were tied to the S.A.S., whose motto is "Who Dares Wins." S.A.S. personnel have been highly effective in disrupting the I.R.A. command structure and infiltrating Protestant paramilitary terrorist organizations.[6]

Essentially, the success of London's antiterrorist campaign is measured by the following significant indicators: (1) reduction in guerrilla strength—approximately 200 terrorists were active in all Northern Ireland in 1979, whereas 700 gunmen were ready for action in Belfast alone in 1972; (2) incarceration of more than 1,200 I.R.A. provisionals as a consequence of arrests, many of which resulted from "tip-offs" from members of the Catholic community; (3) reluctance of the I.R.A. to involve itself in a sustained campaign of operations in Ulster's major cities, Belfast and Londonderry, instead choosing to avoid capture by

---

[5] "Two British Soldiers Facing Murder Charge in Ulster," *The New York Times*, February 2, 1979, p. 5.
[6] "Britain's Secret Army," *Counterforce: The Monthly Newsmagazine on Terrorism* (February 1977): 12–13.

conducting operations almost exclusively in rural areas; (4) a 60 to 70 percent reduction in the number of demonstrators that attend rallies in southern Ireland in support of I.R.A. causes. "We still sing the old I.R.A. songs in the pubs, but that's about as far as most of us want to go in supporting them," remarked one Irishman.[7]

E.T.A. CONFRONTS THE SPANISH POLICE

On May 4, 1979, three thousand additional police officers were assigned to the Madrid area by the Spanish government, to bolster existing security forces in the capital city, and to participate in operations to quell political violence which in 1978 claimed 99 lives—three times more political killings than in 1977. The E.T.A., a socialist and separatist group composed of Basque nationalists, has claimed responsibility for two-thirds of these killings as part of its campaign to secure independence for Euzkadi, the Basque homeland in northeastern Spain. Meaning "Basque Country and Liberty" in English, and written "Euzkadi Ta Askatasuna" in the Basque language, the E.T.A. assassinated one person every 2.1 days during the early months of 1979. Coordinated by a clandestine general assembly comprised of representatives of Basque groups in southern France and northern Spain, the E.T.A.'s tactical operations consist of car bombings and machine-gunning of a target at close range from an ambush position. Approximately 95 percent of the group's targets have been police officers and civil guards.

Strategically, the E.T.A. tries to provoke the conservative military leadership into seizing power and cracking down on the Basque minority, thereby increasing its support in its own provinces, and discrediting the government elsewhere. Although it is not sufficiently powerful of itself to sever its homeland from Spain, the E.T.A.'s atrocities have succeeded in causing unrest in the army and the police forces. On January 6, 1979, King Juan Carlos urged the armed forces to maintain self-control in the face of "these vile attacks by E.T.A." Three days earlier, the military governor of Madrid, Major General Ortin Gill, had been assassinated. Consequently, the Spanish king was anxious to forestall a retaliatory attack against the Basques by the Fuerza Nueva (New Force), a fascist movement that allegedly numbers some police officers in the Basque areas among its members. This group once instigated a riot that caused a force of two hundred police to assemble in a

---

[7] Sean Duignan, "The Troubles in Ulster May, Just May be Easing a Bit," *The New York Times*, October 11, 1977, p. 3E.

small industrial town in the Basque region and move through its empty streets systematically smashing windows and looting.[8]

According to some knowledgeable Spaniards, including José Antonio Martinez Soler, chief economics editor of the Madrid daily *El Pais*, the cycle of terror and counterterror will not end until the participation of the K.G.B. (the Soviet Union's Committee for State Security—Komitet Gosudarstvennoy Bezopasnosti) in the E.T.A., and that of the Central Intelligence Agency (C.I.A.) in the conservative Basque nationalist camp, terminate. Mr. Soler views terrorism in Spain as a permanent destabilizing threat, controlled from Moscow and Washington, and aided by France, where the guerrillas once based their operations. He accuses Paris of being most anxious to see a dictatorship restored in Madrid.[9]

However, since September 1978, the E.T.A. has become the subject of a vast but discreet operation directed by Roberto Conesa, a high-ranking police officer and a specialist under the Franco regime in suppressing leftist organizations. According to Spanish press reports, Mr. Conesa's operatives dismantled 46 E.T.A. cells during the first 4 months of their field operations, under the provisions of an antiterrorist law passed by the Spanish parliament during the summer of 1978.

Spanish antiterrorist legislation is particularly stringent, prison sentences being given to anyone convicted of giving information to or collaborating with a terrorist organization. Imprisonment may also be the penalty for anyone who makes a statement that constitutes an apology for guerrilla acts.[10]

In 1979, raids by Spanish police resulted in the seizure of stockpiles of light weapons, stolen cars, false documents, disguises, and large amounts of pesetas stolen from companies and banks. Another setback for the E.T.A. occurred on December 21, 1978, in the southern French town of Anglet, and involved the assassination of José Miguel Penaran Ordenana. A top-ranking 28-year-old Basque terrorist who operated under the code name "Argala," Mr. Ordenana was killed by a bomb blast in stepping on the accelerator of his car. No one has taken responsibility for the assassination of "Argala."[11]

The antiterrorist operations of Spain's intelligence and police forces

[8] "30 Arrested in Spain in Campaign against Terrorists of Right and Left," *The New York Times*, October 11, 1977, p. 8.

[9] José Antonio Martinez Soler, "Spain's Basque Problem," *The New York Times*, February 2, 1979, p. 5.

[10] "Spain Introduces New Laws in Fight on Urban Guerrillas," *The New York Times*, February 2, 1979, p. 5.

[11] James M. Markham, "Military Governor of Madrid Slain; 2nd Murder of Army Man in 2 Days," *The New York Times*, January 4, 1979, p. 3.

have been facilitated as a consequence of a French move, in February 1979, that ended the Paris policy of granting political-refugee status to Spanish Basques, and the February 1980 deportation of two Soviet agents suspected of being linked to E.T.A. terrorists. Consequently, southern France is no longer being openly used by the E.T.A. to plan operations to be executed in Spain, and clandestine Soviet support of Spanish terrorists is likely to be somewhat reduced. However, the socialists and communists continue to call for the banning of Fuerza Nueva, which they accuse of taking wild revenge against "reds" and "Marxists" in northern Spain and in Madrid. Fuerza Nueva killed eight people during the first 6 weeks of 1980.[12]

Prime Minister Adolfo Suarez, meanwhile, has managed to have formed a constitutional court which has started to sort out the legal anomalies that Spanish civil libertarians find objectionable in the law, and will remove the military from its role in civilian justice.[13]

CONTROLLING TERRORISM IN FRANCE

The French police are engaged in antiterrorist operations targeted on two groups whose existence and activities have received scant attention by the media outside France. Both these groups, the Corsican National Liberation Front (F.N.L.C.) and the Breton Liberation Front, claim to be involved in a struggle attuned to the nationalist aspirations of the peoples they seek to represent, which they do with methods similar to those favored by the I.R.A. and the E.T.A. terrorist organizations.

The F.N.L.C.'s purpose, therefore, is to use terror as a means of ending colonial aggression in Corsica including the big business operated tourist, commerce and transportation agencies, preliminary to the establishment of an independent republic for Corsican people. Consequently, its bombing targets have been banks on the island on Corsica, and airline offices and travel agencies in Paris. Army gasoline storage tanks, and government offices in the Paris area, have also been bombed by the F.N.L.C.

The Breton Liberation Front, committed to the use of terror to establish a separate homeland for Bretons in a Celtic Brittany, has organized the Breton Republican Army to serve as its main operating army. Responsible for 200 bombings, mostly in Brittany, this group on June 26, 1978, placed a bomb in the Palace of Versailles, which exploded and

---

[12] "2 Russians Ousted from Spain as Spies," *The New York Times*, February 17, 1980, p. 7.
[13] James M. Markham, "Reform Zeal Seems to Ebb in Spain as Violence Grows," *The New York Times*, February 19, 1980, p. 4.

destroyed priceless works of art. A police official in Rennes, Brittany, said that several of the suspects accused of the Versailles blast were related to former Nazi collaborators. The basement of the Bazar de L'Hotel de Ville, a Paris department store, also was shattered by a bomb planted by Breton terrorists at a time when it was crowded with customers.[14]

French antiterrorist activities, stepped up during the late spring of 1978, resulted in the rounding up of 23 F.N.L.C. suspects and the arrest of Jean-Paul Roesch, an alleged leader of the Corsican terrorists. On November 30, 1978, French police arrested Lionel Chenevière and Patrick Montauzier, who admitted that they had placed the bomb in the palace of Versailles. However, during January 1980 armed members of the F.N.L.C. took over the Hotel Fesch in Ajaccio, Corsica, to protest police actions against members of their movement. Allegedly, the police were utilizing undercover officers to penetrate the F.N.L.C. that some Corsicans claimed were affiliated with an extreme right-wing terror group known as Francia, a group supposedly protected by authorities.

The French government's reaction to the hotel seizure was swift and overpowering. Hundreds of riot policemen were airlifted to the island, and the local police were reinforced with helicopters, armored vehicles, and automatic weapons. Once the police cordon around the hotel was in place, an officer trained in psychology made his way down from the roof of the hotel, and talked the nationalists into surrendering. Their only demand was to be allowed to march up the main street to the police station singing Corsican nationalist songs under the unfurled banner of their flag: a black Moor's head on a white background.[15]

Meanwhile, Paris has become a shooting gallery for hit teams associated with the Israeli–Arab, the Arab–Arab, and, in 1980, the Iranian–Iranian shadow wars. At least 11 killings have taken place within the confines of the city since 1977 that have been attributed to these conflicts. Issues linked to these assassinations transcend security, as they are political and emotional as well. Historically, France takes special pride in its openness to political exiles, and its constitution states that "anyone persecuted because of his activities in the cause of freedom shall be entitled to the right of asylum within . . . the Republic."[16]

The main French policemen's unions, however, have complained

---

[14] Barbara Slavin, "Bretons Attack the Glory of France," *The New York Times*, July 2, 1978, p. E3, and "One Killed as Bomb Racks Paris Store," *The Star Ledger* (Newark, N.J.), December 3, 1978, p. 23.

[15] Frank J. Prial, "Corsicans, Poor but Proud, Believe Siege Was Futile," *The New York Times*, January 15, 1980, p. 2.

[16] Richard Eder, "Other French Connection Is All Political, Just as Lethal," *The New York Times*, July 27, 1980, p. 4E.

about the violence to which they are exposed while protecting prominent Middle East exiles and diplomats. The police have asked for more arms and equipment and more personnel, although it is estimated that about 10 percent of the Paris force is already assigned to such duties. Although the French government is expected to satisfy the demands of the police unions, it is finding it most difficult to prevent gunmen from utilizing the diplomatic cover of security guards for entering the country. A number of the Paris shootings have been attributed to assassins operating under the cloak of a diplomatic cover.[17]

Action Directe, a terrorist group appearing to have sophisticated knowledge of computer operations, and in close contact with Italy's Red Brigades, is also a target of French antiterrorist operations. During April 1980, 20 members of this organization were taken into custody in a series of raids across France. However, the group is still active, and continues its use of plastic explosives and rocket grenades against government buildings and police stations. One of its bombs tore most of the front off a police station in Toulon. Action Directe has also targeted the Philips Data Systems Company offices in Toulouse, and the C.I.I.–Honeywell–Bull offices in the same city. "They knew exactly how to erase programs from tapes and how to destroy the electronic filing systems," a police inspector said.[18]

ITALY'S RED BRIGADES

The Red Brigades, consisting of 400 to 500 full-time members, are Italy's principal terrorist organization. Built on four main columns, strategically placed in Rome, Turin, Milan, and Genoa, this group was responsible for the coordination of the 54 day operation involving the kidnapping and murder of former prime minister Aldo Moro, which began on the morning of March 16, 1978. Highly mobile, and capable of independent action, each of the Red Brigade's columns is linked to a "central brain" whose operational schemes reflect the input of the writings of the deceased Ulrike Meinhof of West Germany's Red Army Faction (Rote Armee Fraktion—R.A.F.), Uruguay's Tupamaros, and various African and Middle Eastern liberation movements. According to Cristoforo Piancone, an imprisoned member of the Red Brigades, some

[17] Richard Eder, "France Upholds Haven for Exiles," *The New York Times*, July 24, 1980, p. 2.
[18] Frank J. Prial, "Raiders in France Destroy Two Computer Centers," *The New York Times*, April 11, 1980, p. 2.

of these Italian terrorists have received training in Czechoslovakia, and participate in an international terrorist network directed by Abu Nid'ai, head of the pro-Iraqi portion of the Arab Liberation Front. Directed from Egypt, this international coalition also consists of Palestinian terrorists, and some Swiss members of the Red Brigades.[19]

The Red Brigades are believed to have developed sources of information among individuals serving in key positions in the police, security services, and government ministries, who provide the terrorists with early warning relative to the tactical details of Rome's next antiterrorist operation. These contacts also are seemingly used by the Red Brigades as a counterintelligence network, to intimidate officials who advocate harsh antiterrorist procedures, and to keep members of its action cells from using their connection with the group for personal gain. For example, in April 1978, a Red Brigade activist held up a bank in Genoa and demanded 80 million lire (about $100,000). Before withdrawing from the premises, however, the gunman demanded that the manager of the bank provide him with a signed note attesting that he had received the money and nothing more. Italian police officials, generally, are amazed by the efficient managerial and budgetary discipline observed by the terrorists. The intelligent political and psychological assessments that the Red Brigades build into almost every operation indicate that they have access to classified public-security information from command police circles through their supporters and sympathizers. Therefore, many Italian public officials have insisted that their government institute improved methods and procedures relative to internal inspections.

THE ITALIAN "SECRET SERVICE"

The professional use by the Red Brigades of security procedures and methods designed to prevent penetration of their organization by the government's undercover operatives is thought to be responsible for the allegations voiced by some Italians that an unidentified but prominent group of politicians is using the counterintelligence service of Italy's armed forces for its own purposes. The Italian secret service, or counterintelligence service, was originally set up after the Second World War to combat elements who sought to weaken the military forces. Until July 1977, it was solely under the Ministry of Defense.

A conspiracy theory has been a popular device for generations in

---

[19] Curtis Bill Pepper, "The Possessed," *The New York Times Magazine*, February 18, 1979, p. 30.

Italy to explain any calamity that impacts on the country. Many Italians are convinced that the counterintelligence arm, particularly, once had a good knowledge of what the various underground groups were doing, and gave them relatively free rein, so that the public would take fright and deliver law-and-order votes in elections.[20] Until its reorganization in 1977, the counterintelligence service was a relatively small investigative agency, empowered to deal only with the nation's external enemies. For years, this service operated undercover networks at home; left-wing parties and newspapers have long accused it of fomenting terrorism by infiltrating extremist groups for the purpose of inciting terrorist attacks to create a law-and-order backlash.[21]

The Pope's vicar for Rome, Ugo Cardinal Poletti, publicly announced his suspicion "that obscure forces kept the police from fighting violence and terrorism more effectively." Although he did not elaborate on his remarks, the Cardinal was generally regarded to be "denouncing political cynicism and the kind of Machiavellian power play that seemed at times to paralyze the forces created to guarantee law and order in Italy."[22]

Some Italians persist in saying that clandestine right-wing organizations who threaten to execute communists in retaliation for fire bombings and shooting attacks by left-wing groups, such as the Communist Front Line group, are actually police gangs. In June 1978, the Italian news agency ANSA issued a report that supported this position by announcing that it had received a message bearing a skull insignia from a group calling itself "Death Squads for Fallen Policemen," which stated:

> In view of the cowardice of the government which is incapable of meeting the violence of the Red Brigades with violence, death squads have been set up all over Italy of the same type which wiped out political and ordinary crime in Brazil very quickly.[23]

Responding to demands that it improve and expand its secret service to combat crime and terrorism, and attempting to allay the fears of many prominent personalities, including Ugo Cardinal Poletti, Italy's chamber of deputies reached agreement on July 27, 1977, to shake up the Italian secret services and bring them under the direct control of the prime minister. Allegations charged some of their branches with a series of scandals, involving subversive activity, industrial espionage, at least two

---

[20] Paul Hofmann, "Italians Fearful as La Dolce Vita Turns Perilous," *The New York Times*, July 18, 1977, p. 1.

[21] Paul Hofman, "Like The Rest of Italy, Police Are Nearly out of Control," *The New York Times*, March 19, 1978, p. E 3.

[22] Ibid.

[23] "Leftists Step up Terror in Italy," *The Star Ledger* (Newark, N.J.), June 21, 1977, p. 19.

attempted right-wing coups, and a bomb attack in Milan that killed 16 people. Also, Giuseppe Zamberletti, serving as Italy's under secretary of the interior, in July 1977 stated that Italy was "fighting the new spiral of criminality and political terrorism blindly: as a consequence of the narrow operational parameters imposed upon the secret services." Originally established after the Second World War to ferret out elements that sought to weaken the military, the secret service, according to Mr. Zamberletti, "has continued to operate in the same way while the state has developed differently." Commenting further, the Under Secretary claimed that "the new terrorism tends to weaken the institutions set up by the Constitution and even the economic potential of the country. A service linked only to the military does not have the scope to act politically."[24]

Organizational reform of the secret services has included legislation which split the services, once controlled totally by the Ministry of Defense, into military and civilian arms. One branch remains under military control, while the new civilian branch is placed under the Ministry of the Interior; its organization includes a small antiterrorist intelligence service established a few years ago by Mr. Zamberletti's ministry.[25]

Similarly, the United States Secret Service, according to an organizational chart approved April 1, 1977, includes an intelligence division within its Office of Protective Research whose purpose is to provide support to operating elements contained within the Office of Protective Operations. The primary operational objective of the American service, according to the United States code, is still protection, reflecting the original conditions responsible for giving it authority to guard various personages. (In 1901, many Americans were shocked when they learned of the assassination of President McKinley, and noted that no federal law-enforcement agency was assigned the mission of protecting selected public federal officials and distinguished foreign visitors.[26] A secret-service escort for the President was made permanent in 1903.)

CHARACTERISTICS OF THE ITALIAN POLICE

The continuation of terrorism by various Italian extremist groups indicates that the Italian police, although numbering about 250,000, has

[24] "Italy's Chamber of Deputies Agrees on Secret Service Bill," *The New York Times*, July 28, 1977, p. 2.
[25] Ina Selden, "Italy Is to Expand Its Secret Service to Fight Terrorism," *The New York Times*, July 31, 1977, p. 6.
[26] Lyman B. Kirkpatrick, Jr., *The U.S. Intelligence Community* (New York: Hill & Wang, 1973), p. 52.

been unable to control groups responsible for the wave of terrorism that began in December 1969, when a bomb exploded in a Milan bank, killing 16 people, and has since included assassinations, extortions of huge ransoms in numerous kidnappings, frequent bombings, "kneecappings" of criminal-justice officials, and the spectacular abduction of Aldo Moro. Among the major deficiencies attributed by Italian officials to the police are their lack of training and education and their inability to attract candidates to a service that is underpaid and traditionally held in low esteem by the citizens. The Italian police services are composed mostly of people from villages and cities in southern Italy and Sicily, as most young men in the industrial northern regions of Italy look for jobs in manufacturing plants, which pay better wages. Approximately 80 percent of the people now serving in the Italian policing services are southerners—with a good understanding, therefore, of how the Mafia works, but also more likely to become the targets of Mafia influence and pressures. Police officers born and raised in southern Italy, and handicapped by inadequate schooling and a lack of urbanity, find it most difficult to adjust psychologically and sociologically to the conditions prevailing in the industrial regions of northern Italy, where their opposition, the terrorists and sophisticated racketeers, flourish.[27]

Since the Mussolini era, there has been an intense rivalry between the Carabinieri, a military all-purpose elite corps, and the Public Security Police, a uniformed civilian-led force. It seems that the Carabinieri, once used by the kings of Savoy to unify Italy and to establish control over the south, were not trusted by Mussolini, who therefore organized the Public Security Police as a civilian-led counterforce. Consequently, today the Carabinieri and the Public Security Police routinely conduct separate investigations, frequently keeping evidence from each other and witnesses under wraps. Failure to establish close liaison between agencies is a systemic characteristic of the Italian police services, and is responsible for much of the confusion which is evident in the hunt for the Red Brigades terrorists. Unfortunately, politicians and other pressure groups have manipulated and accentuated these divisions, and left-wing parties and newspapers contribute to the divisiveness by keeping up a barrage of criticism based on allegations of illegal covert activities by the police.[28]

In addition to Italy's primary policing agencies, such as the Carabinieri and the Public Security Police, each of which is allocated about

[27] Paul Hofmann, "Like the Rest of Italy, Police Are Nearly out of Control," *The New York Times*, March 19, 1978, p. E 3.
[28] Henry Tanner, "Red Brigades Intimidates Italians but Fails in Effort to Start Civil War," *The New York Times*, May 17, 1978, p. 1.

eighty thousand officers, the Italian government has a number of specialized law-enforcement agencies. Among the most significant of these groups is the forty-thousand-member Finance Guard which, although established to apprehend smugglers and to identify and arrest tax dodgers, is frequently assigned tasks which are not related to fiscal offenses. It is used to curb the narcotics traffic, and to participate in antiterrorist operations. Its exemplary service in the pursuance of all of its assigned missions is responsible for the growing trust that many Italians place in it. The police intelligence networks, dismantled a few years ago in a belated effort to curb Fascist remnants, have never been rebuilt.[29] Consequently, the conduct of antiterrorist operations by Italian police, stymied by rivalry among the various law-enforcement agencies, are also hindered by a lack of background and tactical information on the various terrorist groups.

LEGAL ASPECTS OF ITALIAN ANTITERRORISM

Italy's criminal procedures, revised in the early 1970s to limit powers given to the police during the Fascist era, are commonly regarded as another impediment to the successful conduct of antiterrorist operations. One of the revised laws ruled that a suspect could be questioned only by a judge, and permitted the suspect to have his lawyer present. Although this was modified later to permit questioning of a suspect by the police in the presence of the suspect's lawyer, high-ranking police officials orated that they experienced great difficulty in locating lawyers willing to represent suspects, and consequently lost "the good moment" for interrogation which occurs immediately after the arrest. But Professor Federico Mancini, a socialist member of the judicial council of magistrates, argues that any restrictions of the rights of suspects "involve dangerous powers which could be misused." Although the debate on civil rights and due process continued to rage, during the spring of 1977 the Italian government, supported by the governing Christian Democrats, gleaned support from various groups for its proposal of "preventive arrests," which would allow the police to stop anyone believed to be planning a crime against the state, and hold him incommunicado for 48 hours.[30]

On March 21, 1978, 5 days after the kidnapping of Aldo Moro, the

[29] Hofmann, "Like the Rest," p. E3.
[30] Alvin Shuster, "Italy Seeks to Widen Police Powers," *The New York Times*, June 21, 1977, p. 4.

Italian government had finally mustered enough popular support to issue a decree which expanded the powers of police and magistrates, permitting them to order electronic surveillance without obtaining prior written authorization which would eventually appear in the records on the case, and allowing law-enforcement authorities to question a suspect without any lawyer's being present. This decree also imposed a mandatory life term for perpetrators of kidnappings that result in the death of the victim, and thereby ended the previous practice, whereby the judge was empowered to use his discretion in sentencing persons found guilty of this crime.[31]

On June 12, 1978, the antiterrorist capability of Italy's police was expanded further when it was disclosed that 76.9 percent of the Italian voters in a national referendum favored the retention of a 3-year-old law, the Reale Act, that, *inter alia*, gives the police virtually unlimited power to use firearms.[32] The Italian government has also agreed to allow the police to form a trade union for presenting their grievances, providing they abstain from affiliation with any other trade-union federation. The government has considered reinstating the death penalty for certain terrorist crimes, as an additional antiterrorist measure.[33]

IMPROVED ITALIAN ANTITERRORIST CAPABILITY

Improvements in interagency cooperation among police organizations was regarded as the prime factor responsible for the first significant break in the hunt for the killers of Aldo Moro. On September 14, 1978, a 10-man detail of police antiterrorists, equipped with automatic weapons and bulletproof vests, raided an apartment in a quiet residential neighborhood of Milan and seized Corrado Alunni, alleged to be the mastermind in the kidnapping of the former Italian premier. This action terminated a 6-week police stakeout and surveillance of an apartment building where police anticipated associates of Mr. Alunni might be observed and photographed.[34] Investigating magistrates said that reports of the arrest, intended to be kept secret for at least 3 days to permit the police manhunt for other terrorists to be successfully concluded, were

---

[31] Henry Tanner, "Italians Decree Tougher Penalties for Kidnappings," *The New York Times,* March 22, 1978, p. 5.

[32] Henry Tanner, "Italians Vote Heavily to Retain Law that Widened Powers of the Police," *The New York Times,* March 18, 1978, p. 22.

[33] "Mr. Moro's Fate, and Italy's," ibid.

[34] "Bellissimo! A Terrorist Leader Is Caught," *Time* (September 25, 1978): 47.

leaked within 3 hours by the Interior Ministry in Rome. The roundup of other alleged terrorists who were photographed and filmed at Mr. Alunni's garden apartment was only partially effective. The police, nevertheless, succeeded in arresting two other suspected terrorists, Marini Zoni, 31, a girlfriend of the terrorist leader, and Maria Albernani, 29, of Bologna.

Although terrorism in Italy continues to flare, in April 1980 the Italian police announced the arrest of 45 people on suspicion of being members of the Red Brigades, and hinted that a major breakthrough in the fight against terrorism had been achieved. The police also report that the Red Brigades are experiencing serious difficulties in recruiting new members, and have been compelled to give key missions to untrained young people who were not up to the stress.[35]

WEST GERMANY'S ANTITERRORISTS

After the Second World War, the founders of the Federal Republic of West Germany, committed to check any future internal trend toward fascism, stipulated in their country's constitution that the police function of government be decentralized, and entrusted to the 10 West German states and West Berlin. Prior to the attack by Arab terrorists at the 1972 Olympic Games, therefore, the extent of the Bonn government's antiterrorist support for its states was limited to consultation. Legally, only Bavarian state and municipal police forces, controlled by Bavaria's interior minister, could be used to augment Munich's police for the "Games," while federal forces, consisting of airport and border units, had to be held in reserve, and could be deployed only for emergency use. The shock of the terrorism at Munich, however, prompted some Germans to exert pressure on their elected federal officials to make them consider constitutional revisions to permit federal law enforcement agencies to have a more direct role regarding terrorism and other crimes involving international relations. Privately, government officials responsible for state security acknowledged that "consultation is just not enough," and that expanded central power for the federal government was required. Yet some Germans believe that any federal move toward increased centralization of police power, in addition to its being exceedingly dangerous to the unimpeded operation of democratic processes, could be manipulated by terrorists to represent such a trend as evidence

[35] Henry Tanner, "Red Brigades Reported in Trouble," *The New York Times*, April 27, 1980, p. 14.

of a return to Hitler's police state, which the federal constitution is designed to prevent.[36]

An escalation in the number of assassinations and bombing and incendiary attacks by the Red Army Faction, also known as the Baader–Meinhof Gang, and other extremist elements in the wake of the terrorist incident at Munich eventually required that the West Germans slowly widen the scope of federal law-enforcement agencies to enable them to combat terrorism more effectively. The Bundeskriminalamt (BKA) was permitted to direct the activities of the various state police units assigned to antiterrorist missions. It has assigned approximately 200 hundred officers to a special unit known as TE63. Charged with the task of dealing exclusively with terrorists, TE63 has headquarters at Bad Godesberg, a suburb of Bonn.

Similar to the F.B.I., but with considerably less statutory power, BKA is supported by a strong law-and-order lobby, which actively campaigns for purposes of obtaining increased power and funds for its antiterrorist operations.[37] For example, Dr. Karl Heinz Gemmer, a BKA official, in an address at a policemen's union meeting in April 1978, stated that international policing "with its means and methods was far from being at operative parity" with the international terrorist network. This statement underscores the frustration experienced by many western European law-enforcement commanders who are charged with the conduct of antiterrorist activities. Created in 1951, BKA's original staff of 231 employees had expanded to about fifteen hundred by the time of Andreas Baader's second arrest on June 1, 1972, in Frankfurt. Its present complement is about twenty-five hundred employees, and others are being hired and trained.

The Verfassungschult ("Police Defending the Constitution"), another federal law enforcement agency, has received increased authority, and the 10 West German states and West Berlin have organized their own special police commandos, equipped and trained to function as S.W.A.T. units. Operating budgets for the various state police organizations were increased from about 2.5 billion marks in 1969 to a present peak of well over 5 billion marks.

The key component of the West German police's campaign against terror is a computer, whose primary processing unit is situated within the tightly guarded building occupied by the Interior Ministry at Bonn.

[36] "Killings Expected to Spur Debate on Police Structure," *The New York Times*, September 7, 1972, p. 18.

[37] Paul Hofmann, "West Germany's Capital Seems Gloomier than Ever as It Awaits the Outcome of Schleyer's Kidnapping," *The New York Times*, September 12, 1977, p. 3.

A "crisis center," staffed around the clock and off limits for anyone who does not work there, is situated on the ninth floor of the same building. Additional antiterrorist computer installations are located in TE63's facility in Bad Godesberg, at the main office of BKA in Karlsruhe, and at state police centers in West Germany's 10 states and West Berlin.[38] Constituting a network, this national computer system contains all available historical and present data on what the Germans call "the terrorist scene," and serves both as a data base and as a point of comparison for any and all information gleaned by investigators that may contain clues helpful to antiterrorist forces.

The German police at first anticipated that their computerized network would provide instant and detailed information on persons and events associated with the Red Army Faction (Rote Armee Fraktion, or R.A.F.) and other domestic terrorist organizations. But West Germany is a highly decentralized country, and each of its states has a separate law-enforcement data-retrieval installation; a number of these systems cannot be integrated into the federal government's antiterrorist network. The constitutional safeguards designed to check the centralization of police power in West Germany also restrict the exchange and processing of valuable information required to sustain a nationwide campaign of antiterrorism.

Meanwhile, the antiterrorist computer network continues to function, and from the vast volume of information which it has in storage it occasionally produces information of exceptional value. In May 1978, West German antiterrorist specialists, a few of whom helped Italy search for Aldo Moro, revealed that the Red Brigades, since 1970, have worked with the Red Army Faction and its European sympathizers, and that "new police procedures" had been instrumental in the capture of four of West Germany's most wanted terrorists in Yugoslavia. Brigitte Mohnhaupt, believed to have been in close contact with the murderers of Aldo Moro, was one of the four apprehended.[39]

Some German police officials say that their failure to capture the remaining R.A.F. terrorists is directly attributable to the incompatibility of the computers that some law-enforcement groups are using with systems on which other police investigative units rely.[40]

Constitutional guarantees and the unease expressed by many West

---

[38] Ibid.

[39] "4 Terrorist Groups Feared Linked," *The Chicago Sun Times*, May 11, 1978, p. 70; Robert D. Hershey , Jr., "Yugoslavia Seizes 4 Major Terrorists Long Sought in Bonn," *The New York Times*, May 30, 1978, p. 1.

[40] Paul Hofmann, "West Germany's Orderly Society Proves Vulnerable to Terrorists," *The New York Times*, September 19, 1977, p. 19.

Germans at the first sign of governmental repression have dissuaded some German politicians from advocating additional measures that could be taken quickly by the police and prove extremely effective in a campaign against terrorists. The police are dependent on overt sources of information and the use of computer processing for evaluating and collating data on terrorists, necessitating the use of a nationwide electronic hardware interface for a successful effort. Police officials are only partially correct in stating that their computer network is responsible for their failure to control the Red Army Faction, because the primary limitation on West German antiterrorists is the reluctance of the Bonn parliament to adopt measures which restrict essential freedoms.

Former Chancellor Willy Brandt, speaking at a political convention in the Ruhr during the autumn of 1977, at a time when Hanns-Martin Schleyer, president of the West German Employees and Industry Federation, was a prisoner of the Red Army Faction, cogently expressed the philosophy of the Bonn government's position on antiterrorism by stating that "the community of democrats must prove it is stronger than the perpetrators of the violence."[41] West German law-enforcement officers have been restrained by their government, in using undercover police officers to penetrate the radical groups, although they are legally empowered to use telephone wiretaps and examine mail if there are "factual grounds" for suspicion of high treason or danger to national security.[42]

Although the Red Army Faction's cells are small, and communication between them is effected through "deaddrops" intended to reduce or "cut out" physical contact, entire cells have been eliminated, and others reduced to one or two members, by arrests or fatalities sustained in fierce gun battles with the police. Their operations, however, continue. It is assumed that members for its clandestine cells are recruited from affiliated support groups. In France and Great Britain these have been penetrated by police undercover operatives, whose mission is to ingratiate themselves with the leadership of a terrorist group and be selected to serve as a member of a clandestine cell, thus being able to monitor its activities.[43] Operationally, it appears that the West German police have an excellent opportunity to penetrate the Red Army Faction, as the number of potentially dangerous activists in West Germany has soared to twelve hundred, of whom about 150 are underground. A

[41] Paul Hofmann, "West Germans Urged to Tolerate Dissent," *The New York Times*, September 18, 1977, p. 19.
[42] Jon Bradshaw, "The Dream of Terror," *Esquire* (July 18, 1978): 50.
[43] Frank Kitson, *Low Intensity Operations* (London: Faber & Faber, 1971), pp. 71–72.

terrorist organization's vulnerability increases in proportion to its members. It is quite possible that the terrorists can count also on another six thousand supporters, and fifteen thousand young people, mostly associated with academic life, who are "sympathizers."[44]

Restricted by lawmakers in various areas of covert collection and surveillance, the West German police have been subjected to some harsh criticism regarding the conduct of their antiterrorist campaign, which appears somewhat amateurish to the initiated observer. In September 1978, the police killed Red Army Faction member Willy Peter Stoll in a restaurant in Düsseldorf, but missed three other suspected terrorists living in the same building when they raided his apartment.[45] A few weeks prior to the killing of Mr. Stoll, the police had photographed him and two other suspected terrorists as they were preparing to board a helicopter near Michelstadt, 35 miles south of Frankfurt.[46] The group was allowed to take off, as the police photographic detail claimed to have no knowledge of the trio, which included Christian Klar, who is a fugitive, and wanted for the April 1977 murder of West Germany's federal prosecutor Siegfried Buback and the assassination of Hanns-Martin Schleyer. In addition, Mr. Klar was seen in Rome before and after the Aldo Moro abduction.

On September 24, 1978, during the course of another incident with R.A.F. members, the police surprised three suspected terrorists at target practice in the woods outside Dortmund. A gun battle followed, during the course of which a police officer was killed and two terrorists wounded. The third terrorist managed to escape with the dead police officer's submachine gun.[47]

According to some informed sources, governmental bureaucracies and police organizations are among the most significant obstacles to be overcome during the course of conducting antiterrorist operations in western Europe. A handful of West German police officers in Bonn expressed great irritation with France at the time of the kidnapping of Hanns-Martin Schleyer in the fall of 1977, although they were well aware that the French services—gendarmerie, territorial surveillance organization, and counterespionage agency—have difficulty coordinating within their own borders. According to Bonn police, the French merely

---

[44] Bradshaw, "Dream of Terror," p. 50.

[45] "Manhunt Nets Some Biggies," *The New York Times,* November 6, 1978, p. 50.

[46] Associated Press photograph and caption reading "Suspect German terrorists, from the left, Adelheid Schulz, Willy Peter Stoll and Christian Klar, as they were about to board a helicopter, etc.," *The New York Times,* November 6, 1978, p. 50.

[47] "W. German Police Nab Two Terrorists," *The News World* (September 25, 1978): 2.

went through the motions of hunting for the German businessman in Alsace, where West German officials claimed he was held captive, and where his body was eventually found in the truck of a car parked in Mulhouse, on October 21, 1977. But the West German police, also accused of using shoddy investigative methods in the hunt for Mr. Schleyer, avoid discussing details of receiving information about the location of the businessman's abductors: this proved to be accurate on follow-up investigation, but was not immediately communicated to the proper authorities; and when it was finally transmitted, an important element was omitted from the message.[48]

Horst Herold, head of West Germany's Bundeskriminalamt, acknowledges that "there are piles of the hardest kind of coordinating problems present when it comes to dealing with foreign police departments," regardless of a European Common Market agreement to exchange information on terrorism, regional meetings of law-enforcement officials, and a series of resolutions of the European Parliament endorsing closer cooperation against terrorism.

Elaborating on Director Herold's remarks, Heinz Schwarz, formerly Interior Minister in the West German state of Rhineland-Palatinate, which shares a common border with France, said:

> At the moment the cooperation is mostly on paper and far too restricted to be of much actual use in the event something happens. There is no notion of hot pursuit. If the German police ever ran someone over a border and then shot an innocent bystander, there would be an international hue and cry that no one would ever forget. So while you wait, the suspect vanishes.[49]

Regardless of the limitations which its constitution and parliament have imposed on police antiterrorist operations, West Germany's federal internal security costs amount to some billion marks a year, and an annual budget increase of a further 120 million marks was approved after the death of Hanns-Martin Schleyer.

ANTITERRORIST LEGISLATION IN WEST GERMANY

Measures to combat terrorism by amendments to the penal code have been taken by West German law makers. In January 1976, these were voted by the parliament in response to pressure on its individual members by constituents, some of whom were demanding the enact-

---

[48] John Vinocur, "New Vigor but Big Obstacles in the Hunt for Terrorists," *The New York Times*, May 7, 1978, p. 1.
[49] Ibid.

ment of tough antiterrorist measures, and as a belated first move to combat the operations of urban terrorists. Revisions to the penal code specified fines and prison terms for a maximum of 32 years for perpetrators of bomb hoaxes, publishers of instructional manuals on bomb manufacture and terrorist tactics, authors of articles clearly supportive of serious crimes, and orators speaking on behalf of terrorists and other perpetrators of major violence. Although the Social Democrats and the Free Democrats claimed that the newly enacted measures restricted constitutionally guaranteed freedoms, the conservative Christian Democratic Party took the position that the modifications of the "code" were not harsh enough.[50]

Additional antiterrorist legislation was approved later in 1976, and in 1977. The 1976 laws enabled judges to read letters between jailed terrorists and lawyers, thus permitting authorities to monitor lawyer–client communications, which are privileged in American law. The new legislation also provided for jail terms of up to 10 years for convicted leaders of terrorist organizations. Chancellor Helmut Schmidt's request for a law that would permit judges to monitor private talks between suspects and lawyers, however, was withdrawn.[51]

On October 4, 1977, West Germany's constitutional court rejected pleas by three imprisoned terrorists and four lawyers to declare the enacted prohibitions on lawyer–client communications as unconstitutional, on the grounds that the lifting of the ban would enhance the capability of terrorists to use their lawyers to communicate with one another, and impede the antiterrorist campaign. A few months earlier, the Association of German Judges recommended the drafting of new rules that would bar lawyers "who notoriously belong to circles sympathizing with the terrorist scene" from trials concerning terrorism.[52]

Meanwhile, the wave of terrorism, that has included the assassination and kidnapping of several major West German public figures, continues, unabated by either newly enacted laws or other antiterrorist measures. The respected West German newspaper, *Frankfurter Allgemeine Zeitung*, in 1978 published the results of a survey of 500 students at 33 universities and technical colleges. Some 19 percent of those who were surveyed characterized themselves as active in student politics, and said that they condoned the use of violence against both people and

---

[50] "Terrorism Curbs Enacted in Bonn," *The New York Times*, January 17, 1976, p. 8.
[51] Craig R. Whitney, "Bonn Votes Curb for Terrorists," *The New York Times*, July 30, 1976, p. 5.
[52] "Bonn Courts Upholds Ban on Contact between Terrorists and Lawyers," *The New York Times*, October 6, 1977, p. A15.

property in the pursuit of political goals. Another 36 percent accepted violence directed against property, but not against people.[53]

During a period of crisis caused by a dramatic act of terrorism, it is not unusual for the police to search college facilities for students who are terrorists, or are harboring terrorists. Through August 1977, some half million young Germans were screened in accordance with an old law now called the *Radikalenerlass*, the Radical's Decree, and almost six thousand of those investigated had an entry in the Central State Protection File. The "Radical's Decree" provides for mandatory loyalty screenings for any prospective government employee and bans from the civil service (which in West Germany is 13 percent of the jobs) those deemed potentially disloyal to the constitution. Anyone who walks in demonstrations leading to violence or participates in a demonstration staged in behalf of a radical group could be listed in the Central State Protection File, and the listing subsequently be used to bar the listee from positions "covered" by civil service.[54]

GERMAN PRISON-CONTROL MEASURES

West German authorities regard the 24-hour surveillance of incarcerated terrorists as an absolute necessity, as key prisoners have killed themselves inside German maximum-security prisons. On May 9, 1976, Ulrike Meinhof was found hanged in her cell; and on October 18, 1977, Andreas Baader and Jan-Carl Raspe died of self-inflicted gunshot wounds, and Gudrun Ensslin hanged herself.[55] Kurt Rebmann, West Germany's chief federal prosecutor, later announced that the pistols used by the terrorists to commit suicide had been smuggled into the court building of the Stammheim facility during the spring of 1977, eventually finding their way into the hands of Mr. Baader and Mr. Raspe. Apparently, the weapons that were used, a 7.65 mm and a 9 mm Heckler and Koch automatic, had been secreted inside a sheaf of hollowed-out legal documents and delivered to the prison by Arndt Miller, a lawyer who was arrested during the summer of 1977 on suspicion of assisting an illegal organization.[56]

---

[53] John Tagliabue, "West German Students Anti-Democratic and Prone to Violence?" *The Chronicle of Higher Education* (November 20, 1978): 3.

[54] Jon Bradshaw, "The Dream of Terror," *Esquire* (July 18, 1978): 12–16.

[55] John Vinocur, "Suspicion Festers in Prison Deaths of German Terrorists," *The New York Times*, January 22, 1978, p. 2.

[56] "Bonn Official Says Lawyer Smuggled Guns into Prison," *The New York Times*, January 13, 1978, p. A6.

On November 11, 1977, builders carrying out excavation work on the seventh floor of the maximum-security Stammheim Prison uncovered approximately 14 ounces of explosives and three detonators behind a wall in a cell that was once occupied by another member of the Red Army Faction. About 2 weeks later, prison authorities disclosed that a revolver and a sizable cache of ammunition also were uncovered in the terrorist compound at Stammheim.[57]

West Germany's use of legal prohibitions and construction of modern prison facilities equipped with the latest security systems to restrict communications among terrorists both "inside" and "outside" prison walls needs to be supplemented by other measures of isolating dangerous prisoners from their associates, regardless of the sentiment expressed by Justice Minister Jürgen Baumann: "I am not running a fortress."[58] Until these measures are adopted by all West Germany's prisons, the perfunctory checks, similar to those once customary at the main entrance of Moabit Prison in West Berlin's central district, will not be sufficient to restrict the behavior of isolated terrorists, or prevent their escape.

On May 27, 1978, according to Minister Baumann, two women passed through security checks at Moabit Prison by showing identity cards bearing the names of lawyers who were registered at the facility. Once inside the prison, the women wounded one guard and coerced another into opening an automatic security gate before freeing Till Meyer from his cell and escaping in a van with two other persons.[59]

Mr. Meyer was on trial before the municipal supreme court for the 1974 murder of Günter von Drenkmann, a West Berlin judge, and the 1975 kidnapping of Peter Lorenz, chairman of the Christian Democratic Union and a West Berlin conservative leader. On June 22, 1978, a Moabit Prison guard vacationing in Bulgaria, observed Mr. Meyer, and informed West German authorities. Assisted by West German police, Bulgarian authorities arrested the terrorist and three associates, and quickly placed them on a flight to Bonn.[60]

This brief survey of antiterrorist activities by West European governments indicates that a highly disciplined, well-trained, and profes-

---

[57] "3 in Stuttgart Jail Used a Morse Code System," *The New York Times*, October 21, 1977, p. 3.

[58] Ellen Lentz, "Police of West Berlin Tighten Search for Terrorists," *The New York Times*, June 4, 1978, p. 5.

[59] "2 Women Free Guerrilla from West Berlin Jail," *The New York Times*, May 28, 1978, p. 12.

[60] John Vinocur, "Terror Suspects Seized in Bulgaria, Quickly Handed to West Germany," *The New York Times*, June 24, 1978, p. 1.

sionally led force of police officers, supported by an objective judiciary and reasonably modern laws and prison-control systems, is the vital component needed to control terrorism. Although technology and psychological skills are vital, a reliance on countergangs should be avoided. The precise use of covert police information-gathering methods, undercover operatives, informants, and audiosurveillance are vital for the conduct of antiterrorist operations.

ANTITERRORIST INTELLIGENCE: LIMITATIONS AND APPLICATIONS

Intelligence gathering is a key responsibility of an antiterrorist organi-zation. The United States Senate has insisted, nevertheless, that the activities of the individual law-enforcement officer and intelligence agent assigned to field collection be tightly controlled. In 1978, William H. Webster, Director of the Federal Bureau of Investigation, said that his agency then had 42 informers on domestic intelligence and terrorism matters, whereas it once used approximately thirteen hundred in a single protracted investigation of the Socialist Workers Party. Moreover, the F.B.I. has transferred its responsibility of identifying links between do-mestic terrorist movements and foreign governments from its intelli-gence division to its general investigations branch, where this is handled in the same way as all other criminal cases.[1]

INVESTIGATIVE GUIDELINES

Currently, the level of the F.B.I.'s involvement in all domestic se-curity cases, including terrorism, is regulated by the domestic security guidelines formulated by former United States Attorney General Edward

[1] Nicholas M. Horrock, "Senate Panel Offers Legislation to Curb Intelligence Agents," *The New York Times*, February 10, 1978, p. 1.

Levi in March 1976. These three levels of investigation are: (1) the preliminary investigation, (2) the limited investigation, and (3) the full investigation. Undertaken on "the basis of allegations or other information that an individual or group may be engaged in activities which involve or will involve the use of force or violence," the purpose of the limited investigation is to verify or refute the charge through the use of the F.B.I.'s own files, public records, and newspaper reports. Previously existing informants, physical surveillance, and interviews of persons for the limited purpose of identifying the subject of an investigation may also be utilized during the course of a preliminary investigation. A limited investigation, restricted to determining whether the results of a preliminary investigation warrant a full investigation, permits agents to conduct interviews of a wider scope than those conducted at the first level. However, the Special Agent in Charge (S.A.C.) of a "Bureau" field office must authorize a limited investigation in writing.

Sanctioned only by the F.B.I.'s Washington headquarters in consultation with the attorney general, after preliminary and limited investigations develop specific facts revealing that "an individual or group is or may be engaged . . . in the use of force or violence and . . . the violations of federal law," the full investigation permits agents to use covert collection methods. Court-ordered electronic surveillance, informants, and, pending the approval of the attorney general, "mail covers," may be used during an investigation of this type, although all investigative results are subject to periodic review, and must be reported to the attorney general within 90 days.[2]

State and municipal police activities to control public disorders and terrorism have also been restricted by the proliferation of legislation enacted by Washington and intended to enhance privacy. The Texas Department of Public Safety has ended its use of information obtained from files of a noncriminal nature. Other police departments, including those of New York City, Baltimore, and Los Angeles, have restructured their intelligence files to a point which makes it extremely difficult for a police intelligence unit to provide operational sections with the information needed to control organized crime and terrorism. Specifically, the Freedom of Information Act (F.O.I.A.) is viewed in American intelligence circles as responsible for creating obstacles that impede the collection of information important to the antiterrorist. Frank C. Carlucci, Deputy Director of the Central Intelligence Agency (C.I.A.), in testimony before the United States House of Representatives Intelligence Com-

[2] "F.B.I. Domestic Intelligence Found Curbed," *The New York Times,* November 10, 1977, p. 4.

mittee's legislation subcommittee, stated that his organization is losing significant information because many of its domestic and foreign contacts fear that their identities would be exposed under the provisions of the F.O.I.A.[3]

Providing for public access to government information on demand with the proviso that allows an agency to withhold certain sensitive materials in specified categories, the F.O.I.A. permits even foreigners to submit requests to agencies, including the C.I.A., for data. Mr. Carlucci believes that some of these requests from aliens may be made by "representatives of hostile intelligence services." In his words:

> Recently the chief of a major foreign intelligence service sat in my office and flatly stated that he could not fully cooperate as long as the C.I.A. is subject to the act. . . . They don't say, 'We aren't going to give you X, Y, Z'; that is not the way intelligence services work. But we do know of information in the possession of friendly services that was not given to us.[4]

Although the administration of President Carter assigned antiterrorism a high priority in its intelligence policy, and the C.I.A. adopted measures to facilitate the exchange of information with friendly foreign governments, some American officials believe that the C.I.A. takes an exceedingly cautious reading of prevailing legal curbs on the conduct of covert operations and on the provision of aid to foreign governments. The agency avoided a direct role in helping the Italians deal with the Aldo Moro kidnapping and in assisting the West Germans to respond to the hijacking of one of their airliners. The Hughes–Ryan Amendment of 1974, forbidding the conduct of covert action by the C.I.A. unless the president makes a "finding" that such a response is important to national security and reports it to Congress, and a 1975 amendment to the Foreign Assistance Act, precluding the use of foreign-aid funds to support foreign police activities, were the major factors in the C.I.A.'s decision to reject the requests from Rome and Bonn.

The Italian government had requested that the C.I.A. furnish it with sophisticated audiosurveillance equipment to monitor members of the Red Brigades who were holding Mr. Moro, leader of Italy's Christian Democratic Party, captive. The West Germans had requested the C.I.A.'s assistance in the quick removal of doors on a hijacked airliner on the runway of an airport in Somalia without injuring the passengers held hostage in the compartments. The Italian request for the eavesdropping equipment was denied, and the West German request was stalled in Washington. Meanwhile, a West German police commando unit, sup-

---

[3] "C.I.A. Aide Deplores Data-Release Law," *The New York Times*, April 6, 1979, p. 12.
[4] Ibid.

ported by British technicians who blew off the doors of the hijacked aircraft, stormed through the opening in the fuselage and freed the hostages.[5]

Most American antiterrorist legislation, containing provisions that attempt to obtain an appropriate balance between the need to protect the domestic security and the potential dangers posed by unreasonable surveillance to individual privacy and free expression, mandates the establishment of a legislative oversight committee to control intelligence operations. The House of Representatives is aware, however, of the need to upgrade existing intelligence systems, and to procure new types of equipment to enhance the capability of intelligence units to support field operations. Its Permanent Select Committee on Intelligence, requested a substantial increase for the fiscal year of 1980 over the amount of money that Congress appropriated for intelligence in the fiscal year of 1979.

An appropriation of $13.4 million was earmarked for the continuation of the F.B.I.'s antiterrorist activities, and was used (a) to retain nine "personnel spaces" in the "Bureau's" Headquarters Management Unit, which "performs liaison functions with local agencies in terrorist situations or potential terrorist problems" at public activities, such as the 1980 Winter Olympic Games at Lake Placid, New York; (b) to support two "personnel spaces" in the F.B.I.'s Terrorism Research and Bomb Data Unit, which maintains the agency's data bank on terrorist weapons and methods of operation; and (c) to provide financial support for 74 "personnel spaces" in the F.B.I.'s field offices nationwide. Special agents assigned to antiterrorist field functions are to be detailed to tasks related to operational aspects of the F.B.I.'s program: undercover operations, management of informants, and investigative activities.[6]

ANTITERRORIST INFORMATION GATHERING

American restrictions in the area of information gathering stem from the "Watergate" incident and the subsequent probing of the F.B.I. and the C.I.A. by United States congressmen and others. Covert methods used to identify links between domestic terrorist movements and foreign organizations were the primary target of attack. The leakage of highly

[5] Richard Burt, "C.I.A. Refuses Foreign Bids for Antiterrorist Help," *The New York Times*, June 27, 1978, p. 3.
[6] House of Representatives, 96th Congress, 1st Session, Rept. 96–127 (Part 1): Intelligence and Intelligence-Related Activities Authorization Act, Fiscal Year 1980 (Washington, D.C.: U.S. Government Printing Office, May 8, 1979), pp. 1–4.

sensitive information, in part related to the investigations of the intelligence services by congressional committees, has made it extremely difficult for American agents operating in foreign areas to develop meaningful contacts with people who feel that their identities may one day become public information. Although human intelligence is needed to gain access to motives, intentions, thoughts, and plans, American privacy legislation has prompted the C.I.A. to rely inordinately on technical means of collection. Thus, in January 1979, members of Congress should not have been surprised when the House of Representatives Permanent Select Committee on Intelligence reported that the C.I.A., lacking reliable sources of human intelligence, had produced no assessments pertaining to key opponents of the Shah of Iran for a period of two years ending in November 1977, and produced none in the first quarter of 1978.[7]

Emphasizing earth-satellite photography as the vital element in its ongoing program of modern intelligence research and analysis, the C.I.A.'s earth-orbiting vehicles are capable of transmitting back to the ground the same high level of photographic imagery that the U-2 reconnaissance aircraft provided in the late 1950s. The C.I.A. used intelligence satellites in the 1960s to observe American students engaged in antiwar demonstrations, for the purpose of checking "possible foreign connections" with the American opposition to the war in Vietnam. Referenced in declassified C.I.A. documents as "review of satellite imagery from N.A.S.A. programs to identify photographs too sensitive for public release," this extraterrestrial surveillance operation used cameras capable of taking photographs at altitudes exceeding 100 miles, and accurate enough to record objects the size of a suitcase. Overreliance on satellite intelligence is dangerous, however, since the Soviet Union is becoming increasingly expert in techniques to destroy, blind, or disable reconnaissance satellites. Although satellite enthusiasts boast of orbiting spacecraft whose equipment can read auto license-plate numbers in Red Square, or pick out the warm outline of footprints left by a terrorist band in the snow of the Pyrenees, skeptics inside and outside the "intelligence community" point to an instance a few years ago when the American intelligence officials could not say for certain, based on satellite information, whether an explosion off South Africa was an atomic detonation or not.[8]

[7] Bernard Guertman, "House Blames Intelligence Agencies and Policy Makers over Iran," *The New York Times*, January 25, 1979, p. 1.

[8] "The Motto Is: Think Big, Think Dirty," *Time* (February 6, 1978): 12; Malcolm W. Browne, "U.S. Increases Reliance on Intelligence Satellites," *The New York Times*, October 18, 1979, p. 2.

Antiterrorist planners are obliged to take all precautions to shield their operations from an opponent's reconnaissance satellites. Just prior to launching the helicopters used in the aborted attempt to rescue the American hostages in Teheran, the aircraft carrier *U.S.S. Nimitz* suddenly made a turn and sailed away at top speed, to elude detection by Soviet electronic tracking vehicles. In another instance, during the war in Vietnam an American assault force, training at Eglin Air Force Base in Florida for an operation intended to free prisoners of war being held in a compound near Hanoi, each morning constructed a full-sized wood-and-canvas replica of the prison camp, and each night took it down, to prevent satellites from learning details of the planned raid.[9]

In addition to its "Big Bird," a 12-ton vehicle orbiting at an altitude about 250 miles above the earth, the American information-gathering effort relies on "Blackbird," a fixed-wing strategic reconnaissance aircraft, officially designated the SR–71, for photographic missions. Equipped with three-dimensional filming equipment that is so precise that a mailbox on a country road can be located with ease, the SR–71's cameras can photograph most of the United States in three passes.[10] This aircraft is gradually replacing the U–2, the type used by Francis Gary Powers to fly a spy mission over the Soviet Union. Loaded with photographic equipment for the gathering of intelligence data, Mr. Powers's aircraft was shot down on May 1, 1960, near Sverdlovsk, more than a thousand miles within the borders of the U.S.S.R.

PROCESSING INTELLIGENCE

The clandestine-collection methods available for use by American antiterrorists, are closely controlled and regulated by the courts. Consequently, it is imperative that personnel assigned to analytical functions be instructed in the techniques used to evaluate and interpret information derived from overt sources, so as to limit their dependence upon informants, undercover operatives, audiosurveillance, and other forms of covert collection. Furthermore, clandestine-collection methods, even when properly managed, are politically sensitive, hazardous, and expensive. These methods should be used sparingly, but not excluded; sometimes critical data required to control offenses dangerous to human

[9] Richard D. Lyons, "Soviet Launches a Spy Satellite to Track U.S. Ships," *The New York Times,* May 2, 1980, p. 3.
[10] "The Motto Is: Think Big, Think Dirty," *Time* (February 6, 1978): 12.

life, such as bombings and arson, are not available through other means.[11]

Newspaper clippings and other public sources of information are an indispensable input into any analytical investigation of terrorist matters. Intelligence analysts have long been aware that a seasoned reporter performs functions markedly similar to their own. During the Crimean War, the Czar, Nicholas I, referring to the investigative journalism of the British reporter William Howard Russell, commented as follows: "We have no need of spies, we have *The Times*."[12]

A civilian, Berthold Jacob, wrote a little book, published in 1935, which shocked Hitler: it contained an accurate description of the German Army's order of battle. The material in the book had been assembled entirely from information discovered in obituary notices (which invariably contain a list of mourners), wedding announcements, (whose contents include a listing of invited guests), and notices in military journals intended to inform interested persons of promotions, assignments, and retirements. Colonel Walther Nicolai, one of Hitler's advisors on intelligence matters, regarded Jacob to be "the greatest intelligence genius I have ever encountered in my thirty-five years in the service."[13]

Contemporary examples of outstanding investigative reporting include a listing of secret electronic-surveillance bases operated by the Norwegians for the United States, pieced together by an editor for an Oslo publishing house from information listed in telephone directories, and an article in the *New York Times* that revealed how the Weather Underground Organization (W.U.O.) operated in the United States as secret agents of a foreign power, Cuba. The W.U.O. was, thus, a legitimate target for the F.B.I.'s counterintelligence operations.

Using simple but proven research tools—a pair of scissors, a pot of glue, and a file of index cards—investigative reporters and others are able to write reports which simultaneously alarm and inform the intelligence community. An antiterrorist analyst should identify the reporters who seem knowledgeable in his particular area of investigation, verify the details in their stories for accuracy and reliability, and then use their information to reevaluate the general principles and specific details con-

[11] Herb Jaffe, "Hyland Says Wiretap Law Protects Privacy," *The Star Ledger* (Newark, N.J.), May 29, 1977, p. 5.

[12] Jock Haswell, *Spies and Spymasters* (London: Butler & Tanner, 1977), p. 83.

[13] Ladislas Farago, "Research and Analysis: The Chief Components of Usable Intelligence," in William E. Dougherty and Morris Janowitz, *A Psychological Warfare Casebook* (Baltimore: The Johns Hopkins Press, 1968), p. 514.

tained in his particular area of concentration. The basic elements of the processing system utilized by both the investigative reporter and the analyst are the same: a controlled and systematic information flow intended to insure a maximum amount of relevant facts within established parameters, a file arranged by categories with a cross-indexing capability, and a person with a capacity and predilection for analysis.

An analyst must read newspapers, periodicals, and other published materials to glean information on the variables, factors, relationships, and trends associated with a particular area of investigation. Significant articles are clipped from the printed materials by the analyst, and pasted to index cards which have been annotated in accordance with an established scheme. Experienced analysts are able to assess rapidly the significance of open information of this type and exclude extraneous data from their files. A clogged file makes it impossible for an analyst to come to any conclusion about anything.

The use of clipping services should be avoided; the analyst assigned to the antiterrorist investigation is the only person knowledgeable enough to insure that the correct materials are clipped and that relevant items are not overlooked.

Another task for the analyst is to provide directions for the information gatherers (collectors) who have been assigned to obtain information for him from their field contacts. Only the analyst knows exactly what information needs to be gathered from a particular place or subject within a specific time frame. Intelligence, if it is to be effective, must be directed and controlled centrally.

Occasionally, however, there is a need for placing a clandestine contact in a designated area for the purpose of reporting anything which he or she thinks might be of interest. Unfortunately, operations of this sort usually result in the contact's providing either a flood of worthless information, or no information at all.[14]

Stemming from the mission of the antiterrorist analyst are three key areas of responsibility: (1) to identify and define existing conditions conducive to the development or enlargement of terrorist activity by a particular group; (2) quickly to assess changing conditions which impact both upon the behavior of a specific terrorist group and the antiterrorist methods intended to control it; and (3) to forecast the path to be followed by an assigned terrorist group from existing conditions.

It is imperative that quantitative and qualitative performance indicators be devised and used by managers of analytical personnel to meas-

[14] Haswell, *Spies and Spymasters*, p. 16.

ure the performance of their subordinates in the three key responsibility areas of an antiterrorist analyst.

Managerial utilization of a performance-appraisal system for such analytical personnel tends to force the development of a work product which is measurable by realistic standards of quantity and quality, thereby enhancing managerial control, and contributing to the viability of the analytical function as a consequence of having indicated both its need and use.

ANALYTICAL TASKS AND TOOLS

Analysts associated with an antiterrorist intelligence module are involved in tasks relating to the seemingly endless culling of file cards for the purpose of extracting bits of information relative to the targets, philosophy, antecedents, organization, connections, and prospects of a particular terrorist group. Target analysis, an integral part of this analytical process, is an especially useful study, as its purpose is to develop the intelligence required to protect targets from attack by terrorists. It is concerned with the following tasks: (a) defining the target, (b) identifying the conditions that cause it to be attacked, (c) assessing the posture of the target toward threatening conditions affecting it, and (d) estimating the vulnerability of the target to terrorist action.[15]

Antiterrorist analytical personnel should also be involved in assessing the societal conditions which a particular group of terrorists regards as being manipulative for their own ends, such conditions in consequence being advantageous to their total operational, organizational, and psychological capability and objectives.[16] For example, toward the end of its reign of terror the Symbionese Liberation Army adopted a policy of property bombing, because it had lost through attrition the black leadership that had formulated its policy of assassination. It recognized that these killings were no longer attuned to a level of violence "acceptable" to the group for which it was seeking to characterize certain actions taken by the government, businessmen, or property owners as illegal acts against the people.

Since terrorist operations are primarily propaganda intended to influence the political behavior of a target through the skillful application

---

[15] Department of the Army, *Psychological Operations*, FM33–5 (Washington, D.C.: U.S. Government Printing Office, 1961), p. 52.

[16] Arturo C. Porzecanski, *Uruguay's Tupamaros: The Urban Guerrilla* (New York: Praeger Publishers, 1973), p. 11.

of bombings, kidnappings, assassinations, etc., they can be analyzed through the use of a formula represented as SCAME: analysis of Source, Content, Audience, Media, and Effects.[17] An analyst studying the Puerto Rican terrorist group, Fuerzas Armadas de Liberacion Nacional (F.A.L.N.), could use this formula to determine the probable identity of the terrorist group responsible for an incident by examining its nature, the symbolic bombing of a corporate office building owned by a firm which has financial interests in the Caribbean area; its intended audience, extremist members of the "independista" communities of New York and Chicago, or right-wing groups who prefer to see Washington's tie with Puerto Rico severed; its media impact and coverage, as determined by time and space factors derived from newspaper and television reports; and, finally, the effect that a terrorist bombing has on the target audience for whom it was detonated.

Developed through a three-phase process, as depicted in Figure 2, a link diagram is a useful analytical tool. The steps in its development are: (a) the organization of raw data into logical order, (b) the construction of an associational matrix for the purpose of detecting evidence of a link between individuals, places, and things identified with the subject of an inquiry, and (c) the charting of the assembled information in graphic form. A skilled analyst utilizes the link diagram to chart rapidly and to examine graphic relationships, for the purpose of further substantiating logically his conclusions and predictions concerning the terrorist activity depicted.

Analysts conducting an investigation of terrorist activity should recall this passage from Michael Crichton's best-selling novel, *The Andromeda Strain:* "At first glance, they were as different as possible; they were at opposite ends of the spectrum sharing nothing in common. And yet there must be something in common."[18] Analysts must, nevertheless, beware of using theory in their work; theory tends to channel an investigation along certain lines, bias observation by reducing the parameters of an inquiry, limit its users to one consistent set of definitions and assumptions, adjust concepts by the use of calculation, and lead to overgeneralization of its specific conclusions. Even so, an analyst, after recognizing these pitfalls, must utilize theory during an investigation, as a guide to the formulation of an hypothesis, and as a way of looking for facts which may not be readily apparent.[19] Also, theory serves as an

---

[17] *Psychological Operations,* FM33–5, p. 58.
[18] Michael Crichton, *The Andromeda Strain* (New York: Dell Publishing Co., 1970), p. 151.
[19] John B. Wolf, *The Police Intelligence System* (New York: The John Jay Press, 1978), pp. 24–26.

instrument of control for the manager of an antiterrorist analytical section, as it indicates which investigations are crucial, and facilitates their systematic progress.

Managers of antiterrorist analytical personnel must be aware of the policies and procedures used by their counterparts in other disciplines, who direct the work of analysts using theory in their investigations. For example, the national Center for Disease Control, situated in Atlanta, Georgia, promulgated "Eleven Commandments" as guidelines for epidemiologists assigned to track "legionnaires' disease," a respiratory condition that broke out among people who had attended an American Legion convention in Philadelphia in July 1976.

The first three of these commandments are to (1) determine the existence of an epidemic (terrorist threat), (2) verify the diagnosis (analysis), and (3) specify that a quick survey of both the known cases of disease and the community situation be undertaken in a manner markedly similar to the analytical practices utilized by an antiterrorist analyst engaged in assessing the impact of armed propaganda on the targets and audience of a particular terrorist group.[20] Managerial adherence to these commandments facilitates the decision to commit resources to a particular antiterrorist investigation, the quality and quantity of the resources assigned, and the probable duration of the research effort.

The remaining seven "commandments" describe standard practices recommended for use by all analytical personnel who use theory in their research. They are as follows: (4) formulate a tentative hypothesis, (5) plan a detailed epidemiological (antiterrorist) investigation, (6) conduct the systematic collection of data, (7) analyze information obtained from all sources, (8) test the hypothesis, (9) formulate conclusions, (10) put control measures into operation or, as in the case of an antiterrorist analyst, recommend control measures, and (11) make a report.[21]

Acting in accordance with these "commandments," David Scondras believes that it is possible to predict whether a building is "arson prone" by studying the history of its sales transactions and its housing-code and rent-control violations, as well as back taxes owed. "We're developing a diagnostic tool for another type of cancer," he says; "once it is diagnosed, we believe it can be cured." Mr. Scondras is director of a project in Boston, funded by the United States Fire Administration, the objective of which is to develop a computerized system that will help

---

[20] Gwyneth Cravens and John S. Marr, "Tracking Down the Epidemic," *The New York Times Magazine*, December 12, 1976, pp. 34–36 & 98–109.
[21] Ibid.

Figure 2a

Figure 2a–c. Analytical tool: (a) Associational matrix. ○, Overt information, representing the Essential Elements of Information (E.E.I.'s) to be verified for accuracy, reliability, and pertinence. ●, Overt information, verified for accuracy, reliability, and pertinence, (b) a section of an associational matrix illustrating linkage, and (c) assembled information in graphic form. (Prepared by John B. Wolf. © 1979 John B. Wolf. All rights reserved.)

		J. Smith	J. Jones	C. Martin	XYZ Club	ABC Inc.
		1	2	3	4	5
1	J. Smith	●	●			●
2	J. Jones	●	●	●	●	●
3	C. Martin		●	●	●	
4	XYZ Club		●	●	●	
5	ABC Inc.	●	●			●

Figure 2b

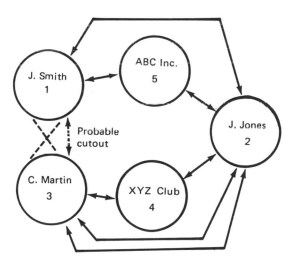

Figure 2c

officials of American cities gain foreknowledge of whether a building is likely to be intentionally burned.[22]

A similar data base is already being exploited by analysts responding to incendiary attacks attributed to the F.A.L.N. These investigators are aware that this group's modus operandi includes the following: (1) using relatively low-yield incendiary devices for daylight attacks, (2) targeting department stores near the noon lunch hour, and (3) placing the explosive devices in public areas of the store selected. The purpose of the F.A.L.N. fire-bombings, according to intelligence officers familiar with the terrorists, is to have their arson attacks publicized by the press because of the apparent lunacy and drama associated with the location and timing of the ignition of their Improvised Explosive Devices (I.E.D.).

A spate of fires during the months of June and July 1979 in New York City department stores were believed to have been set—accidentally or intentionally—but were not attributed to the F.A.L.N., for the following reasons: no accelerants or fuels had been used, all the fires were relatively small, there was no attempt to disable sprinkler devices, and the fires in question were ignited in "areas where customers could have had access, but probably didn't."[23]

Although the usefulness of antiterrorist analytical operations is evident, they are destined for oblivion unless those who manage them recognize the indispensable role of analysis in the processing of collected information. It is sad, but it seems that an organization which has devised untold innovations and methods in the analytical area does not view analysis in its proper perspective. Recently, the C.I.A. placed an advertisement for personnel in a major newspaper, stating: "We're looking for men and women with special talent. *The primary task of the Central Intelligence Agency is to gather information abroad to help protect and guide the international interests of the United States.*" This notice supports the contention, frequently voiced in intelligence circles, that Americans are "the world's best collectors of information but the world's worst analysts."

[22] "9 Try to Devise Computer to Predict Arson Targets," *The New York Times*, May 6, 1979, p. 51.
[23] "Accidents or Arson Cited in 5 Store Fires," *The New York Times*, July 21, 1979, p. 23.

10

A FRAMEWORK FOR THE STUDY AND CONTROL OF TERRORISM

Terrorism is a result of human actions. The general principles of the scientific method are relevant to its analysis. A procedure for approaching a question, situation, person, or idea according to a definitely established, logical, and systematic plan, the scientific method includes the following nine stages: (1) data collection, (2) statement of the problem, (3) analysis of the problem, (4) selection of the aspects to be studied, (5) use of induction to observe, describe, and classify specifics, (6) statement of the hypothesis, (7) use of deduction to formulate and test assumptions, (8) clarification of the relationship between the original problem and the hypothesis, and (9) generalization to other situations. Utilization of these procedures has facilitated the development and refinement of an analytical framework for the study and control of terrorism.

ITERATE (an acronym for International Terrorism: Attributes of Terrorist Events) is a computerized data base used as a research tool by the C.I.A. to demonstrate the feasibility and utility of summarizing terrorist trends, comparing terrorist campaigns, and evaluating policy prescriptions for crisis management. "It has also been used in other government-sponsored research to test hypotheses about deterrence and the effects of publicity on terrorist behavior, and to devise general profiles of terrorist behavior in hostage bargaining situations." The

C.I.A. and other agencies are currently developing more advanced systems.[1]

The analytical framework described in this chapter, however, consists of primary category groups that are derived solely from the observable and factual descriptions of those who use terror to alter the status quo. Furthermore, this framework has been designed to serve as a guide for use primarily by police and other security personnel serving in the capacity of intelligence analysts who seek to obtain specific details from designated individuals—investigators, confidential informants, undercover operatives—assigned to collect field information regarding an agitational or small-scale type of terrorist group. Utilizing this framework an intelligence analyst can be supported by an entire patrol division which he has alerted through organizational channels to detect and report on a specific element of information which he needs to facilitate his continuing progress with an investigation.

The framework assumes that first a plan, then a doctrine, and finally a system composed of principles, values, and objectives precedes the perpetration of an act of agitational terrorism. Separate and primary categories are included in the framework for ideology and propaganda whose objectives can be discovered and observed—they are facts, too. An assessment of the magnetism, longevity, and manipulative quality of an ideology is an important task for the intelligence analyst. The framework, however, includes only facts which are used to indicate relationships from which abstractions and developed theories are derived. Uncorroborated information is excluded. Thus, the framework is fit for use by a police intelligence analyst when undertaking a specific and inductive inquiry into a situation involving a matter of agitational terrorism.

CATEGORIES EXTRACTED FROM THE ANALYTICAL SYNTHESES

The analytical framework described in this chapter is intended to be used only as a tool to analyze information which has been previously collected, collated, and evaluated, and which pertains exclusively to agitational terrorism. The structure of its primary subdivisions was established by examining various syntheses of the significant literature which describes this phenomenon. The results of this study indicate that

[1] Richard J. Heuer, Jr., *Quantitative Approaches to Political Intelligence: The C.I.A. Experience* (Boulder, Colo.: Westview Press, 1978), pp. 127 & 145.

the characteristics of agitational terrorism may be separated into eight major coded categories.[2] These coded categories are:

- *Code Category 01:* Information relative to an international, national, or internal (domestic) symbolic act, executed in a particular locale on a specific date and at a specific hour and time of day
- *Code Category 02:* Information which provides an associable basis between the terrorist act and a stage of a revolutionary process: planning, action, consolidation
- *Code Category 03:* Information relative to the perpetrating organization and its membership, its foreign or domestic criminal associations, and particularly its clandestine apparatus to help members prepare and execute direct action and propaganda operations and cover them when tasks are completed
- *Code Category 04:* Information relative to the ideology of zealous and resolute individuals who are intractably committed to a cause which they believe just
- *Code Category 05:* Information relative to techniques utilized by a terrorist group to influence political behavior, thereby permitting them to manipulate the population and to fight effectively with few resources
- *Code Category 06:* Information relative to the extranormal tactics used by terrorists (kidnapping, bombings, assassination, etc.), and their weapons
- *Code Category 07:* Information relative to the targets attacked by terrorists: specifically, aspects of target vulnerability, the adverse impact that target destruction or restriction will have on a specific group, and the positive impact that the destruction of a specific target will have on the image of the group responsible for assaulting it
- *Code Category 08:* Information pertaining to the propaganda goal of a terrorist group: specifically, how it is manipulated to enhance the public visibility of a terrorist group, or used to create an atmosphere of perpetual, widespread, and ever-increasing fear in a particular segment of a population, or in a population at large

CATEGORIES INCLUDED IN THE ANALYTICAL FRAMEWORK

An analytical framework constructed for operational use by law-enforcement agencies has been derived from the categories mentioned

---

[2] Martha Crenshaw Hutchinson, "The Concept of Revolutionary Terrorism," *Conflict Resolution*, XVI, no. 3 (March 1974): 383–96.

above. It consists of ten primary categories and an assortment of sub-category groupings. It is anticipated that additional subcategories will be added to the framework as law-enforcement research regarding agitational terrorism expands. The categories included in the framework are:

- *Code Category 01: Type and Nature of the Operation*
  - A. International, transnational, internal
  - B. Region and country of operations
  - C. Characteristics of the environment (i.e., urban, rural, etc.)
  - D. Day and date of the week, hour of the day
  - E. Mode of transportation
  - F. Route(s) of transportation
- *Code Category 02: Relationship to a Revolutionary Process as Exhibited by:*
  - A. Speeches
  - B. Demonstrations
  - C. Armed robberies and other violations of criminal statutes
  - D. Recruitment of a political following
  - E. Cause articulation, as expressed in handbills and related literature
  - F. Significant political support
  - G. Mob techniques
  - H. Labor associations
  - I. Terror
  - J. Urban guerrilla warfare
- *Code Category 03: Organization*
  - A. Name, membership, number, type, etc.
  - B. Associations, foreign and/or domestic
  - C. Logistics and support apparatus
  - D. Safehouse networks
  - E. Clandestine apparatus
  - F. Potential for public disorder
- *Code Category 04: Ideology*
  - A. Extremist, right-wing
  - B. Extremist, left-wing
- *Code Category 05: Propaganda Classifications*
  - A. Overt, white
  - B. Overt, black
  - C. Overt, grey
  - D. Covert, white

    E. Covert, black

    F. Covert, grey

    G. Disinformation operations

    H. Deception operations

- *Code Category 06: Tactics*
  - A. Kidnapping
  - B. Barricade and hostage
  - C. Bombing
  - D. Armed assault or ambush
  - E. Hijacking (airplane, boat, train, etc.)
  - F. Assassination
  - G. Incendiary attack or arson
  - H. Other
- *Code Category 07: Weapons*
  - A. Handgun
  - B. Shotgun
  - C. Rifle (automatic or other)
  - D. Knife
  - E. Explosive device
  - F. Other
- *Code Category 08: Targets*
  - A. Material
    1. Corporate building type and affiliation
    2. Residential building type and affiliation
    3. Transportation facility
    4. Airplane, boat, train, etc.
    5. Utility system
    6. Other
  - B. Personal (selected individual)
    1. Affiliation
    2. Official title
  - C. Personal (indiscriminate act)
- *Code Category 09: Audience*
  - A. Sympathizers
  - B. Nonsympathizers
  - C. Neutrals
- *Code Category 10: Media Coverage*
  - A. Newspaper
  - B. Magazine
  - C. Television
  - D. Radio

The coded category subdivisions listed above have been designed to assist intelligence analysts, and the detectives with whom they work, to answer essentially two general questions about a case involving agitational terrorism: Why did it happen? and In what circumstances is it likely to happen again? These are the same two questions that detectives try to answer when investigating other crimes. Both the intelligence analyst and the detective, on receiving answers to these questions, may be interested in further explanations and predictions, and therefore consider such questions as: What motives would explain a specific type of crime? Where is a given type of crime likely to occur? Information carded, coded, recorded, and filed in accordance with the category subdivisions mentioned above will facilitate obtaining answers to these questions and others which are asked about aspects of agitational terrorism for the purpose of its control.[3]

COMPUTER-ASSISTED ANALYSIS

The computer offers great assistance to the analyst. One purpose in assigning codes to each category listed in the analytical framework is to enable a computer to make basic associations and correlations that the analyst, without computerized assistance, would laboriously have to make by himself. In particular, a computerized file will assist in the development of new patterns and trends relative to agitational terrorism. Codes are also used to organize information to respond to predetermined or programmed questions. An analyst, for example, is aided in his probing of the subject of terrorism by making inquiries into a data bank containing the information included in the primary coded categories which compose the analytical framework described above.

ANALYTICAL PROJECTIONS

From an analysis based on this framework, an intelligence analyst should make a projection concerning particular aspects of his investigation. This projection should include one or more of the following:

1. Purpose, reason, or cause of the event
2. Nature of the situation
3. Groups and/or individuals involved
4. Number of persons expected

[3] William B. Sanders, *The Sociologist as Detective* (New York: Praeger Publishers, 1974), pp. 1–17.

5. Locations affected
6. Time and/or duration of the event or situation
7. Potential for disorder
8. Effect on the law-enforcement agency, the jurisdiction it services, visiting dignitaries, other individuals, etc.
9. Significance of the event or situation
10. Evolving patterns and trends
11. Recommendations for consideration of the law-enforcement agency's top management concerning possible actions to be taken

ANALYTICAL FRAMEWORKS AND PUBLIC ORDER

There is an additional advantage realized by the use of an analytical framework to control terrorism, in that it supports any police agency's efforts to preserve public order. A framework considered from this perspective is an analytical device which provides an intelligence analyst with the information he requires to assist an agency in discharging its duty to maintain public order, protect life and property, and insure the orderly functioning of a city and its services. An analytical framework is thus used by an analyst as a guide for his recommendations relative to those events or situations in which, after a reasonable exercise of police judgment, it is concluded that there is a substantial possibility of the lawful rights of a citizen being interfered with or disrupted.

Essentially, the analytical framework is not a device for monitoring the political and personal beliefs or preferences of any individual, group, or organization. That kind of surveillance is the concern of a police department only when its activities substantially threaten to result in public disorder.[4] The analytical system formulated in this chapter is intended as a guide for the development of measures for controlling terrorism and thus freeing society from the constraints on civil liberty which uncontrolled terrorist activity necessitates. Lacking this proactive system, a government may unleash a campaign of indiscriminate violence against a handful of terrorists and their real or imagined supporters, thereby forgoing its mandate to govern. Rather, this system is designed to prevent the dire effects not only of fear but, even more, of "the fear of fear."

[4] Los Angeles Police Department, *The Los Angeles Police Department Public Disorder Intelligence Division Standards and New Jersey State Police Central Security Unit Manual Delineating the Scope-Functions and Operations* (West Trenton, New Jersey, February 10, 1976), pp. 1–27. (Note: The Intelligence Guidelines mentioned in this footnote are not confidential, and are available to citizens on receipt of a written request.)

PART III
APPENDIXES

APPENDIX A

Terrorist activities attributed to or claimed by the most active groups mentioned in the preceding chapters during the period July 1, 1979, through June 30, 1980, are here listed.

Irish Republican Army (I.R.A.)

July 23: Towns in Ulster adjacent to the border with the Irish Republic. Some 150 terrorists participated in operations that blocked roads with hijacked vehicles in a dozen towns along the border with the Irish Republic. A freight train was also seized by armed guerrillas.

August 19: Newbutler, Northern Ireland. Two policemen were injured when a bomb planted by terrorists on a country road exploded.

August 27: Mullaghmore, Ireland. Earl Mountbatten of Burma, one of the heroes of modern British history, was killed when his fishing boat was blown up in the sea a 1/4 of a mile off the coast, by terrorists. His 14-year-old grandson and a 15-year-old passenger were also killed, and four other passengers, including his daughter, were seriously injured.

August 27: Warrenpoint, Northern Ireland.   An I.R.A. bomb, hidden in a parked civilian truck loaded with straw, exploded and killed 18 British soldiers as the troops were traveling in a truck convoy between two army bases. A second remote-controlled bomb exploded, damaging a helicopter and injuring two more soldiers who were trying to pick up the dead and injured.

August 29: Brussels, Belgium.   A bomb planted by the I.R.A. or "people sympathetic to their aims" under an open-air stage where a British army band was preparing to give a concert injured at least 15 persons, including four bandsmen, and caused extensive damage.

September 11: Cloughhogue Bridge, near Newry, Northern Ireland.   Masked I.R.A. terrorists hijacked a 16-car freight train and sent it careening driverless down the main Belfast–Dublin line. The driver and a guard were released unharmed.

September 20: Belfast, Northern Ireland.   Two I.R.A. gunmen assassinated an assistant governor of Crumlin Road Prison in Belfast in his car near the jail. The gunmen approached the car when it stopped at a traffic light.

October 6: Newry, Northern Ireland.   Two warehousemen, formerly members of the British Army's Ulster Defense Regiment, were the targets of a machine-gun attack as they parked their car. The I.R.A. gunmen opened fire from a nearby vehicle, killing one of the workers and seriously wounding the other.

October 15: Rosslea, Northern Ireland.   Two I.R.A. terrorists machine-gunned a delivery man to death in front of a group of young schoolchildren. The victim was a part-time member of the Ulster Defense Regiment.

November 7: Belfast, Northern Ireland.   A prison guard was shot dead at a bus stop. The Irish National Liberation Army, an ultraleftist splinter group of the I.R.A., took responsibility for the killing.

November 23: Belfast, Northern Ireland.   A prison officer was found shot dead in his home. The I.R.A. claimed responsibility for the killing.

November 27: Belfast, Northern Ireland.   At least 21 bombs exploded in Belfast and other Northern Ireland centers. Police described the bombings as a "coordinated blitz" by the I.R.A.

December 6: Lisburn, Northern Ireland.   Two bombs exploded in the offices of the pro-British Ulster Unionist Party, setting fire to the building and damaging three nearby stores. A third bomb started a fire in a hardware store, and a fourth damaged offices. Lisburn is the headquarters for British Army forces.

December 16: Dungannon, Northern Ireland.   A land mine exploded and ripped through two British army vehicles on rural patrol, killing four members of the 16th Air Defense Regiment. Containing some 500 pounds of explosives and hidden in a culvert on a country road, the bomb was exploded by remote control. The I.R.A. claimed responsibility.

December 17: Belfast, Northern Ireland.   An I.R.A. gunman, firing from a sedan, killed a prison guard as he left a bar after lunch to return to work at Crumlin Road Prison.

February 5: Belfast, Northern Ireland.   Six I.R.A. terrorists burned down an auction salesroom, holding the staff at gunpoint and planting three firebombs. Several valuable antiques were destroyed.

February 17: Bielefeld, West Germany.   Colonel Mark E. Coe, 44 years old and a senior staff officer at First Rhine Army Corps in Bielefeld, was fatally shot outside his home by a man and a woman. German police were investigating the possible involvement of the I.R.A.

March 8: Belfast, Northern Ireland.   A car bomb seriously injured a part-time member of the Ulster Defense Regiment.

April 9: Belfast, Northern Ireland.   I.R.A. terrorists seized a house adjacent to a library, holding its occupants hostages. The gunmen lured the police into an ambush by reporting a break-in at the library. On responding in an armor-plated Land Rover, the police and their vehicle were riddled by gunfire from at least three American-made M–60 machine guns. One policeman was killed, and three others were wounded.

April 11: Belfast, Northern Ireland.   Two I.R.A. terrorists, one thought to be a teenaged girl, shot and killed a part-time police officer as he walked into the offices of the Northern Ireland Housing Executive. The assailants escaped on a motorcycle.

April 19: Newry, Northern Ireland.   Utilizing a time switch, I.R.A. terrorists fired a salvo from the tubes of homemade mortars buried in a mound of sand on the back of a truck at the police station. Twenty persons were injured.

May 14: Crossmaglen, Northern Ireland.   Policemen and soldiers discovered the body of a man that the I.R.A. said was a police informer. The victim had apparently been taken to a guerrilla refuge in Ireland and questioned before being shot in the head. His body, the head in a hood, was dumped on the outskirts of this town, which is situated in the southern reaches of county Armagh, almost astride the frontier with Ireland.

June 8: Londonderry, Northern Ireland.   A car bomb exploded and damaged a studio of the British Broadcasting Corporation, a telephone headquarters, two banks, and a score of shops and offices.

June 9: Dungannon, Northern Ireland.   A bomb exploded and badly wounded a British Army bomb expert who was trying to defuse the device.

Euzkadi Ta Askatasuna (E.T.A.—The Basque Separatist Organization)

July 4: Fuengirola, near Malaga, and Torremolinos, Spain.   Bombs exploded in a tourist hotel in Fuengirola and the state-operated inn, or parador, in nearby Torremolinos. Warned in advance by telephone, the police emptied both buildings, and no one was injured. The E.T.A. threatened to continue to plant explosives in tourist spots along the Costa del Sol unless its demand for the transfer of 100 Basque terrorist suspects from jails in central Spain to prisons in their northern home regions was granted.

July 28: Bilbao, Spain.   Firing machine guns from a speeding car, E.T.A. terrorists killed two policemen at a roadblock.

July 28: San Sebastian, Spain.   The E.T.A. raked a police station with machine-gun fire, wounding three policemen.

July 29: Barajas Airport Terminal, Madrid, Spain.   A powerful bomb, planted in a suitcase in a baggage area, caused the roof of the domestic-arrivals building to collapse, and spewed glass shards into a taxi waiting zone. The E.T.A. claimed credit for the blast.

July 29: Madrid, Spain. Synchronized explosions were detonated in suitcase lockers situated in the Chamartin and Atocha railroad stations. Approximately 115 people were wounded by flying glass shards. An anonymous caller to a Basque news agency said that the E.T.A., the Armed Organization of the Basque Revolution, had placed the bombs.

August 4: Eibar, Spain. Two E.T.A. machine-gunners shot and killed a member of the Spanish Civil Guard outside his home as he was getting into his car to go to work.

August 13: Bilbao, Spain. Three hooded E.T.A. gunmen assassinated a municipal policeman as he directed traffic in an industrial suburb.

August 17: Lasartein, Spain. Using a stolen car for transport, E.T.A. gunmen shot and critically wounded a policeman patrolling a dark street.

September 19: Bilbao, Spain. An army colonel and a major were ambushed by E.T.A. terrorists and shot to death. Their driver was gravely wounded. Submachine guns were used in the attack.

September 23: San Sebastian, Spain. Brigadier General Lorenzo Gonzalez-Valles Sanchez, the military governor of Guipuzcoa Province, was shot to death as he took a Sunday walk with his wife. The E.T.A. assassins escaped in a stolen car.

October 8: San Sebastian, Spain. E.T.A. terrorists sprayed a bar frequented by policemen with gunfire, wounding 11 people.

October 8: Pamplona, Spain. A police inspector was murdered by E.T.A. gunmen as he drew his weapon in self-defense.

October 9: Santander, Spain. E.T.A. terrorists killed two sergeants of the paramilitary Civil Guard and badly wounded a third.

October 24: Barcelona, Spain. Police uncovered a tunnel resembling the digging used by an E.T.A commando unit which on December 20, 1973, assassinated Admiral Luis Carrero Blanco. This tunnel contained empty bags of ammonium nitrate, a crucial component of any explosive charge, and led to a military housing compound of more than 600 military apartments. Joaquin Bellock, civil governor of Barcelona, said, "Only the technical details for the wiring of explosives were missing. The plan was almost ready to go."

October 27: San Sebastian, Spain. The E.T.A. killed a member of the Basque Socialist Party who had actively campaigned for a referendum to restore limited autonomy to the Basque provinces. Although the E.T.A. called the referendum illegal, 88.78% of the 921,550 votes cast favored the statute proposed by the Madrid government.

October 31: Bilbao, Spain. A member of the paramilitary Civil Guard was shot to death as he left his home in Portugalete, a suburb of Bilbao. The police said that the murder bore all the marks of an E.T.A assassination.

November 12: Madrid, Spain. The E.T.A. claimed responsibility for the kidnapping of Javier Ruperez, the foreign-affairs secretary of the governing Union of the Democratic Center. An opponent of Spain's entry into the North Atlantic Treaty Organization (N.A.T.O), Mr. Ruperez in 1978 traveled to Algiers to obtain the release of Spanish fishermen who had been kidnapped by the Polisario guerrilla movement. Supported by Algeria, the Polisario movement is fighting for the independence of Western Sahara, formerly a Spanish colony.

November 15: San Sebastian, Spain. Lieutenant Colonel Tomas Lopez de Diego, an infantry officer, was gravely wounded by E.T.A. gunmen as he left his home in the morning.

November 16: near Mondragon, Spain. E.T.A. gunmen, using submachine guns, killed an office worker as he passed a crossroads on his way to work.

November 16: Bilbao, Spain. Police at a control point escaped injury by throwing themselves to the ground as E.T.A. terrorists poured gunfire into their roadblock.

January 10: Vitoria, Spain. Jesus Maria Velasco Zuazola, commander of the autonomous police force of Alvara Province, was shot to death as he stopped his car at a red light on his way to work. The authorities said that the attack was in the style of the E.T.A.

January 14: Elorrio, Spain. A member of the paramilitary Civil Guard was walking home in civilian clothes when he was hit by a volley of submachine-gun fire unleashed by E.T.A. terrorists. He died within minutes.

January 20: Bilbao, Spain. A bomb blast in a bar frequented by the paramilitary Civil Guard killed four people and injured 19. Police blamed the E.T.A., but said that no organization had avowed responsibility, possibly because the dead included a woman and the father of five children.

January 23: Bilbao, Spain. A bar owner, linked with ultrarightist groups in a magazine article, was killed by E.T.A. gunmen.

January 25: Bilbao, Spain. A gravedigger, said to hold right-wing views, was killed by the E.T.A.

February 1: Lequeitio, Spain. Firing more than 100 rounds from submachine guns and using hand grenades, E.T.A. terrorists killed six members of the paramilitary Civil Guard in a highway ambush.

April 6: San Sebastian, Spain. E.T.A. gunmen killed two men and wounded another in two shooting incidents. One of the dead men was a paramilitary Civil Guard.

April 13: Vitoria, Spain. Eugenio Lazaro, a municipal police chief, was killed by the E.T.A. shortly after he left Mass at a local church. The killers had stolen a taxi earlier, and told the driver they were members of the E.T.A.

May 15: San Sebastian, Spain. The E.T.A. killed two national policemen and wounded a third as they were having breakfast in a bar.

May 29: San Sebastian, Spain. Four policemen were wounded in an attack by the E.T.A. on two police patrol cars.

June 25: Vitoria, Spain. The manager of a Michelin tire plant was killed as he was about to enter his home. Michelin has been a frequent target of the E.T.A. because of its role in a series of labor disputes.

June 25: Alicante, Spain. The E.T.A. claimed credit for a powerful blast that exploded in an empty room on the fifth floor of the 547-room Hotel Melia. About 500 foreign tourists had been evacuated from the hotel before the explosion, because the terrorists had informed the police that the hotel was a possible target.

June 25: Javea, Spain.   An E.T.A. bomb went off at a country house at a tourist complex. No casualties were reported, as the device apparently exploded in a garden.

Red Brigades and Prima Linea (Front Line)

July 13: Rome, Italy.   Lieutenant Colonel Antonio Varisco, of the paramilitary Carabinieri police, was shot and killed by the Red Brigades as he drove along a busy street near the Tiber River. Driving up to the colonel's car, the killers tossed a tear-gas grenade into the passenger compartment, and blasted their victim in the head with a shotgun. The terrorists announced afterward, "We have executed the right hand of General Dalla Chiesa." The general was the commander of Italy's police antiterrorists.

September 21: Turin, Italy.   A Fiat executive was killed by terrorists linked to Front Line as he was leaving his home in the morning to drive to work. Front Line is a terrorist group connected with the Red Brigades.

November 16: Turin, Italy.   Detectives of an antiterrorist squad said that a powerful rocket shattered windows at the Lamarmora military barracks. The Red Brigades claimed responsibility for the attack.

November 21: Genoa, Italy.   Members of the Francesco Berardi Genoa column of the Red Brigades killed the crew of a police patrol car as they stopped for coffee near their barracks. The killers followed them into a café and opened fire with pistols.

November 24: Turin, Italy.   Red Brigades fired a rocket and submachine guns at an armored police car and police. The authorities said that the shootings caused no casualties.

December 7: Rome, Italy.   A policeman was ambushed and killed in a Rome neighborhood. His assailants shot him nine times, and then fled in a car.

December 11: Turin, Italy.   About 30 terrorists of the Front Line organization stormed the Business Administration School of the University of Turin, swarmed through classrooms and libraries, and gathered together about 200 students and faculty members who were in the building when they attacked. Ten carefully selected victims were then shot systematically in the legs. The terrorists claimed that the school was targeted because it caters to people who will serve as "instruments of the forces in power."

December 14: Turin, Italy.   Fiat, after dismissing 61 workers on charges of "lack of discipline, intimidation, and violence in the factory," was the target of a group of the Red Brigades, who invaded three of the factories. A $600,000 payroll was stolen from one of the plants, and a foreman and a guard were shot and wounded in the other plants. "We have suspended this Fiat foreman," the Red Brigades said in a telephone call. "If he shows his face at the factory again, we will kill him."

December 21: Rome, Italy.   Terrorists raided the office of a business consultant and shot him in the legs.

December 21: Milan, Italy.   Three people tied and gagged two male nurses at a hospital, and shot them above the knees.

December 21: Turin, Italy.   Two terrorists ambushed a foreman of a Fiat plant and shot him in the legs.

January 8: Milan, Italy.   The Red Brigades, using submachine guns, ambushed and shot three policemen to death. Dressed in plain clothes and riding in an unmarked car, the three officers were on routine patrol when they found their way through a narrow street blocked by a car whose driver pretended to have had a breakdown.

January 19: Rome, Italy.   A 6.6-pound bomb, planted by the Red Brigades in a police barracks, destroyed a first-floor dormitory where about 20 officers serving with units of the antiterrorist police were asleep. Eighteen officers were injured.

January 25: Genoa, Italy.   Front Line terrorists in a speeding car opened fire at three men sitting in a police car, killing two and wounding one. The dead persons were a police commander and his driver, and the wounded person was an army colonel.

January 29: Venice, Italy.   The manager at the Italian chemical group Montedison's Porto Marghera plant was shot to death as he left home for work. The Red Brigades terrorists fired five bullets into his chest from close range.

January 31: Genoa, Italy.   The Red Brigades said that it was responsible for the ambush killing of Lieutenant Colonel Emanuell Tuttobene, a senior state-police officer, and his driver, on January 25. Additionally, the terrorists stated that an army colonel in the same car had been deliberately spared. Submachine guns were used in the attack, which took place at a site near the deceased colonel's home.

February 5: Monza, Italy.   Front Line ambushed and killed the chief engineer of the Icmesa chemical plant owned by Hoffman–La Roche, a Swiss company. The victim was one of several people charged with culpability for an explosion at the plant, just outside Seveso in northern Italy, in July 1976. About 4.4 pounds of Dioxin, a highly toxic chemical, polluted a vast area. The area around the plant is still closed to the public, as more than 600 children developed skin diseases.

February 6: Rome, Italy.   A policeman on routine patrol duty near the Lebanese embassy was killed by terrorists firing from a motor scooter. The killers were members of Front Line.

February 7: Milan, Italy.   "We have killed the squealer Waccher," Front Line terrorists announced after shooting William Waccher, a suspected police informer, outside his home. Police believe that he was killed to prevent him from testifying at a forthcoming trial of Front Line terrorists.

February 11: Milan, Italy.   The manager of a scientific consulting company was pushed back into his seventh-floor apartment by two Red Brigades terrorists posing as newspaper vendors, and shot in the leg. Before leaving, the terrorists painted their 5-pointed-star symbol on a wall.

February 12: Rome, Italy.   Vittorio Bachelet, a law professor, was shot dead by members of the Red Brigades on a staircase at Rome University a few moments after he had completed a lecture. The victim was a colleague of the assassinated premier Aldo Moro, vice president of Italy's Superior Council of Magistrates, and president of the Catholic Action church service organization. The terrorists used a silencer-equipped pistol, and fired at point-blank range into the chest of their target. As the professor fell, mortally wounded, down a staircase, a female terrorist ran down the stairs after him, and fired another round into his neck.

March 16: Salerno, Italy.   Nicola Giacumbi, chief prosecutor of this southern Italian city, was shot to death in front of his home by the Red Brigades as he returned from a walk with his wife.

March 18: Rome, Italy.   Girolamo Minervini, a judge of Italy's highest court of appeals, was shot and killed as he rode to work on a bus in a residential quarter behind the Vatican. The Red Brigades took responsibility for the killing in a phone call to a news agency.

March 24: Turin, Italy.   Three members of Italy's elite paramilitary police, the Carabinieri, were shot dead in a suburban bus. The Red Brigades took responsibility for the killings of the policemen, who wore civilian clothes and carried automatic weapons.

March 24: Genoa, Italy.   At the University of Genoa, an economics professor was shot in the legs by the Red Brigades as he entered the hall where he was scheduled to lecture.

May 7: Rome, Italy.   Pericle Pirri, head of the state Labor Office, was shot several times in the legs by the Red Brigades.

May 8: Rome, Italy.   The Red Brigades shot Guido Passalacqua, a journalist specializing in reports on Italy's political crime, in both knees.

May 12: Mestre, Italy.   Alfredo Albanese, head of the Italian antiterrorist police force in the Venice region, was murdered in classic Red Brigades style. The terrorists used their car to block the passage of Mr. Albanese's vehicle through a busy street shortly after he had left home. Three men and a woman then gunned him down. The "hit team" escaped in a waiting car driven by an accomplice.

May 19: Naples, Italy.   Pino Amato, a Christian Democratic politician, was shot to death on a narrow street after terrorists blocked his car with their own. The four Red Brigades terrorists involved in the ambush surrendered after a brief gun battle with Mr. Amato's bodyguard–driver and police. They told the police that they were "political prisoners," and would not answer questions.

May 28: Turin, Italy.   Walter Tobagi, a prominent newspaper reporter who specialized in the coverage of political terrorism for *Corriere della Sera* of Milan, one of Italy's leading newspapers, was shot at close range in the back and neck by a Red Brigades terrorist who ambushed him on the sidewalk outside his home. He was on his way to work. Mr. Tobagi and Giorgio Bocca were coauthors of a recent book investigating the psychology of political terrorism.

Corsican National Liberation Front (F.N.L.C.)

October 25: Paris, France.   The F.N.L.C. bombed an army gasoline storage tank in the suburb of La Courneuve, a government building, a second gasoline station storage tank, a depot of the state-run Sieta Tobacco Company, and a railroad car. Five separate explosive charges were placed.

January 9: Ajaccio, Corsica.   About 20 F.N.L.C. terrorists, carrying shotguns, seized the Hotel Fesch and demanded the release of autonomists detained by the French police.

January 10: Corte, Corsica.   Approximately 30 F.N.L.C. terrorists occupied the town hall. Elsewhere on the island, a riot policeman and two civilians were shot to death in three incidents, and five people were wounded.

May 14: Paris, France.   An F.N.L.C. terrorist drove a sedan slowly up the tree-lined Avenue d'Iéna to the front of the Iranian Embassy, which is guarded by police on foot and in a parked bus. A terrorist sitting in the front passenger's seat wound down his window and lobbed a fragmentation grenade at the police. Almost simultaneously, a submachine gun started firing out of a rear window at the bus. Three policemen were hit in the legs, and a fourth sustained head injuries.
   According to an F.N.L.C. caller who telephoned the police, the early-morning raid was directed against "the oppressors of the Corsican people," not the Iranian Embassy.

Fuerzas Armadas de Liberacion Nacional (F.A.L.N.)

October 18: Chicago, United States.   The F.A.L.N. Puerto Rican terrorists planted three bombs set to detonate about midnight. One bomb exploded in a Chicago office building that contains city and county government offices, and another went off at the Great Lakes Naval Training Center north of the city. A third bomb was found by a cleaning woman in a downtown office building, and dismantled by the police.

October 18: New York City, United States. Pipes, a timer, and a propane tank were found in the Democratic and Republican Committee headquarters in Manhattan. The F.A.L.N. took credit for the placement of these objects, called "scare devices," by the police.

November 25: Chicago, United States. Three bombs exploded in this midwestern city the previous night and early the following morning. The first explosion occurred just before midnight in the washroom of a U.S. Marine recruiting station on the second floor of an office building. Forty-five minutes later another explosion sheared a steel door off its hinges at the Naval Reserve Armory on Lake Michigan. A third explosion damaged a military recruiting office in the northwest section of the city. The F.A.L.N. sent a communiqué to the Federal Bureau of Investigation (F.B.I.), but the authorities refused to discuss the contents of the note.

Omega–7 (An Anti-Castro Group of Cuban Exiles)

October 27: New York City, United States. Omega–7 claimed credit for exploding a bomb shortly before 10 P.M. that damaged a side entrance to the Cuban Mission to the United Nations on Lexington Avenue at 38th Street. Three persons in the area were slightly injured, and 160 windows were shattered by the explosion.

November 25: Union City, New Jersey, United States. Eulalio J. Negrin, who negotiated for release of political prisoners in Cuba and whose travel agency in an adjacent city was bombed by anti-Castro terrorists, was shot to death in the street by one or two men wearing ski masks. "We will continue with these executions until we have eliminated all of the traitors living in this country," a man with a Spanish accent and representing Omega–7 told Associated Press.

December 7: New York City, United States. An Omega–7 terrorist carrying a smoking bomb in a shopping bag eluded police guards and placed it at the Cuban Mission to the United Nations, situated at Lexington Avenue and 38th Street in Manhatten. Fifteen windows were shattered by the bomb when it went off about 11:30 P.M. Two police officers were treated for possible ear damage caused by the blast.

December 12: New York City, United States. A bomb believed to consist of 12 sticks of dynamite exploded at the Soviet Mission to the United Nations, located at 136 East 67th Street in Manhattan. Omega–7 claimed credit for the blast that injured two mission employees and

four city policemen. The explosion also damaged the mission building, and shattered hundreds of apartment windows in the area.

January 13: New York City, United States.   The store-front windows of the
Soviet airline Aeroflot were blasted out by a bomb which was heaved
into the building it occupies at 545 Fifth Avenue, near 45th Street.
The explosion, occurring about 6 P.M., also cracked the windows of
Qantas Airways and British Airways across the street. A caller to
United Press International took responsibility on behalf of O-
mega–7. However, the Jewish Defense League also claimed credit
for the blast.

January 14: Miami, United States.   Omega–7 bombed the Padron Cigars
factory in the Little Havana section at 12:40 A.M., causing "significant
damage."

March 26: New York City, United States.   Omega–7 planted an explosive
device under the car of Dr. Raul Roa Kouri, the Cuban delegate to
the United Nations. The car was parked in front of 12 East 81st
Street, the residence of the diplomat. However, the bomb was discovered by a bodyguard, who called police. After retrieving the
device from a garbage truck (Sanitation Department employees
mistook it for a trash bag), police bomb-section officers said that the
device was made of plastic explosives and was contained in a plastic
trash bag. A caller to Associated Press said that Omega–7 intended
to keep trying to kill Dr. Roa Kouri.

APPENDIX B

A CHRONOLOGY OF APPREHENSIONS AND CONVICTIONS
OF TERRORISTS LINKED TO WEST GERMANY'S
BAADER–MEINHOF GANG (DECEMBER 1977 TO JULY 1980)

After the abduction and murder of Hanns-Martin Schleyer, a West German industrial leader, in Cologne on September 5, 1977, western European leaders announced that they would organize new antiterrorism measures. The center of the new operation, according to a French source, is the computerized files of West Germany's criminal police. The thousands of records contained in these files have supported the police efforts to apprehend the killers of the German industrialist and other members of the Baader–Meinhof gang and its affiliates. A chronology of the West German antiterrorist operation, conducted in close cooperation with Paris and London, follows.

December 20, 1977: Bern, Switzerland. Swiss customs guards arrested two German terrorists who drove into Switzerland from France. When they were ordered to leave their car for an identity check, one of the terrorists pulled out a pistol and began shooting. Two guards were wounded at the border by the terrorists, who were finally taken into custody at a roadblock outside Delemont. Miss

Gabriele Krocher-Tiedemann, sentenced to prison in West Germany for the attempted murder of a policeman in 1973 but freed in 1975 with other terrorists and flown to Aden in exchange for the release of the West Berlin leader Peter Lorenz, was one of the terrorists captured by the Swiss guards. Christian Moller, a bank-robbery specialist who joined the terrorists in 1976, was also arrested.

December 28, 1977: Stuttgart, West Germany.   Verena Becker, a member of the Baader–Meinhof terrorist group, was sentenced to life imprisonment for armed robbery and attempted murder. Arrested in the summer of 1976 in southern West Germany after a shootout with police, Miss Becker was among 11 jailed West German terrorists whose release was demanded in October 1977 by plane hijackers and the kidnappers of Hanns-Martin Schleyer.

September 7 or 8, 1978: Düsseldorf, West Germany.   Willy Peter Stoll, a prime suspect in the murder of Hanns-Martin Schleyer, was killed by police in a Chinese restaurant.

September 15, 1978: London, England.   Astrid Proll, a founder member of the Baader–Meinhof gang, was arrested. Fleeing to England in 1974 while her trial in West Germany was adjourned because of her ill health, she worked in London as a garage mechanic, and married an Englishman, Ronald Puttick, under a false name.

September 24, 1978: Dortmund, West Germany.   Angelika Speitel, a leader of the Red Army Faction, more widely known as the Baader-Meinhof gang, and Michael Knoll, another terrorist, were captured by police after a gun battle in the woods. A third terrorist, a man, escaped. On March 21, 1979, the West German prosecutor Kurt Rebmann announced that Miss Speitel would stand trial for the murder of one policeman and the wounding of another during the course of the "fire fight" in the woods. On November 30, 1979, she was sentenced to two life prison terms for her part in the shootings.

June 9, 1979: Frankfurt, West Germany.   Rolf Heissler, a principal suspect in the abduction and murder of Hanns-Martin Schleyer, was wounded and captured by police who had staked out his apartment.

November 5, 1979: Karlsruhe, West Germany.   Stefan Wisniewski, arrested in France in May 1979 and extradited to West Germany a year later, was charged by the federal prosecutor's office with murdering Mr.

Schleyer's bodyguards, kidnapping, attempted extortion, coercion, and forging documents.

May 6, 1980: Paris, France.   French police, acting in cooperation with West German authorities, raided a Paris apartment and over-powered two women believed to be among West Germany's most wanted terrorists. The apartment was in the Latin Quarter, near the Sorbonne. The seized women were identified as Sieglinde Hoffman, wanted in connection with the 1977 murder of Jürgen Ponto, a leading West German banker, and Ingrid Barabass, who was sought in connection with several bank robberies and the kidnapping of an Austrian industrialist, Walter Palmers. Three other women, none of whom had known terrorist connections, were arrested in the apartment. Additionally, officers found 240 pounds of explosives, and a remote-control device for model airplanes that could easily be adapted for use in detonating a bomb. The I.R.A. uses this device to trigger bombs by remote control.

July 25, 1980: Stuttgart, West Germany.   Horst Herold, chief of the federal police, said that officers seized four automobiles that they believe were used by terrorists, and license plates for four other cars. The vehicles were impounded following a traffic accident on a country road near Stuttgart. Juliane Plambeck, sought in connection with the abduction of Mr. Schleyer and with the 1977 murders of a former chief prosecutor, Siegfried Buback, and a prominent banker, Jürgen Ponto, was killed when her car collided with a truck. A companion and suspected terrorist, Wolfgang Beer, also died in the crash.

September 5, 1980: Düsseldorf, West Germany.   A state court sentenced Christof Wackernagel, 28 years old, and Gert Schneider, 31, to 15 years in prison for their part in the slaying of Mr. Schleyer. The two terrorists were wounded by Dutch police on November 10, 1979, as they tried to shoot their way out of a public telephone booth in an Amsterdam suburb near Schiphol Airport.

The court's finding was issued 3 years to the day after the kidnapping of Mr. Schleyer.

APPENDIX C

INVESTIGATING THE ASSASSINATION OF ALDO MORO

Aldo Moro, one of Italy's most influential politicians, was kidnapped on March 16, 1978, in Rome by the Red Brigades who killed all five of his bodyguards in a bloody street ambush. His body was found in a parked car in Italy's capital on May 9, 1978, fifty-five days after his abduction. A chronology of key developments in the protracted hunt by Italian antiterrorists for evidence to arrest and convict the killers of Mr. Moro follows.

May 16, 1978: Rome, Italy.   Police found, under a surface of a garden, a waterproof 10 by 13 foot cell that received air and dim light through a window facing on the inside of a well. Plants and garbage bags concealed the entrance to the stairs leading down from the garden. This subterranean room is located in Rome's Primavalle working-class suburb about 2 miles from the scene of former Premier Aldo Moro's abduction, and the police said that they believed that it may have served as his prison. His abductors could have reached the garden easily before police roadblocks went up 45 minutes after the kidnapping.

May 18, 1979: Rome, Italy. Police raided a Red Brigades hideout in a suburban Roman printing and photocopying shop. Equipment seized in the shop may have been used to prepare the terrorists' communiqués to the government during Mr. Moro's captivity. A number of suspects were taken into custody, and large quantities of guns, false documents, and Red Brigades leaflets were seized.

May 20, 1978: Rome, Italy. Four of the ten persons arrested in the printing shops on May 18 were released, and five others were charged with membership in an armed band. The tenth person was still being held, pending a decision on his status.

June 5, 1978: Rome, Italy. Enrico Triaca, the 25-year-old owner of the print shop raided by police on May 18, and five other suspected terrorists, were formally charged with complicity in the kidnapping and slaying of Mr. Moro. Mr. Triaca's mimeographing equipment was used to print Red Brigades literature, and his apartment was used as a base for the urban guerrilla organization.

September 13, 1978: Milan, Italy. Corrado Alunni, believed by police to be the mastermind behind the kidnapping and killing of Mr. Moro, was captured when officers who had been watching his garden apartment for a week moved in. Weapons, leaflets, $36,000 in cash, and documents linking the Red Brigades to other Italian terrorist groups were also seized. Mr. Alunni was considered the heir to the Red Brigades leadership after its founder, Renato Curcio, was captured in 1975.

January 21, 1979: Turin, Italy. Police discovered a Red Brigades hideout on the outskirts of Turin.

February 2, 1979: Milan, Italy. Four suspected terrorist hideouts were raided by police. Five pistols, false license plates, forged documents, and a supply of Red Brigades literature were seized by officers. Four persons were arrested at the hideout locations, and charged with illegal possession of weapons and participation in armed bands.

April 7 and 8, 1978: Rome and Milan, Italy. After months of investigation, during which the telephones of many suspects had been tapped, heavily armed plainclothes police officers wearing bulletproof vests searched a number of homes and offices of far-left groups, and seized large quantities of materials. At least 16 leftist extremists were arrested, including Antonio Negri, a political-science professor at Padua University. A Leninist, Professor Negri was suspected of being the chief ideologist, and possibly the secret leader, of the Red Brigades.

April 10, 1979: Rome, Italy.   Investigators said that they had evidence, including a voiceprint, linking Professor Negri to the murder and abduction of Mr. Moro. The tape was a recording between the abducted politician's wife, Eleonora, and a caller who said that he was speaking on behalf of the abductors. Prosecution experts said that they were convinced that the voice was Professor Negri's. The recording had been examined with advanced techniques at the West German Federal Criminal Bureau in Wiesbaden.

April 16, 1979: Rome, Italy.   Twelve suspects, including Professor Negri, were incriminated as accomplices in the Moro case by documents and statements from witnesses. No further details were available.

April 24, 1979: Paris, France.   It was announced that a clandestine "strategic headquarters" of Italy's Red Brigades was uncovered in a language school in Paris as a consequence of an investigation conducted by the French secret services. Reportedly, terrorist ringleaders telephoned instructions from Paris to fellow conspirators in Italy, unaware that their conversations were being monitored by French and Italian intelligence agents.

May 30, 1979: Rome, Italy.   Valerio Moruci, 28 years old, and Adriana Faranda, 29, were arrested in Prati, an upper-middle-class area near the center of Rome. The police said that the couple's apartment was a Red Brigades hideout, and contained the following items: (1) a Czechslovak Skorpion 7.65 mm. machine pistol of the type used in the slaying of Mr. Moro; (2) signs used by security forces to stop vehicles at roadblocks; (3) bulletproof vests of the type used by terrorists in an attack in Rome; (4) radio-monitoring equipment; (5) an incendiary grenade and three pistols: a Smith & Wesson, a Luger, and a Beretta.

June 8, 1979: Rome, Italy.   Three employees of *Metropoli* magazine were arrested in connection with the murder of Mr. Moro.

August 31, 1979: Rome, Italy. Italian authorities formally charged Franco Piperno, a 36-year-old physics professor, with the murder of Mr. Moro. The ultraleftist college professor was arrested in Paris on August 18, 1979.

September 3, 1979: Rome, Italy. Italian investigators identified three other chief suspects in the killing of Mr. Moro being sought in France as Lanfranco Pace, Nanni Balestrini, and Laura Barbiani.

September 14, 1979: Paris, France. Lanfranco Pace, a 32 year-old Marxist magazine editor and a former professor of philosophy, was arrested outside a Paris hotel by French police. Mr. Pace and Mr. Piperno— leaders of the ultraleftist Autonomous Workers Movement formerly headquartered in the northern Italian city of Padua—were charged with involvement in the murder of Mr. Moro by the Italians.

October 18, 1979: Rome, Italy. Franco Piperno was extradited from France to face charges that he helped the Red Brigades kidnap and kill Mr. Moro.

November 12, 1979: Rome, Italy. Ballistics experts announced that the Czechoslovakian-made Skorpion machine pistol found in a Red Brigades hideout in Rome on May 30, 1979, was the weapon used to murder Mr. Moro.

March 29, 1980: Paris, France. French police announced the arrests in Toulon of Franco Pinna and Enrico Bianco, sought in connection with the kidnapping and slaying of Mr. Moro. The French police action also netted about twenty-eight other people suspected of ties with a group, called Direct Action, which claimed responsibility for a machine-gun attack on government offices in Paris. It is also suspected of having ties with the Red Brigades.

April 14, 1980: Rome, Italy. Italian police created the impression that the leadership of the Red Brigades in the Turin area had been wiped out, as they were making arrests on the basis of information provided by confessed Red Brigades members already in jail. Previously, suspected terrorists refused to cooperate with the investigating magistrates. Apparently Patrizio Peci, arrested in February 1980 in Turin, is suspected of giving authorities information about other terrorists. Mr. Peci was the head of the Red Brigades Turin "column," and is alleged to have played an important role in the kidnapping and murder of Mr. Moro.

April 15, 1980: Rome, Italy.   Patrizio Peci reportedly confessed that he played a part in the kidnapping of Mr. Moro. His confession was the first in the two-year-old case. It was also revealed that Mr. Peci directed antiterrorist squads of the Carabinieri, Italy's elite police force, to an apartment in Genoa where they surprised four members of the Red Brigades on March 28, 1980. Riccardo Dura and Lorenzo Betassa, members of the Red Brigades Central Command, and two other terrorists, were killed in the ensuing gunfight.

Only two known members of this central leadership, which once included Mr. Peci, are at large. One is Mario Moretti, whom Mr. Peci was said to have named as the man in charge of the Moro operation, and the other is Barbara Balzarani, who is believed to have taken part in the killing of Vittorio Bachelet at Rome University on February 12, 1980.

According to published information received from investigating magistrates, Mr. Peci had been in an emotional crisis, and had called his mother periodically during the weeks before his arrest. Once he started talking, the investigators were able to persuade other alleged terrorists, of both the Red Brigades and the Front Line, "to do the same."

APPENDIX D

THOUGHTS AND STRATEGIES OF ISLAMIC GUERRILLA WARFARE IN THE UNITED STATES

On November 29, 1979, members of the United States Senate were warned to take precautions against possible attacks by religious fanatics and nationalist terrorists, as a consequence of information contained in a document distributed in Washington, D.C., entitled "Thoughts and Strategies of Islamic Guerrilla Warfare in the United States." The arrests on November 16, 1979, in the Baltimore–Washington International Airport of eight Iranians carrying high-powered rifles, ammunition, scopes, and a street map of Washington with embassy buildings marked supplemented the message contained in this document.

At the time, Senator Barry Goldwater remarked, "We are going back to an uncivilized condition in a large part of the world. I am not ruling out," he added "such problems in our own nation's capital and in this country. We hope and pray that it doesn't happen."

The contents of the document distributed in Washington, D.C., are printed on the following pages (it is a literal, *uncorrected* copy of the original).

Thoughts and Strategies of Islamic Guerrilla Warfare in the United States

The divine parameters of Al-Islam as a universe of spiritual and intellectual thought and continual religious discipline include community and individual opinions, attitudes and positions on political issues as they might directly relate to the interests of the Islamic Jummat, nationally and internationally. Thus, when political issues develop which affect the Islamic community in part or in whole, the entire Islamic community have involvement towards the resolution of the issue.

Muslims in America should not consider themselves an isolated community from the rest of the Islamic world; we have a special responsibility to Allah and to our consciences to come to the defense of Al-Islam in no uncertain terms, methods and resources to represent the determined stance of Al-Islam when America is involved in a political situation or an on-going cold war that concern or threatens the safe interests of the Islamic community.

As well, the rest of the Islamic community, leaders and 'Arab-Islamic' countries around the world must have the knowledge that there are active Muslims in the United States who are willing and able to come to the defense of Al-Islam when any part of the community is threatened; as well they must be supportive of our efforts in real terms. Further, a so-called Muslim who does not understand that our community is a very important segment of the whole Islamic society is himself or herself a threat and dangerous element of the community.

Thus, because Al-Islam is a total way of life, we must be prepared and willing to defend our lively interests and future with rhetoric, demonstrations, coordinated policies, and physical warfare if necessary if the mission is given from the almighty Allah to engage in warfare in the interest of Islam and there occasionally comes a time throughout history by Allah when warfare by Muslims in defense of the community as a whole is the most intelligent method, both spiritually and politically.

The United States has threatened the Islamic community with the use of their military 'option' in what it considers in the interests of the American people and country. Such threats have been recently targeted at the Islamic Republic of Iran where our fellow Muslim brothers and sisters are active in the Islamic Movement behind the cry "Allah-u-Akbar," God is Great. And indeed God is Great.

Muslims in America can not any longer tolerate such arrogance by the U.S. and must now prepare to stand behind Islam in warfare in the United States. At the point when the United States initiates military action against our community, measures must counter until the whole of our community is safe. One must also remember that the U.S. is indirectly endangering our community by their military and financial support of the so-called state of Israel.

However, Islamic guerrilla warfare in the United States must not be unplanned. Strategies must be thorough, e.g. targets must be chosen intelligently and realistically, weapons should be chosen in correlating targets/persons in mind, timing nocturnal encounter considerations, personal safety, retreat methods, etc. But most importantly, it is also necessary for a Muslim to sacrifice himself or herself in such efforts.

Muslims should not limit themselves to conventional guerrilla weapons, e.g., shotguns, handguns, gasoline bombs, but other weapons which can be utilized with a no noise factor, e.g., daggers, razors, solid steel clubs, etc. With a relatively no-noise factor involved in an attack, the Servant or Servants of Allah can vacate the location of the encounter unnoticed or inconspicuous.

Because U.S. foreign policies are made by individuals some targets may exist as high-ranking persons; although, any American citizen can be targeted. However, all successful encounters must be later anonomously announced and publicized with the statements left at the encounter, messages to the press (domestic & foreign), etc. (Any American can be targeted and no American is innocent as long as U.S. foreign policies are to the detriment of the Islamic community.) By Allah's mercy, Muslims will place fear in the hearts and minds of the kafir.

Since Zionists are influential in U.S. policies, the targeting of zionist females in American can be effective towards our cause if these continued guerrilla strategies are made known to the U.S. public and government.

Our holy Quran gives us comfort with the revelation that the kafir are hypocrites, criminals of the earth and the believers and non-believers are of the same calibre in the sight of God Almighty. The Quran reveals that Victory is with the Islamic community, however, Muslims must not think that simply because our final victory is indeed within the future we can sit back comfortably and relax. If Muslims in the United States are not prepared and actually will to come to the defense of Al-Islam, the WRATH OF ALLAH will surely come to our community by the efforts of the kafirs.

May Allah bless our community, our members and may Allah give some of our leaders more strength to be more publically outspoken and supportive of the Islamic World Movement, or may they be replaced.

AS-SALAAM-ALAIKUM

(*Community Instructions:* Duplicate, Disseminate, Circulate.)

APPENDIX E

MANIFESTO 1980 OF THE W.E.B. DU BOIS
REVOLUTIONARY ARMY

W.E.B. Du Bois was a black American leader who founded the National Association for the Advancement of Colored People (N.A.A.C.P.) and edited this group's magazine, *The Crisis*, from 1910 to 1934. His writings contain his views regarding the impact of oppression and of American egalitarian values in creating ambivalent loyalties toward race and nations in the minds of Afro-Americans.

Adopted on March 10, 1980, by a group calling itself the Governing Body of the W.E.B. Du Bois Revolutionary Army, and circulated surreptitiously during the spring of 1980 in California, a 20 page document entitled *Manifesto 1980–?* purports to speak for oppressed people everywhere.

It is reproduced as follows.

"MANIFESTO" 1980–?

WHEREAS, it is now apparent that non-violent methods are completely ineffectual in implementing programs that would bring about the amelioration of the plight of the masses and,

WHEREAS, the systematic genocide of the masses by the various law enforcement agencies on behalf of the ruling classes continues unabated,

THE W.E.B. DU BOIS REVOLUTIONARY ARMY

after long and painful consideration has adopted the following manifesto for the upcoming decade.

Succinctly stated, unless our demands are met we will institute a program of terror focusing on the affluent ruling classes in which we will harass, torture, and kill "targets of opportunity" with the ruling classes being our primary targets selected on a basis of random selection within this class group.

Our manifesto is composed of the following parts:

PART I—SITUATION

PART II—MISSION

PART III—EXECUTION (no pun intended)

Our movement embodies the aims of the following revolutionary groups:

Black Consciousness Movement	Montoneros
Popular Democratic Liberation Front	Movimiento de Liberacion Nacional
Spartacist League	Euzkadi Ta Askatasuna
Baader–Meinhof Group	Grupo de Resistencia
Sekigun	Antifascista Primo de Octubre
Black September Group	Brigate Rosse
Popular Front for the Liberation	Prima Linea
of Palestine	Armed Forces of Puerto Rico National
Provisional Irish Republican Army	Liberation
Ejercito Revolucionario del Pueblo	

The following brigades of the W.E.B. Du Bois Revolutionary Army have unanimously adopted this manifesto:

Geronimo Pratt Brigade	Carlos Washington Brigade
Jane Fonda Brigade	Joanne Little Brigade
Roland T. Price Brigade	Emmett Till Brigade
Eulia Love Brigade	Henry Lee Johnson Brigade
William Gavin Brigade	Murry Weiss Brigade
Philip Agee Brigade	Jane Margolis Brigade
Bob Avakian Brigade	Frank Hicks Brigade
Kevin Moore Brigade	Jeff Rooney Brigade
John Levers Brigade	Tom Hirschi Brigade
James Lee Campbell Brigade	Cedric Steward Brigade

Adopted on March 10, 1980, by the governing body of the W.E.B. Du Bois Revolutionary Army on behalf of oppressed peoples everywhere.

A detached statement regarding our approach to terrorism might serve a useful purpose at this point. Violence, such as is evidenced by the police forces, begets violence; this is not a statement of morality but a simple truth, demonstrated throughout history. At times it is a well hidden truth because the incubation period may extend over centuries. Eventually some irresistible precipitating chain of events proves to be the catalyst. Politicians and the majority of media commentators do not study world history. They seem unaware of the long memories dormant with depressed peoples everywhere and they are always ready with phrases such as "unparalleled in human history" and the "greatest outrage ever recorded." Human history is long on outrages though and the adjective "greatest" is better avoided. Even the effort of Germany to exterminate the Jews of Europe was not sui generis. The Germans themselves also tried to exterminate the gypsies. They allowed 2.5 million Russian P.O.W.'s to die of starvation. Earlier, the Spaniards in the Americas annihilated millions and wiped out whole nations. Little Belgium was responsible for the deaths of as many as ten million Congolese. At this very moment, Brazil is eradicating the Indians of the Amazon. On a lower level of violence, the English had a good go in their time at erasing the Irish as a nation. The French state, newly liberated by the allies in 1945, killed 10,000 or more Algerians in the spring uprisings of that year and eventually they left at least a million Algerians killed. They left, as they had earlier left Indochina and as the U.S. in turn left Indochina, not through a change of heart but because the price of staying became too high. The Western nations, including the U.S.A., have a charming habit of regularly blowing the whistle on themselves, declaring the board swept clean and a whole new ball game is begun. Then they decide to forget everything they have done before, and expect the rest of the world, including the surviving victims, to do the same. This is precisely the situation obtaining in regard to the racists and their apologists. However, as far as the genocide practices are concerned these are not past history as is plain from the current evidence at hand.

A good example of failing memory is the English who declare themselves appalled at the Irish Republican Army outrages in Ulster against the local majority. They have completely forgotten that the Protestant majority of Ulster was planted there by force and violence. The land was expropriated and an Irishman could be driven off his property even by his own son provided the son converted to Protestantism.

In the Basque country, Franco's Spain ordered the execution of some 10% of the local population and workmen were sent into the graveyards to eradicate Basque names from the tombstones. When Basque terrorists kill a Spanish business man who grew rich under Franco they are called mad dogs by every well-meaning politician.

In Germany, the violence of the state in recent history does not need further elaborating, although a different term is used for those Germans of 40 years ago; they were "Nazis," not Germans. The entire West German state apparatus, though liberally sprinkled with mayors and cabinet ministers once closely involved in the appalling schemes of the Third Reich, was stunned, virtually overwhelmed, when the German Terrorist Red Army made its appearance. It was as if those former army officers, S.S. men and Gestapo officials had never heard of using bombs, machine guns, rifles and pistols.

In Iran's bloody and unsavory history, massacres under the recent Shah have been laid at the door of the U.S. at least since 1953, the year the C.I.A. overthrew Premier Mohammed Mossadegh. The massacres were not on television but other events were. The Shah's sister, appearing on B.B.C. television, when asked about the dissidents responded, "Oh, we roast them a bit, maybe, like toast, you know." Her fawning sycophantic entourage chuckled at her wit. The V.I.P.'s and the jet set of the West, from Vogue editors to Prince Bernhard and Henry Kissinger, flocked to the Shah's extravaganzas paid for by a starving peasantry.

The point of this introduction is not to boast or applaud terrorist violence per se but to merely point out that terrorism has its place when all else fails and this is the situation in which the masses find themselves at the moment. When one class of individuals through their power positions are able to spend more on their pets or their hairdressers than the working classes spend for essentials something is obviously wrong. We are not psychopaths, no more than the patriots of Iran, Ireland or the West Bank are psychotics, whose only desire is to kill men, women and children and throw away our own lives in the process. The seeds from which this violence springs have been planted in us by the ruling classes who have consistently turned a deaf ear to our cries of anguish. Except for a different turn of the wheel of fate they might have been the oppressed who when denied justice would have inevitably turned to terrorism as a last resort.

PART I—SITUATION

First, let us examine the conditions now existing in regard to the black, brown, red and yellow masses. Fifty million people starve to death each year; 450 million show signs of serious malnutrition and almost one quarter of the world's population have too little to eat. Wheat surpluses from the U.S. go first to the nations able to pay the highest prices rather than to the needy. Voluntary programs to alleviate this condition will never be developed in a capitalistic country concerned only with profits.

The Great Emancipator in his first inaugural speech said, "The country belongs to all the people and if the citizenry are dissatisfied with their government it is their right to revolt."

Most of Jimmy Carter's state of the union message delivered on January 23, 1980 was just so much tired political rhetoric and as long as he refuses to reduce the $650,000.00 per year that the First Lady spends for her office no one should take his economy pledges seriously but in his speech he made one statement that was the truth. He said, "In an oppressed country violence is the only outlet for popular frustrations."

Angela Davis said in a recent address at San Diego, "I see no real hope for the masses."

These three statements put things in their perspective and Jesse Jackson was right when he stated when talking of the struggle for human rights in the 1980's, "It will be an active struggle involving direct action; if rewards aren't won it could mean going back to the streets."

The study of the history of non-white minorities in America is a depressing experience particularly when one realizes that the plight of the minorities has improved little in certain areas. America's so called free enterprise system is immoral because its one tenet is the oppression and the exploitation of the masses so as to bring profit to those who hold power. We say here and now: we will submit no further to the brutal indignities being practiced against us; we will not be intimidated, and most certainly not eliminated. We claim the ancient right of all peoples, not only to survive unhindered but also to participate as equals in man's inheritance here on earth. As far back as 1829 David Walker said, "Remember Americans that we must and shall be as free and as enlightened as you are." He was, of course, addressing white Americans.

After twenty years of civil rights legislations and fifteen years of poverty programs discrimination and oppression continue to define black existence in America. Conditions in the black community are still intolerable. The black ghettos are a breeding ground for crime, dope and suicide and ever increasing scenes of police brutality which can only be characterized as contemplated genocide.

The black unemployment rate is higher than it was twenty five years ago when the Supreme Court first lifted the burden of legal inequality from the backs of the blacks.

Once the classic method of lynching was the rope. Now it is the policeman's bullet. To many an American the police are the government, certainly its most visible representative. We submit that the evidence suggests that the killing of blacks has become police policy in the United

States and that police policy is the most practical expression of government policy under the direction of the white power structure.

We can cite some typical cases from voluminous evidence. Here in Oakland, California during 1979 nine blacks were gunned down by the police department which is two thirds white and we have already had one more killing in 1980 only three days before black residents packed the Oakland City Council to demand action against the escalating terror campaign against Oakland blacks.

Among those killed in 1979 was 15 year old Melvin Black shot to death by three white undercover policemen. One of these officers, Glenn Tomak, also shot another black, Talmadge Curtis, to death in December.

One notorious racist officer, Robert Fredericks, who has been involved in five other shootings, shot to death Charles Briscoe, a shop steward for the IAM. One of Fredericks's victims was Brother Bobby Hutton of the Black Panther Party. Fredericks's most recent exploit involved shooting Briscoe four times with a shotgun. Not satisfied with this result he returned to his squad car, grabbed a .357 magnum and emptied six more rounds into Briscoe.

Racist police repression is an old story here in Oakland and continues without respite since the police, many of whom are recruited in the South, have nothing to fear in the way of punishment for their acts.

From the police vendetta against the Panthers to the cases of Tyrone Guyton, a black 14 year old shot to death by the police in 1973 and 23 year old Floyd Calhoun, cut down by Oakland police in 1975, the wanton killings by these gunmen in uniform are notorious.

Down south in Los Angeles the situation is the same with both the L.A. Police Department and the L.A. County Sheriff's department in competition.

In reflecting on the accomplishments of the L.A.P.D. one must give them credit for that one glorious moment in their history when they managed to eliminate the S.L.A. They managed to dispatch this poorly equipped, miserably trained group of misfits and only used 410 officers, 321 vehicles and 2 helicopters. They fired 5,371 rounds of ammunition 75 tear gas rockets and 8 tear gas cannisters. The F.B.I., who were straining at the leash on the sidelines, got into the act when the L.A.P.D. actually ran out of tear gas rockets.

Contrast this with the lack of success which the L.A.P.D. had in the attack on the Black Muslim Mosque in South Central Los Angeles.

We will discuss under Part III—Execution our plans for the Oakland P.D., the L.A.P.D. and other law enforcement agencies including the vaunted F.B.I.

In 1978 and 1979 the L.A. County Sheriff's Department was involved in 77 shootings and 27 of these involved fatalities and not one single officer was reprimanded. The most recent two examples are indicative of the type of shootings which the Sheriff's department engages in.

One demented individual, brandishing a knife according to police witnesses, was surrounded by 18 sheriff's deputies and 5 L.A. City policemen. Tired of sparring with this mentally ill black they finally shot him 13 times because they felt "the deputies were in danger because of the knife." In records going back to 1907 there had never been a law enforcement officer seriously hurt with this type of weapon.

In the most recent case a teenage black was shot in the back of the head while lying face down on the pavement with one handcuff on. He was unarmed. Sheriff Peter Pitchess has refused to consider the possibility that the officers in either case were wrong. Naturally if given the opportunity Mr. Pitchess would be very high on our priority list.

One case involving the L.A.P.D. will suffice and that is the celebrated Eulia Love affair in which this woman was shot 11 times over a small utility bill. Police Chief Gates vigorously defended the shooting. Neither of the two officers involved was reprimanded and one of the officers was actually promoted. It was the first shooting for one of the officers, Lloyd O'Callagan but the other officer, Edward Hopson has been involved in at least three other shootings which has undoubtedly helped his macho image around the station. We will, of course, file these names away along with many others for future reference in high hopes of meeting them under somewhat different circumstances.

As the Black Panther Party of Oakland stated long ago, "Black people have already judged you, America, and condemned you to death and we also know that history has selected us, your slaves and chief victims, to be your executioners, the instrument of your destruction." The present political structure has perpetuated and protected racism and as far as the black masses are concerned is bankrupt.

The nature and character of the struggle of blacks in America coincides with the struggles of the oppressed and the exploited now sweeping the Third World and as our martyred Brother Shabazz once said, "It only takes a single spark to light a fuse."

Another statement of Brother Shabazz also comes to mind, "You can't operate a capitalistic system unless you are a vampire; you must have someone else's blood to suck. Show me a capitalist and I'll show you a bloodsucker."

White power is so formidable, so entrenched, so callous that it cannot be attacked legally in a non-violent manner. It is our opinion that any black person, except for the extreme Uncle Tom (and there aren't many of them left) or those of our black brothers (of whom there are many) who have willingly donated themselves to the white power structure, is ready for violence if necessary. We will light the fuse.

Vic Solomon of CORE said years ago, "We hold no love for non-violence; it is a philosophy that was bankrupt long ago. We simply don't believe in having our people slaughtered by the police. We must fight from a position of strength."

Ours is a well financed, superbly trained, closely knit group impossible to infiltrate and our patience learned by observing the mistakes of other groups is our greatest strength.

PART II—MISSION

Our twofold mission is simply this:

1. Prevent for all time the genocide being systematically carried out against minority groups.
2. Implement a plan for the redistribution of wealth through the establishment of a trust fund administered by distinguished black Americans such as Donald McHenry, Vernon Jordan, Julian Bond, Jesse Jackson, Benjamin Hooks, Shirley Chisholm etc.

Donations to this trust will be realized through assessments of all sectors of the affluent power structure including but not necessarily limited to the following: (a) banks, (b) insurance companies, (c) brokerage firms, (d) all industrial and retail organizations, (e) doctors and the medical profession in general, (f) the legal profession which includes most of the present political figures, (g) entertainment industry, including movies, television, the music industry, and particularly professional sports in which so many of our black brothers have become willing pawns.

These must be more than token assessments; there must be an effective redistribution of wealth. During the time when the average worker is denied a 6% salary increase because it is "inflationary" why should some mediocre baseball, basketball or football player earn hundreds of thousands of dollars for playing what is essentially a kid's game for half a year?

How this trust fund is administered will be the responsibility of the Trustees.

PART III—EXECUTION

If the explanation as to how this ambitious program will be forced on the power structure appears to be unusually long it is because it is essential that the law enforcement agencies and others understand that we have the expertise, the resources and most of all the ruthless resolve to implement our plan or to die in the process (along with many others).

Our most potent weapon is simply terror. We do not believe that any responsible law enforcement official in the country would claim that it is possible, even in a police state, to prevent attacks against "targets of opportunity," selected at random from among the affluent groups mentioned above.

As Brother Eldridge Cleaver once said (before he was born again) "We do not claim the right to indiscriminate violence." This is true in our case unless we are forced to go to Phase 2 which will be explained later. Initially, we will limit our attacks to "targets of opportunity" from the white power structure and those of our black brothers, i.e. athletes and rock stars, who have become willing pawns of the oppressors.

Brother Shabazz stated years ago, "We will use whatever weapon we have at hand; at the start we will use the Molotov cocktail; then the hand grenade, progressing to whatever other advanced weapons we find necessary."

Although we have long since passed the primitive, but effective, Molotov cocktail stage, we still realize that many of the most potent weapons, i.e. fire, gasoline and other volatile fuels are all around us to be used if required. Our instructors, some of whom gained valuable instruction at Lumumba University in Russia, but also in Cuba and North Korea have imparted the true revolutionist's skills to work with what is at hand. As any knowledgeable law enforcement agent knows the manufacture of napalm, fire fudge, even TNT is relatively simple and requires nothing that is not readily available on the open market.

Affluent areas such as Hillsborough, Hope Ranch, Montecito, Beverly Hills, Bel Air and Rancho Santa Fe are ideal areas for disastrous fire. All the arsonist has to do is be patient and wait until conditions are ideal.

Any weapon in the world is available if the terrorist has adequate funding and the right connections. This includes everything from the AK–47 and the M–16 to fragmentation grenades and hand held rockets. In Phase 2 we will discuss more diabolical weapons but for now we think you will get the broad picture.

Poison, normally thought of as a woman's weapon, will not be excluded. There is presently available a new highly efficient system capable of delivering poison through clothing subcutaneously, without the victim's knowledge because it is both silent and painless. The poison we use, we can promise you will not be the mild laxative type drug that the F.B.I. introduced into oranges and sent to the Black Panther party headquarters in Jersey City ostensibly from the Oakland Black Panther Party.

As a matter of fact we have had a particular interest in the F.B.I. since 12/4/69 when at the instigation of the F.B.I. fourteen members of the Chicago police department, armed with machine guns, entered an apartment on 2337 Monroe St. at 5 A.M. Minutes later Fred Hampton and Mark Clark lay dead, their bodies riddled with machine gun bullets. Five other people were seriously wounded. The F.B.I.'s Judas, William O'Neal was paid an additional $300.00 for his "uniquely valuable services" to quote J. Edgar Hoover, in setting up our black brothers, Hampton and Clark.

Should some misfortune befall any agents of the "new" F.B.I. it will simply be, to quote Brother Shabazz, "a case of the chickens coming home to roost."

The F.B.I.'s own files, surrendered very reluctantly in compliance with the Freedom of Information Act demonstrate clearly to anyone who is objective that the "old" F.B.I. (and a leopard never changes his spots) was one very small step removed from the Gestapo.

Let us consider the F.B.I.'s role in the assassination of Martin Luther King, Jr. Arthur Murtagh was a member of the F.B.I.'s intelligence unit at the time that Dr. King was killed. According to Murtagh the unit was known throughout the Bureau as the "Get King" squad. Now King was from Georgia; so were Jimmy Carter and Andrew Young. J. Edgar Hoover, the late Director, was a venomous individual who ruled the Bureau with an iron hand. He is usually depicted as an uncontrollable eccentric who, as architect of the F.B.I. and the collector of files on everyone, had entrenched himself so deeply that he was not only autonomous but in the words of the TV Series, "Untouchable." This naive description of the F.B.I. ignores the fact that, despite any bureaucratic aberrations, the F.B.I. is and always has been a disciplined organ of ruling class violence created by the capitalistic state. It is a special national police force, which reflects not only the venality and eccentricity of its director but also the attitudes of the decisive sections of the financial world which easily has within its power the ability to dispatch any director, even Hoover, if he seriously steps out of line. We do not suggest that everything is just one big conspiracy with the F.B.I. as its executive action arm nor do we suggest that the F.B.I. polls the capitalist on every move. We merely suggest that they are comfortable bed fellows.

Now F.B.I. files indicate clearly that Hoover was conducting a vendetta against King, using fair means or foul. It has been suggested and there is hard evidence from the F.B.I. files to support this contention that Hoover tried to drive the civil rights leader to suicide. Jimmy Carter ran a racist campaign with his running mate, Lester (AXHANDLE) Maddox and served with this avowed racist as Lt. Governor without incident. Andrew Young in the meantime was a Democratic Congressman. Carter continued his racist policies while governor of Georgia. He supported his church in excluding blacks, proclaimed a holiday for Lt. James Calley, strongly supported Atlanta police Chief, John Inman at a time when the black community was demanding his removal for dozens of random murders of black youths. He also strongly backed the racist Law Enforcement Assistance Administration.

With this record is it natural to assume that Carter would turn over a new leaf and appoint an anti-racist UN Ambassador like Andrew Young and consistently defend him against his critics? We suggest it was in payment for past favors. What were these favors?

Consider the following facts. Martin Luther King, Jr. was not a revolutionary. He preached non-violence to the oppressed masses while rarely, if ever, demanding that the ruling class disarm. This tactic plays into the hands of the ruling class because it helps lull the oppressed who are politically inexperienced, and naive who desire social change to be as peaceful as possible into conferring the right to violence on the ruling classes. King acted as a brake on the rebellious segment of Black America. However, throughout the nation the swing was away from King and his non-violence which served the ruling classes and toward the more militant leaders. King had outlived his usefulness to the capitalists, the charismatic leader was out of control of the movement.

As long as the capitalists patronized King, who served their purposes effectively, he was provided ample protection although other sections of the ruling class had made attempts on his life. But when he failed to keep the Memphis workers non-violent his fate was sealed. King came to Memphis for only one evening on very short notice. Supposedly, James Earl Ray, the convicted assassin, had never been in Memphis before. Although King was not staying at his usual motel the assassin found out exactly where he was staying. We suggest that he received assistance since an assassination of this type is virtually impossible without specific knowledge.

James Earl Ray had four forged Canadian passports and had spent considerable sums of money before being apprehended indicating an organization of considerable sophistication.

Who pointed the finger at King? Our candidate is his close friend and associate, Andrew Young, who along with Ralph Abernathy and Jesse Jackson, was nearest to King when he was shot and who assisted the assassin in escaping by giving false directions as to where the shot came from.

Frank Holloman, Director of the Memphis police and a former high ranking F.B.I. agent made his contribution by reducing the twelve man detail guarding King to just two men.

When A.D. Williams King, brother of Martin Luther, was found drowned in 1969 Andrew Young was on hand to assure the press, before any autopsy had been performed, that "no evidence of a crime existed" and "it was just one of those freak things."

When the King brothers' mother, Alberta Williams King, was shot to death in 1974, law enforcement agencies were back at the media microphones to proclaim the "no conspiracy" theory. The assassin said he was a Hebrew and the enemy of all Christians and that is why he decided to travel all the way from Dayton, Ohio to Atlanta, Georgia to kill one. Believe that and you will undoubtedly believe anything.

It is our suggestion that it was all the work of Andrew Young who became chief apologist for U.S. imperialism and would have continued in this role had he not had the misfortune of irritating the Zionists. This was a tragic miscalculation on his part. We have no love for the Zionists but on the other hand we cannot tolerate the perfidy of an Andrew Young either.

Those black brothers who willingly aid the capitalist cause, and there are many of this ilk around, will be sought out and will be exterminated whenever the opportunity presents itself. In dwelling at great length on the ills of California we do not want to create the impression that ours is a local organization. It is a national organization that has ties worldwide. We have communicated with and have received instruction from many of the revolutionary groups now engaged in the worldwide struggle for determination. In the interest of security, which is naturally of paramount importance to our cause, we have kept our contacts with these groups at a minimum and except in one instance (that being the assassination of Colonel Yosef Alon 7/1/73) we have not cooperated with any other group in conducting revolutionary operations.

As William Webster, the head "honky" of the F.B.I., recently stated the F.B.I. depends on intelligence (translated informer) to thwart the efforts of terrorist groups. This is why such great emphasis is placed on security of our organization.

There are several reasons why so much planning time has been devoted to California. The moneyed, the powerful, and the famous are here, making this area a prime target for large scale kidnapings, assassinations, and terrorist activities in general. Those who enjoy the good life (at other people's expense, of course) are the most vulnerable because they have the most to lose.

It is the most populous state, epitomizes the decadence of the nation as a whole, has an inordinate percentage of affluent, corrupt, individuals who feel that the "good life" is their birthright no matter who picks up the tab and are especially vulnerable to terrorist activities because of their softness.

Affluent targets are easy to locate; one does not need a sophisticated intelligence network to locate these leeches tooling around with their Rolls Royces or Mercedes, adorned by the personalized vanity license proclaiming their importance to all the world.

As one self proclaimed expert on terrorism stated, "The terrorist has a lot going for him. He picks his target; he picks his time; he picks his weaponry and WHAM ! ! ! "

Our victims will be selected at random from those groups we listed in the beginning. Detailing of our intentions would be too lengthy so we will confine our comments to one segment of the "new" elite—the professional athlete.

Our colleges and universities have become training camps for professional sports. Athletes in most institutions do not worry in the least about grades and in some instances it has been reported that the graduates of a four year college were actually illiterate. They are instant millionaires for engaging in spectacles which contribute little to the betterment of mankind. Who can afford to pay these pampered kids such astronomical salaries? It is obviously the very rich, who if their team is a losing proposition write it off as a tax loss with the rest of the taxpayers picking up their share so that they can mingle with the "jocks." To show a profit the prices of admission and concessions are beyond the reach of the working class. One might argue that you aren't forced to attend the sporting events and superficial reading of the facts might even suggest that this is true. However, what is less obvious is the fact that it is the advertising on television that brings in the most revenue and of course the cost of this advertising, which is truly unbelievable, is borne by the housewife who buys the products. It is a rich man's game in which the athletes are willing pawns for obvious reasons: money. Many athletes will be singled out for special treatment as the opportunities present themselves.

Among these are:

Bill Walton (who once gave lip service to our cause) who has been drawing a salary of $700,000.00 per season for the past two years without setting foot on the court until recently. He is now out for the rest of the season. What other class of worker(?) would be afforded this opportunity?

Jack (Call Me Assassin) Tatum—the reason is obvious.

Charles White, who upon winning the Heisman Trophy stated that this was the greatest honor that could ever come to any man in his lifetime. The next time he is modeling furs for his Zionist friends in Beverly Hills perhaps we will drop around to show him what the game of life is really all about.

O.J.—we would have to include the juice because he represents "pimping" at its worst. Perhaps the next time he appears at the bookstore we will be there to discuss black philosophy on our terms.

Mohammed Ali—We can't forget Ol' Motormouth, who we felt showed some courage in resisting the draft and not only twisting Honky's tail but having him ask for more. Now it appears that Ali has turned diplomat and has been fronting for the racist Carter group in Africa. There is nothing worse than a turncoat and punishment should be meted out accordingly.

Incidentally, those fawning flacks and inarticulate "ex-jocks" who have pumped up this special class of individual to the point of adoration will not be neglected.

These are but a few of those who deserve special attention and in our estimation are most vulnerable.

You may recall the case of the alphabet bomber who had gone through A & B and everyone was wondering about target "C". Was it the Colosseum or the Forum where they were having a concert? Attendance at both the Colosseum and the Forum was only a third of the number expected.

Can you imagine what a little c4 or some fragmentation grenades would do if we were forced to go to Phase 2 which would include public spectacles and indiscriminate targets? Even smoke grenades at the Rose Bowl would result in thousands of deaths just from confusion.

We sincerely hope we won't be forced to even contemplate heinous acts such as these. However, unless our aims and demands are given serious consideration at the highest level you can be sure that these acts are in our game plan. More about Phase 2 later.

Naturally, a great deal of time has been spent in formulating plans for those sports dominated by the whites such as the auto racing circuit, the playground of the "good ole boys," the golf circuit which has an inordinate percentage of southerners and the tennis circuit which has always been the darling of the ruling class.

In the case of the professional athlete we do not actually have to kill in order to render obsolete a valuable piece of machinery. We could borrow some of the techniques favored by our Red Brigade comrades and the I.R.A. patriots and shoot a few of these pampered darlings in the kneecaps. Wonder what their contracts would be worth then? Would the ruling class who "owns" them renegotiate their contracts? This seems to be very fashionable these days. There is a virtual army of Zionist negotiators urging the athletes to pressure the owners even though their clients are operating under valid and overly lucrative contracts, to up their salaries. This is what happened to Brother Jabbar. What a target he would make! ! !

The practices and mores of other members of the establishment, the bankers, brokers, doctors, lawyers etc. are particularly odious and, except to comment on the role of attorneys in the misapplication of the criminal code, we will say no more.

Throughout history one or more of the professions have dominated the ruling class. We passed through the witch doctor stage, the priest stage, the warrior stage, the church stage, the robber baron stage and now we are in the legal profession stage. Most of our lawmakers are attorneys, important law enforcement officials are attorneys, the judiciary are attorneys and more importantly at the street level the attorneys are responsible for the inequitable application of the laws.

While our black, brown, red and yellow brothers languish in prisons coast to coast, often framed (in the case of Geronimo Pratt) or in many cases convicted of minor crimes, the affluent white offender goes free.

Consider the following cases characteristic of thousands:

A famous movie executive, already earning almost half a million dollars per year, pleads guilty to embezzlement and does not spend one night in jail. Was there stigma attached to his guilt? Apparently not, because he was rewarded by being named to head one of the largest studios in the world. This makes him interesting to our cause on two counts: the obvious miscarriage of justice which should be corrected and his position as part of the power structure. The fact that he is a regular on the Hollywood party circuit has been duly noted.

A well connected tycoon, intimate friend of presidents, steals almost thirty million dollars from his bank and is given straight probation. Convicted of income tax evasion he has yet to go to jail and his horses continue to race and win at Santa Anita and he is much sought after in compiling any party list. Although his wife owes the stockholders seven million dollars and claims to be bankrupt she still managed to transfer land worth three million dollars to her son. Because of his age we will probably not consider this man a high priority target (let him die a winner) but we will add the names of the members of his family to our list.

Policemen in San Francisco plead guilty to extortion (normally a very heavy beef) and receive 6 months in jail, served on weekends, given sick leave and are back on the force.

A university official, who had already been convicted of drunken driving, rear ends a car while drunk and causes two elderly women to die a horrible death by fire. The power structure all came to his assistance and he, predictably did not receive one day in jail.

A law enforcement officer in Ventura County, driving under the influence runs down and kills a pedestrian. He is not suspended or fired from his job nor is his license to drive suspended. While intoxicated he kills a second pedestrian. He was this time suspended from the force but was found innocent of manslaughter.

As a matter of fact, as long as the law enforcement agencies, and the judges and the public as a whole take such an insouciant attitude toward the drunken driver who kills approximately 25,000 people per year why should they worry about a little terrorist? One death from terrorism is worth more to the media than a dozen hit and run deaths.

After eighteen months of testimony in the Korea bribery scandal the net result was three congressmen were "reprimanded." What are the odds for any convictions resulting from ABSCAM?

Blacks go to prison for stealing bread; GSA employees received three months for stealing untold millions. To rub salt in the wound the GSA is trying to demote the investigator who initiated this massive fraud scheme.

A white former city councilman across the bay kills two people with premeditation and receives a relatively short sentence for a lesser offense.

The list could go on and on but we think this demonstrates our point. It is time for black vigilantes; to correct these injustices and to hunt down and exterminate the known racists such as the KKK.

If evidence is not forthcoming from the media that our plan is being given serious consideration at the very highest levels and unless there is evidence in the media that an honest attempt is being made to correct some of these obvious injustices we will harass, torture and murder "targets of opportunity" selected at random from the power structure. To regard this manifesto as the ravings of a few maniacs would be fatal. No other message will be forthcoming from us. The next evidence will be a crime of such enormity that it will focus the attention of the whole world on our cause. You can count on that.

Phase 2

If we have no success with Phase 1 in which our operations would be limited to "targets of opportunity" selected at random from the affluent sector we will forced to go to Phase 2 which is unthinkable at the moment.

Lengthy discussions of weaponry are pointless except to point out what is most certainly of great concern to every antiterrorist squad in the country and that is simply that as weapons become more and more sophisticated, more and more miniaturized and more and more powerful the task of protecting the tremendous crowds of the frenzied fans that now attend the sporting events and the rock concerts is virtually impossible.

With adequate financing any weapons are available including those hand-held weapons capable of bringing down aircraft.

Even nuclear weapons are within the capabilities of today's resourceful terrorist. Building an atomic bomb is like building any other except that the nuclear material is more difficult, but by no means impossible to obtain. So much weapons grade nuclear material is missing from some of the nuclear installations that in one case they are contemplating closing the facility. The agencies charged with the responsibility of accounting for nuclear material completely lost track of the whereabouts of hundreds of kilograms of plutonium and enriched uranium.

Of course, the government refuses to disclose the amounts of missing nuclear materials but it is interesting to note that a recent General Accounting Office report focuses on the lax security measures, the amount of missing materials and points out the fact, well known to us, that it would be easy for fissionable materials to come into the hands of terrorists. With so much nuclear material missing and unaccounted for you can be sure that some of it is for sale. To prepare for every eventuality, as thorough planners do, it is reasonable to assume that we would avail ourselves of the opportunity to purchase some of this material.

Three requirements must be met in order to construct a nuclear device: (1) a design for the device (many undergraduate and not particularly bright college students have submitted papers that demonstrate how simple it is to obtain the information needed to formulate a workable, fairly efficient, design); (2) a reasonable level of skill in handling high explosives, nuclear materials and fuses (well within the capabilities of most experienced bomb builders with the skills developed in Southeast Asia); (3) sufficient quantity of fissile materials (5 kilograms of plutonium or 15 kilograms of uranium–235).

The indiscriminate use of nuclear weapons, nerve gases, contamination or poison in the water supply of the cities are especially repugnant to us but it will be used if we are forced to go to Phase 2.

A reiteration of our plans is as follows:

If we do not see evidence in the media that our demands, which we feel are just, are being given serious consideration at the highest level; if this manifesto is regarded as the ravings of a group of demented individuals we will kill numbers of people selected at random from the affluent segment of the citizenry.

If this tactic fails we will go to Phase 2 in which we will deploy more diabolical weapons on the general population.

We have no intention of adding our names to the long list of black martyrs stretching back to antiquity; therefore, from this date on you will have no more communiqués from us.

Our deeds will speak for themselves; the blood of the ruling class and their lackeys, especially the white power structure, will be on your hands.

LONG LIVE THE REVOLUTION! ! !

APPENDIX F

REMARKS BY ROBERT A. FEAREY

Robert A. Fearey was special assistant to Secretary of State Henry A. Kissinger during the administration of President Gerald Ford, serving as coordinator for combating terrorism. His office was a headquarters for antiterrorist information gathering, and provided policy direction, relying on the resources of other United States government agencies. Mr. Fearey's speech before the Los Angeles World Affairs Council and the World Affairs Council of Orange County, delivered February 19, 1976, is reproduced here, as his remarks relative to the future of terrorism were most prophetic.

Remarks by Robert A. Fearey, Special Assistant to the Secretary of State and Coordinator for Combatting Terrorism, before the Los Angeles World Affairs Council and the World Affairs Council of Orange County February 19, 1976

INTERNATIONAL TERRORISM

First let me say how much I appreciate your invitation to be here today. The World Affairs Council is a widely known and highly respected forum. I welcome the opportunity to discuss how our Government views the problem of international terrorism and how we are meeting it. And

I hope you will give me an idea of how you feel about the problem in the question period.

My topic is *international* terrorism. I shall not be specifically addressing the indigenous, or national form of terrorism, such as we see in Northern Ireland, Argentina and many other countries and which accounts for most terrorism today. Nevertheless a good deal of what I shall say about international terrorism will apply also to the indigenous form.

Definition

What precisely is "international terrorism"? It has three characteristics.

First, as with other forms of terrorism, it embodies an act which is essentially criminal. It takes the form of assassination or murder, kidnapping, extortion, arson, maiming or an assortment of other acts which are commonly regarded by all nations as criminal.

Second, international terrorism is politically motivated. An extremist political group, convinced of the rightness of its cause, resorts to violent means to advance that cause—means incorporating one of the acts I have just cited. Often the violence is directed against innocents, persons having no personal connection with the grievance motivating the terrorist act.

And third, international terrorism transcends national boundaries, through the choice of a foreign victim or target, commission of the terrorist act in a foreign country, or effort to influence the policies of a foreign government. The international terrorist strikes abroad, or at a diplomat or other foreigner at home, because he believes he can thereby exert the greatest possible pressure on his own or another government or on world opinion.

The international terrorist may or may not wish to kill his victim or victims. In abduction or hostage–barricade cases he usually does not wish to kill—though he often will find occasion to do so at the outset to enhance the credibility of his threats. In other types of attacks innocent deaths are his specific, calculated, pressure–shock objective. Through brutality and fear he seeks to impress his existence and his cause on the minds of those who can, through action or terror-induced inaction, help him to achieve that cause.

An example. On September 6, 1970, the Popular Front for the Liberation of Palestine (P.F.L.P.) hijacked three airliners flying from Europe to New York, diverted them to airports in the Middle East, and moments after their passengers had been evacuated, blew them up. The terrorists' purposes were:

1. To attract world attention to the Palestinian cause.

2. To convince the world that the Palestinians could not be ignored in a Middle East settlement, or there would be no lasting settlement.

3. To demonstrate that they had destructive powers which they were prepared to use, not just against Israel but far afield against other governments and peoples, until their aims were achieved.

Another recent and vivid example. Last December 21 five professional international terrorists—a Venezuelan, two Palestinians, and two Germans—took control of the OPEC ministers and their staffs in Vienna, killing three persons in the process, demanded and received publicity for their "Arab rejectionist" cause over the Austrian national radio, and finally released the last of their understandably shaken hostages in Algeria. Their purpose appears to have been to pressure the more moderate Middle East governments into tougher oil and anti-Israel policies.

Historical Origin

Terrorism as a form of violence for political ends is as old as history, probably older. It is said to have acquired its modern name from the French Reign of Terror of the mid-1790s. The first use of international terrorism is hard to pinpoint. However, the historians among you will recall the Moroccan rebel Raisuli's kidnapping of an American and an Englishman in 1904 in a successful attempt to force the American and British governments to pressure France into compelling the Sultan of Morocco to comply with Raisuli's ransom, prisoner release, and other demands.

Perhaps the opening phase of the international terrorist threat we face today, though itself a reaction to oppression and terror, was the hijackings by freedom-seeking escapees from the eastern European communist countries in the middle and late forties. In the early sixties the stream of hijackings from the United States to Cuba commenced. Terrorist groups around the world saw the potential for publicity in hijackings and began to use them for attention-getting political objectives. Beginning in about 1968 Palestinian and other violence-oriented political groups in several parts of the world began to extend their terrorist activities to countries—or to the diplomats of countries—not directly involved in the dispute giving rise to the violence.

Modern Terrorism

The years since 1968 have seen a progressive development of the employment of international terrorism for the attainment of national, ethnic or world revolutionary political goals. They have also marked development of intelligence, training, financial and operational collaboration among terrorist groups in different parts of the world. And they have seen such groups take increasingly telling advantage of technological advances which afford the terrorist opportunities he never had before.

Air Transport. Two or three individuals can take control of a large airplane with two to three hundred passengers, divert it wherever they wish, and blow it up when they get there, with or without its passengers aboard. Or a loaded aircraft can be downed by a bomb placed in its hold. Little wonder that the airplane has figured in so many terrorist acts of the last fifteen years.

Communications. Today's television, radio and press enable a terrorist to achieve an almost instantaneous, horrified, attention-riveted audience for his action. Since public attention to his cause is usually one of his key objectives, communications advances have been critically valuable to the terrorist.

Weapons. New types of weapons are constantly adding to terrorists' capabilities. A leading example—the Soviet SA-7 heat-seeking rocket equivalent of our Red Eye, easily portable by one man, capable of bringing down commercial aircraft. Two of these weapons were found in the hands of Arab terrorists at the end of a runway in Rome in 1973. Fortunately they were found in time. Another key terrorist weapon—plastic explosives.

Targets. Finally, our complex and interdependent modern world society presents a plethora of vulnerable, damaging targets for terrorists. Large aircraft are one such target. But there are also super-tankers, electric power grids, gaslines, nuclear power plants, and others. Modern terrorists can cause destruction far beyond anything possible in earlier, simpler ages.

The U.S. Response

So beginning about 1968 our government faced a clear problem of terrorist use of aircraft, of modern communications media, of powerful, light-weight precision weapons, and of cooperation among terrorist groups in different countries, all to achieve political shock effects in an increasingly interdependent and vulnerable world. The danger grew, with a mounting series of kidnappings, bombings, murders, and shootouts, by Palestinians, Croatians, Tupamaros, Cubans, Turks, and others. In September, 1972, eleven Israeli athletes were killed, along with five terrorists, at the Munich Olympic Games before an appalled TV audience of hundreds of millions.

Our government had until that time pursued a number of antiterrorist efforts, mainly in the hijacking area. But with Munich, President Nixon and Secretary of State Rogers decided to adopt a more systematic approach. The President directed Secretary Rogers to chair a "Cabinet Committee to Combat Terrorism," and also to establish an operating arm of the Committee called the Cabinet Committee/Working Group. The Working Group originally consisted of senior representatives of the ten Cabinet Committee members, but twelve other agencies concerned with different aspects of terrorism have since been added.

The Cabinet Committee and Working Group have a broad mandate to devise and implement the most effective possible means to combat terrorism at home and abroad. The Cabinet Committee meets as required and the Working Group has met 101 times. It is the coordinating forum for the entire United States Government's anti-terrorism effort. When a terrorist abduction of an American abroad or of a foreigner in the United States occurs, we set up and run a task force in the State Department's Operations Center. A similar, complementary task force is established in the concerned American embassy abroad. We have, unfortunately, gained considerable experience in coping with such incidents after hostage cases in Port-au-Prince, Khartoum, Guadalajara, Cordobas, Santo Domingo, Kuala Lumpur, Beirut, and other places.

Means of Combating Terrorism

What have we learned from our study of terrorism and from our practical experience with it? How does one combat terrorism? Basically in three ways:

Intelligence. If you can learn his plans ahead of time, you can sometimes forestall the terrorist. It was through intelligence that the terrorists armed with SA–7's were apprehended at the edge of the airport in Rome before they could destroy their intended Israeli Airlines target. The C.I.A., the F.B.I., and other intelligence agencies coordinate their anti-terrorist efforts through the Cabinet Committee/Working Group.

Physical Security of Target Installations and People. Here again we have improved our position significantly since 1972. United States civil airport security has been strengthened to the point where, in combination with bilateral and multilateral anti-hijacking convictions, we have not had a successful commercial hijacking in the United States in three years, though there was of course, the recent terrible bombing at La Guardia. The security of our diplomatic posts abroad has been upgraded with armored limousines, more Marine guards, closed-circuit TV systems, careful briefing of personnel, etc.

Apprehension and Punishment of Terrorists. To achieve this key objective we seek international cooperation. The threat is international and can be met only by international means. A major focus of United States effort and initiative with other nations has been in the anti-hijacking area. We took the lead in negotiating in the International Civil Aviation Organization (I.C.A.O.) three conventions on hijacking and aircraft sabotage. The general idea of all these conventions, now ratified or adhered to by about seventy countries, is to deter terrorists by internationalizing their criminal acts and thus providing legal means of apprehending and punishing them.

But we have not been altogether successful in this purpose. Hijacking has declined sharply, but more because of improved airport security than the anti-hijacking conventions—except for our highly effective bilateral agreement with Cuba. Too few countries are willing to arrest, try, and *severely* punish international hijackers and saboteurs, or indeed international terrorists of any kind. United States efforts for the adoption of enforcement mechanisms to give the international aircraft hijacking and sabotage conventions sanctions teeth by denying air services to non-complying countries, have been completely unavailing. A United States-proposed convention in the 1972 United Nations General Assembly which would have obliged participating states to prosecute or extradite international terrorists coming under their control, at safe haven destinations or in other ways, won the support of only about half a dozen nations. It did, however, serve as the genesis of the UN convention to protect diplomats and foreign officials adopted in 1973 but still awaiting the necessary ratifications to come into effect.

The RAND Corporation recently calculated, on the basis of experience since 1968, that there is an eighty-percent chance that an international terrorist involved in a kidnapping will escape death or capture. The terrorist kidnapper has a close to even chance that all or some of his ransom demands will be granted. World-wide publicity, normally an important terrorist objective, is achieved in almost every case. For all crimes of terrorism (as opposed to just kidnapping) the average sentence for the small proportion of terrorists caught and tried is less than eighteen months. In a word, outside the hijacking area, our and a small but hopefully growing number of other governments' efforts to make terrorism unprofitable for the terrorists have made little headway.

So these are the ways we seek to combat terrorism: intelligence, physical security, and apprehension and punishment of terrorists. In addition, and very importantly, we encourage and assist other nations to alleviate the inequities and frustrations from which international terrorism mainly—through by no means entirely—arises. Unfortunately, effective action to reduce these inequities and frustrations is in many instances a very long-term proposition. The trend in most countries and regions is the other way. The awakening political consciousness of oppressed, poverty stricken or otherwise frustrated peoples on every continent threatens an increasing resort to terrorism in areas not relatively free of it.

U.S. Policies in Terrorist Incidents

From time to time Americans abroad are assassinated or abducted by international terrorist groups. What are our policies in such incidents?

With respect to assassinations, we seek to deter or thwart such attacks through intelligence warning and physical security, both in cooperation with the host government. If an American is nevertheless assassinated, we do our utmost to ensure that the murderer is brought to justice and that intelligence and security measures in that country affecting American citizens are intensified.

With respect to abductions, our policies were made very clear by Secretary Kissinger in Vail last August. He said:

> The problem that arises in the case of terrorist attacks on Americans has to be seen not only in relation to the individual case but in relation to the thousands of Americans who are in jeopardy all over the world. In every individual case, the overwhelming temptation is to go along with what is being asked.
>
> On the other hand, if terrorist groups get the impression that they can force a negotiation with the United States and an acquiescence in their demands, then we may save lives in one place at the risk of hundreds of lives everywhere else.
>
> Therefore, it is our policy . . . that American ambassadors and American officials not participate in negotiations on the release of victims of terrorists, and that terrorists know that the United States will not participate in the payment of ransom and in the negotiation for it.

The following month, at Orlando, the Secretary said:

> When Americans are captured, we are always in great difficulty because we do not want to get into a position where we encourage terrorists to capture Americans in order to get negotiations started for their aims. So our general position has been . . . that we will not, as a government, negotiate for the release of Americans that have been captured. . . . We will not negotiate . . . because there are so many Americans in so many parts of the world— tourists, newsmen, not only officials—that it will be impossible to protect them all unless the kidnappers can gain no benefit from it.

For these reasons, the United States Government has not and will not pay ransom, release prisoners or otherwise yield to terrorist blackmail. Nor will it negotiate with respect to any of these matters. We urge the same policy on other governments, private companies and individuals. We rely for the safe return of American hostages on the responsibility under traditional international law of a host government to protect all persons within its territories, including the safe release of hostages. We consider it the host government's sovereign right to decide during an incident how it will fulfill this responsibility.

This may sound somewhat cold and unfeeling. But you may be sure that those of us charged with managing cases of Americans abducted abroad feel keenly both the plight of the hostage and our government's legal and moral responsibility to exert every appropriate effort for his safe return. The local American embassy abroad, and the task force at home, go to work with all the experience, energy, and imagination they can muster. They stay in close and continuous contact with the host government, supporting it with all practicable intelligence, equipment, technical services, and other assistance and advice it may request, except advice on how it should respond to demands from the abductors. This decision we consider to be the exclusive responsibility of the host government, taken in awareness, however, of our own government's policy not to accede to terrorist demands.

Sometimes a host government proves unwilling or unable effectively to discharge its responsibility to secure the hostage's release, perhaps because he has been seized by a rebel or outlaw group within the country. In such cases we do not wring our hands helplessly. We may nominate an intermediary to the host government, we may enlist the assistance of a third government, or we may ourselves conduct discussions with the abductors. But if we hold such discussions they are strictly confined to such matters as the well-being of the hostage and to humanitarian and other factors arguing for his unconditional release. There are no negotiations. The host government is kept closely informed.

So we do not allow ourselves to be rendered helpless as a result of our no-concessions policies or the failure of a host government to fulfill its obligations under international law. Sometimes the terrorist has decided in advance to execute the hostage, or stubbornly holds to his demands to the point of fulfilling his threat to execute. But in the more typical case the terrorist is not anxious to kill the hostage and when he sees, usually over time, that he is not going to succeed in his blackmail effort, he will begin to have second thoughts and events will move toward release. We recently witnessed this process in the Netherlands, British, and Irish governments' patient but firm handling of the Moluccan, Balcombe Street, and Herrema incidents. The year 1975 saw an encouraging trend of greater firmness by a number of NATO governments in their handling of terrorist incidents. It also saw a welcome trend of a higher level of terrorist arrests and trials and of sterner laws against terrorism, notably in Germany.

Some argue that we are misreading the situation—that acceding to terrorist demands to save an American hostage's life would have no, or insignificant, effect on the safety of other Americans abroad or on our effort to combat international terrorism. Such reasoning is tempting, but I for one would be reluctant to assume the responsibility of following it. On the other hand, we have repeated, convincing evidence that our government's no-negotiations, no-concessions policies are widely known by terrorist groups abroad, that they are believed, and they are having an important deterrent effect.

The United States has not yet had to face seizures or attacks within its own territories by international terrorist groups. Would our government, as a host government responsible for dealing with such incidents at home, practice the same, firm no-concessions policies it has urged on other governments, including when our own citizens have been abducted abroad?

The answer is yes. We are convinced of the soundness of these policies. And we have seen other governments, faced with a series of terrorist incidents of a type we have thus far been spared, arrive by hard experience at the conclusion that firmness is the only course. We have dealt as firmly as the law allows with domestic terrorist organizations, such as the Black Panthers, Symbionese Liberation Army, Weather Underground, and Puerto Rican Liberation Armed Force. I do not think you will find your government wanting if, unhappily, the international terrorist menace reaches our shores.

I have discussed the international terrorist threat and the United States response to that threat. What are the principal issues and requirements as we look to the future?

International Cooperation Against Terrorists

First, how are we to achieve more effective international cooperation for the apprehension, trial, and punishment of international terrorists?

This objective is as intractable as it is central. Most countries apparently remain unwilling to apply strict legal sanctions to international terrorists. In the Third World, where most of the difficulty lies, many countries sympathize with the political aspirations of groups which practice terrorism. There is the sympathy of Arab governments for the Palestinian cause, including approval of terrorist attacks on Israel and, in the case of the radical Arab governments, approval and support of Palestinian terrorist attacks in Europe and elsewhere as well. There is the sympathy of newly independent countries, many of which used terrorism to help achieve their freedom, for anti-colonial terrorist groups. And there is the sympathy of practically all Third World governments for terrorists striking against repressive, authoritarian regimes, particularly in the developed world. Third World governments generally accept the terrorists' argument that the weak and oppressed, with their pleas for justice unheeded, and lacking the means for conventional war, have no alternative to terrorism—that terrorism in a perceived "just" cause is not criminal but patriotic and heroic.

We, with our Judeo-Christian tradition, can understand this reasoning, up to a point, but we can never accept it. We believe there can be no justification, in any circumstances, for the deliberate killing of innocent individuals. We recognize that the alternatives to terrorism, centering on peaceful protest, constructive proposals and negotiation, often involve frustration and delay. But we believe that in an interdependent world attempting to move away from violence before it is too late they offer the only acceptable means of change.

For different reasons than those put forward by Third World countries, most advanced countries are also disinclined to commit themselves to clear and unequivocal sanctions against terrorists. Sometimes they are inhibited by political or commercial interests from offending governments that support or condone terrorism. Or they are concerned that if they convict and imprison terrorists this will attract more terrorists to their territories seeking, through further violence, to free their comrades. Or they are reluctant to see rights of political asylum weakened. The Communist giants, the Soviet Union and China, appear to share our conviction that hijacking, aircraft sabotage and other forms of international terrorism are a criminal threat to civilized society and should be stopped. But they also share the Third World's belief that terrorism as an instrument of "wars of national liberation" is acceptable, and they support such terrorism.

A succession of major international terrorist incidents during 1975, culminating in the seizures in Vienna and the Netherlands, appears to have somewhat enhanced awareness of the common danger presented by international terrorism. Venezuela and Colombia have jointly proposed a new consideration of the problem by the General Assembly in the fall. Our government earnestly hopes that this increased awareness and concern is widespread, and that antiterrorism proposals in the 1976 General Assembly will find a different atmosphere and reception from that accorded the convention we proposed in 1972. In an address in Montreal last August Secretary Kissinger urged the United Nations once again to take up and adopt our 1972 proposals, or some similar convention, as a matter of the highest priority. In December our representative on the UN 6th Committee reiterated this position. All stand to suffer if the present apparently heightened interest in the control of international terrorism is allowed to die without result and has to be reawakened by further terrorist acts of even more serious proportions than those suffered in 1975.

Effectiveness of Terrorism

A second question. How effective has international terrorism been for the terrorists' purposes?

Clearly international terrorists have had tactical success, as recently at Kuala Lumpur and Vienna, achieving their objectives of publication or broadcasting of manifestos, release of imprisoned comrades, or extortion of ransom. And these successes have been achieved at small cost to the terrorists—most have escaped to safe havens, or, if caught, have later been rescued by comrades or served very short terms. On the other hand, international terrorist groups have fruitlessly suffered suicidal losses in attacks within Israel. And such groups operating in Europe and elsewhere have in a number of cases suffered heavy casualties while achieving none of their purposes, except dubious publicity, as in the Baader–Meinhof seizure of the German Embassy in Stockholm last April or the earlier mentioned South Moluccan, Balcombe Street, and Herrema incidents.

How about terrorist groups' attainment of their fundamental political goals—the causes their abductions and attacks are intended to serve?

Here too the overall record is hardly a source of encouragement for terrorists. Certainly the Baader–Meinhof Gang and the Japan Red Army have not succeeded in advancing their nihilist, world revolution cause significantly. The kidnappings and murders of United States and other diplomats in Brazil, Guatemala, Argentina, and elsewhere have won the terrorists no discernible political gains. The terrorism perpetrated by South Moluccan extremists in the Netherlands achieved world publicity, as sensational crimes are wont to do. But the terrorism was essentially negative in its consequences for the South Moluccan cause, embarrassing the group's responsible members and outraging the Netherlands government and people.

As for Palestinian terrorism, the Palestinian cause is unquestionably more widely known as a result of Palestinian terrorism than it otherwise would be. But against this must be set the revulsion of all civilized peoples over the crimes committed by Palestinian terrorist groups at Lod, Munich, Khartoum, within Israel, and elsewhere. And terrorist attacks have contributed importantly to the hatred and bitterness which impede a Middle East settlement from which the Palestinians might hope to achieve their goal of a Palestinian state. The decline in the

Palestinian terrorism within the past two years suggests that the more moderate Palestinian leaders have come in part, at least, to share the view that terrorism is counter-productive to the attainment of Palestinian objectives.

International terrorism, in short, is no success story, for the Palestinians, the South Moluccans or any other group.

Seriousness as a World Problem

A third question, then, is how deeply need we be concerned about international terrorism as a world problem?

Up to now international terrorism's toll in dead and wounded and property damage has been relatively small. This is true of all forms of terrorism, compared with the casualties and property losses of even the most minor conventional wars. But it is particularly true of international terrorism. It has been estimated that some eight hundred people have been killed, including terrorists, and some seventeen hundred injured, in all international terrorist incidents from 1968 through the present. Year by year this is no more than the crime rate of one moderate-sized American city—intolerably high as that rate is. Property damage, principally in destroyed aircraft, has been equally limited.

But international terrorism's limited toll in lives and property thus far is only part of the story. There are a number of things we should note and ponder:

- Most of the world's airports are now manned by guards and inspectors, aided where possible by expensive X-ray machines. Even so, no air traveller is secure from terrorist attack.
- United States and other nations' embassies in Beirut, Buenos Aires, Nicosia, and many other capitals are heavily guarded in sharp contrast with, and derogation of, their diplomatic function. Diplomats can no longer go about their business in any capital without varying degrees of fear of being kidnapped or killed.
- The world's leading statesmen work and travel under costly and inhibiting restrictions.
- Mail received at potential target addresses, such as my own government department, must be x-rayed for explosives before delivery.
- State authority is weakened as governments accede to terrorist demands for release of prisoners, ransom, and publicity.
- The principles and standards of justice are impaired as the perpetrators of horrible acts of violence are given short sentences or let free.

None of these conditions has reached critical proportions. But in combination they signal a potential for mounting, serious erosion of world order if we do not succeed in bringing the international terrorist threat under control.

Future of Terrorism

So, finally, what of the future?

I just noted terrorism's, particularly international terrorism's, relatively small toll in killed and wounded and property damage. This could soon begin to change. New weapons are constantly enlarging terrorists' destructive capabilities.

Particularly rapid advances are being made in individual weapons development as we and other advanced nations seek to equip our foot soldiers with increased, highly accurate firepower. There is obvious risk of growing quantities of these weapons coming into the hands of terrorists, weapons which are as capable of being employed against civil aircraft, super-tankers, motorcades and speakers' podiums as against military targets. The Soviet SA–7 heat-seeking, man-portable missile has already, as I mentioned, been found in the hands of terrorists.

And there are more serious hazards. As nuclear power facilities multiply, the quantity and geographical dispersion of plutonium and other fissionable materials in the world will increase greatly. The possibility of credible nuclear terrorist threats based on illicitly constructed atomic bombs, stolen nuclear weapons, or sabotage of nuclear power installations can be expected to grow. Even more plausible would be threats based on more readily and economically produced chemical and biological agents, such as nerve gas and pathogenic bacteria.

Would terrorists actually use such weapons? Probably not. They could already have attacked cities with toxic aerosols, for example, but have not done so. Terrorists, at least the rational ones, fundamentally seek to influence people, not kill them. The death of thousands, or tens of thousands, of persons could produce a tremendous backlash against those responsible and their cause. But the possibility of credible nuclear, chemical and biological threats, particularly by anarchists, is real. Though the chances of such threats being carried out may be small, the risk is there and must be met.

There is a further danger, one of international terrorist groups for hire, which we may already be seeing in an incipient stage. A government might employ such groups to attack, alarm or subvert another government or international organization. Powerful pressures might be brought to bear through a small, deniable expenditure by the aggressor government.

The future, some believe, holds a prospect of reduced resort to open warfare but of a high level of subversive and terroristic violence and insecurity originating with governments or sub-governmental elements using, or threatening to use, against our vulnerable modern societies, the frightening small, or even more frightening mass effect, weapons I have cited. A world of many Ulsters might be statistically safer for the average man than the world of the past sixty years of repeated major conflicts. But it would be a more nerve-racking and unsettled world of continuing low level violence and threatened mass destruction terrorist attack.

Conclusion

In conclusion, man's inhumanity to man is not confined to war. Terrorism too inflicts brutal suffering on the innocent. We see its toll daily in atrocious acts of indigenous or international terrorism.

To combat the latter the United States presented to the 1972 General Assembly the carefully formulated draft convention for the Prevention and Punishment of Certain Acts of International Terrorism which I mentioned earlier. The idea of the convention was simple. States, we felt, should be left to deal themselves under their domestic law with acts of terrorism against persons within their own territories, except diplomats and other internationally protected persons. However, when terrorists sought to export terrorism by blackmailing states through acts committed on the territory of other states or in international air or waters, international law should impose obligations on the states' parties to the convention to prosecute or extradite such territories coming under their control. Had this convention come into force with a full range of parties, international terrorism would have been dealt a heavy, perhaps fatal blow. There would today be no safe havens.

Instead our proposal foundered in a discussion of definitions and of the causes of international terrorism. It was argued that we had ignored the problem of terrorism practiced by repressive governments—state terrorism—to which group terrorism is often a response. It was further argued that international terrorism practiced in a just cause, such as the self-determination of peoples and human rights, could not be considered criminal.

Our reply to the first of these arguments was, and is, that there is a wealth of existing law and on-going effort in the field of state action, including state terrorism. Though these laws and effort have not given us a perfect world, mixing of the problem of international terrorism with the problem of state terrorism would not assist the reduction of either.

With respect to the causes of terrorism, we have pointed out that none of the many states which have won their independence the hard way, including our own nation, engaged in the type of international violence which our draft convention seeks to control. Our proposal is carefully restricted to the problem of the spread of violence to persons and places far removed from the scene of struggles for self-determination. We have further noted that even when the use of force may be legally justified, there are some means which must not be used, especially when directed against innocents. This principle has long been recognized in the rules of war. Certainly, if a state acting in a situation where its very survival may be at stake is legally precluded from resorting to atrocities, individuals or groups purportedly seeking to advance some self-determined cause should be similarly limited.

Terrorism is an affront to civilization. Like piracy, it must be seen as outside the law. In Secretary Kissinger's words last August in Montreal, "It discredits any political objective that it purports to serve and any nations which encourage it." The United States is not wedded to its 1972 proposal, but it is firmly wedded to that most precious of human rights, the right of the innocent person to life. It is time—past time—for the international community genuinely to address the affliction of international terrorism and to take effective action against it. The technological interdependence of the modern world enables the terrorist to carry out and publicize acts of terrorism in ways that were beyond reach a few decades ago. The international community must catch up with this modernization of barbarism before it is victimized by acts of terrorism as yet only imagined.

SELECTED BIBLIOGRAPHY

Adelson, Alan. *SDS: A Profile*. New York: Charles Scribner's Sons, 1972.

Aron, Raymond. *Peace and War: A Theory of International Relations*. New York: Frederick A. Praeger, 1968.

Barzun, Jacques, and Graff, Henry F. *The Modern Researcher*. New York: Harcourt, Brace & World, 1970.

Beaufré, André. *Strategy of Action*. New York: Frederick A. Praeger, 1967.

Becker, Jillian. *Hitler's Children: The Story of the Baader–Meinhof Terrorist Gang*. Philadelphia: J.B. Lippincott Co., 1977.

Begin, Menachem. *The Revolt*. New York: Nash Publishing, 1978.

Bouza, Anthony V. *Police Intelligence: The Operations of an Investigative Unit*. New York: AMS Press, 1976.

Burton, Anthony M. *Urban Terrorism: Theory, Practice and Response*. New York: The Free Press, Macmillan Co., 1976.

Camus, Albert. *The Rebel: An Essay on Man in Revolt*. New York: Random House, Vintage Books, 1956.

Camus, Albert. *Resistance, Rebellion and Death*. New York: Modern Library, 1960.

Caroz, Yaacov. *The Arab Secret Service*. London: Corgi Books, Transworld Publishers, 1978.

Combined Operations: The Official Story of the Commandos. New York: Macmillan Co., 1943.

Conrad, Joseph. *The Secret Agent: A Simple Tale*. London: Doubleday & Page, 1907.

Crozier, Brian. *A Theory of Conflict*. London: Hamish Hamilton, 1974.

Daley, Robert. *Target Blue: An Insider's View of the N.Y.P.D.* New York: Delacorte Press, 1973.

Daughtery, William E. *A Psychological Warfare Casebook*. Baltimore: The Johns Hopkins Press, 1958.

Garson, G. David. *Political Science Methods*. Boston: Holbrook Press, 1976.

Goldman, Peter. *The Death and Life of Malcolm X*. New York: Harper & Row, 1973.

Gross, Feliks. *Foreign Policy Analysis*. New York: Philosophical Library, 1954.

Haney, William V. *Communication and Organizational Behavior*. Homewood, Ill.: Richard J. Irwin, 1973.

Haswell, Jock. *Spies and Spymasters: A Concise History of Intelligence*. London: Thames & Hudson, 1977.

Henissart, Paul. *Wolves in the City: The Death of French Algeria*. St. Albans, Hertfordshire: Paladin, 1973.

Heuer, Richard J., Jr. *Quantitative Approaches to Political Intelligence: The C.I.A. Experience*. Boulder, Colo.: Westview Press, 1978.

Jackson, Sir Geoffrey. *Surviving the Long Night: An Autobiographical Account of a Political Kidnapping*. New York: Vanguard Press, 1974.

Kedward, Roderick. *The Anarchists: The Men Who Shocked an Era*. New York: American Heritage Press, 1975.

Kirkpatrick,, Lyman B., Jr. *The U.S. Intelligence Community: Foreign Policy and Domestic Activities*. New York: Hill & Wang, 1973.

Kitson, Frank. *Low Intensity Operations*. London: Faber & Faber, 1971.

Laqueur, Walter. *Guerrilla: A Historical and Critical Study*. Boston: Little, Brown & Co., 1976.

Lawrence, T.E. *Seven Pillars of Wisdom: A Triumph*. London: Jonathan Cape, 1935.

Le Carré, John. *Tinker, Tailor, Soldier, Spy*. New York: Alfred A. Knopf, 1974.

Le Carré, John. *Smiley's People*. New York: Alfred A. Knopf, 1977.

Le Carré, John. *The Honourable Schoolboy*. New York: Alfred A. Knopf, 1977.

Le Carré, John. *The Spy Who Came in from the Cold*. New York: Coward, McCann & Geoghegan, 1978.

Lenin, V.I. *On the Unity of the International Communist Movement*. Moscow: Progress Publishers, 1966.

LeVine, Victor T. *Political Corruption: The Ghana Case*. Stanford, Calif.: Hoover Institution Press, 1975.

Macdonald, John M. *Bombers and Firesetters*. Springfield, Ill.: Charles C Thomas, 1977.

McLellan, Vin, and Avery, Paul. *The Voices of Guns: The Definitive and Dramatic Story of the Twenty-Two-Month Career of the Symbionese Liberation Army*. New York: G.P. Putnam's Sons, 1977.

Mao Tse-tung. *On Guerrilla Warfare*. New York: Frederick A. Praeger, 1961.

Mao Tse-tung. *On Practice: On the Relation between Knowledge and Practice, between Knowing and Doing*. Peking: Foreign Language Press, 1964.

Marighella, Carlos. *Minimanual of the Urban Guerrilla*. Havana: Tricontinental, 1970.

Merkl, Peter H. *Political Continuity and Change*. New York: Harper & Row, 1967.

Michel, Henri. *The Shadow War: European Resistance 1939–1945*. New York: Harper & Row, 1972.

Moss, Robert. *The War for the Cities*. New York: Coward, McCann & Geoghegan, 1972.

Myagkov, Aleksei. *Inside the K.G.B.* New Rochelle, N.Y.: Arlington House, 1976.

Orlov, Alexander. *Handbook of Intelligence and Guerrilla Warfare*. Ann Arbor: The University of Michigan Press, 1972.

Porzecanski, Arturo C. *Uruguay's Tupamaros, The Urban Guerrilla*, New York: Frederick A. Praeger, 1973.

Rogers, Everett M., and Agarwala-Rogers, Rekha. *Communications in Organizations*. New York: The Free Press, Macmillan Co., 1976.

Sanders, William B. *The Sociologist as Detective: An Introduction to Research Methods*. New York: Frederick A. Praeger, 1974.

Sanger, Richard S. *Insurgent Era: New Patterns of Political Economic and Social Revolution.* Washington, D.C.: Potomac Books, 1967.

Seymour, Gerald. *Harry's Game: A Novel.* New York: Random House, 1975.

Steiner, George A. *Strategic Planning: What Every Manager Must Know.* New York: The Free Press, Macmillan Co., 1979.

Tanham, George K. *Communist Revolutionary Warfare: From the Vietminh to the Viet Cong.* New York: Frederick A. Praeger, 1968.

Thompson, Sir Robert. *Defeating Communist Insurgency: The Lessons of Malaya and Vietnam.* New York: Frederick A. Praeger, 1970.

Thompson, Sir Robert. *Revolutionary War in World Strategy 1945–1969.* New York: Taplinger Publishing Co., 1970.

Trinquier, Roger. *Modern Warfare: A French View of Counterinsurgency.* New York: Frederick A. Praeger, 1964.

Trotsky, Leon. *The Russian Revolution: The Overthrow of Tzarism and the Triumph of the Soviets.* Garden City, N.Y.: Doubleday, Anchor Books, 1959.

Tullock, Derek. *Wingate in Peace and War.* London: Macdonald & Co., 1972.

Wilensky, Harold L. *Organizational Intelligence: Knowledge and Policy in Government and Industry.* New York: Basic Books, 1967.

Wolf, John B. *The Police Intelligence System.* New York: The John Jay Press, 1978.

Wolfe, Bertram D. *Communist Totalitarianism: Keys to the Soviet System.* Boston: Beacon Press, 1961.

INDEX